Contents

Acknowledgments

We acknowledge our great debt to the insatiable curiosity of professional programmers, and their amateur counterparts, affectionately known as "hackers," for the stimulus to write this book. We note Messrs. Kernighan and Ritchie who, under the sponsorship of Bell Laboratories, created and defined the C language, deserve a special place in a Computer Hall of Fame which has not yet been created.

Prentice-Hall helped pioneer the popularity of the C programming language by publishing (in 1978) the Kernighan and Ritchie book *The C Programming Language* when there were few people who could understand C—and just a few really cared. It should be specially noted that the Robert J. Brady Company, a division of Prentice-Hall continued the pioneering effort by encouraging us to write this book.

Also, to Dr. Mark Scott Johnson, formerly assistant professor in computer sciences at San Francisco State University and member of the research staff of Hewlett-Packard, we sincerely express our thanks for his constructive (and corrective) guidance in refining the C structures that form one of the most important elements of this book. Special notice is deserved by Paul Brest of Stanford University's School of Law, and the late Mr. James B. Johnstone, a professional writer and computer user. They generously devoted considerable time to reviewing and critiquing the text and to tirelessly entering, testing, and verifying the numerous source-code examples which are important parts of this book.

There is a group of people—selected by Mr. David T. Culverwell, Editor-in-Chief, his splendid editorial assistant, Mrs. Jessie Katz, and Mr. Chris Williams, Western Editor of the Robert J. Brady Company—who fulfilled a very important and useful function in the preparation of this book. They are known as "reviewers." Their function was to critically examine and comment on all the text and code this book contains. Their efforts and comments are very much appreciated.

With tongue in cheek, we acknowledge our own typing efforts. The numerous lines of code were entered and edited by ourselves using **WordStar** and **VEDIT**. These were printed out on an **NEC Model-7710 Spinwriter** with a **PICA-10** thimble. We had to make a choice among the printer's thimbles with respect to the numeral "1" and the lowercase letter "l," and the zero and the uppercase letter "O." We elected to clearly distinguish between the numeral "1" and the lowercase letter "l." The same distinction could not be achieved between the numeral "0" and the uppercase letter "O." This is a tradeoff we hope you will find acceptable. The original printouts were used as artwork in the production of this book. This was not done for economic reasons but rather to eliminate the distinct possibilities of typographic errors in transferring the extensive groups of C code from the manuscript pages to the printed pages.

Proofreading, and the very difficult and critical task of creating the index, and attending to the complex logistics requirements of acting as primary liaison with the production staff at the Robert J. Brady Company (vitally important functions that would have driven us up the wall if we'd had to do them ourselves) were bravely undertaken by Dorothy F. Wortman.

Last in our mentions but among the first in our minds are the authors and publishers of C compilers who contributed their disks and documents to us for evaluation without demanding or even suggesting that we print anything but our own viewpoints and responses to their work.

Leon A. Wortman
Thomas O. Sidebottom

Palo Alto, California
November 1983

Introduction

"C." What a strange name for a computer programming language. Is it really a name? If so, was there ever an "A" or a "B?" How did "C" come about? Why was it created? And what can it do that other languages cannot do, or what can it do better than others?

Perhaps you've done some work with BASIC; may even have written some useful programs in this exceptionally popular language. Perhaps you've gone on to work with higher-level languages such as Pascal, or PL/I. But "C" strikes you as being something else!

It is "something else!" It is rapidly building a following among professional programmers and among those who enjoy the fruits of the intellectual exercises built into constructing a program in the "C" language.

It seems that C was preceded by B which was derived from the "Basic Cambridge Programming Language" (BCPL) in the early 1960's. There is no evidence that, as far as programming languages go, there ever was an A. C was created in the late 1960's as a general purpose programming language and, because it was developed along with the UNIX operating system, it is strongly associated with UNIX.

The original UNIX operating system, an assembler, and several utility programs were written in assembly language. This made UNIX machine- or hardware-dependent. In fact, UNIX ran only on one particular type or brand of computer. To escape from this dependency, the programs were rewritten in a language called "B" that was developed specifically for transportability.

The B language was modified by Dennis Ritchie of Bell Laboratories. The new language created was named C. Ritchie then rewrote the UNIX software in this new C language. As a result, it can be moved, transported or run on a great variety of brands and models of computers. Most happily for those who do not have access to mini- or mainframe-computers, programs written in the C programming language run very well indeed on microcomputers under a wide variety of operating systems.

You may have been more than just a bit discouraged by what you've seen of source codes for programs written in C. Those who have written programs in high-level languages and who see C source code for the first time report that C code does look strange or hard to read. Admittedly, C is a difficult programming languge to take on in a self-teaching mode. Very few programmers, amateur and professional alike, dare try to learn the C programming language without having ready access to someone who is already an experienced C programmer. However, where do you find such a knowledgeable person who also has teaching skills?

If your interest in C has been high enough to pursue or investigate, you probably already own a copy of the highly intriguing, tantalizing book, *The C*

Programming Language, published by Prentice-Hall. It was co-authored by Dennis M. Ritchie and Brian W. Kernighan of Bell Laboratories.

In your search for assistance, instruction, and reading matter on the language, you also may have learned there is virtually no other authoritative C text available to you. Even the computer journals and periodicals are short of articles. Very few have been published concerning this language. Compilers, assemblers, and linkers are commercially available for C. However, none offers or claims to offer in its software documentation anything remotely resembling a tutorial on how to write useful C source code. Examples of C programs are relatively rare, cutting off this avenue as a means for learning by emulation.

There are prerequisites to gaining full, meaningful benefits from this book. They are not difficult prerequisites. You, the reader-student, should have a reasonably good foundation in programming in a high-level language such as those we've already mentioned: BASIC, Pascal, or PL/I. Any of the numerous variations of BASIC and Pascal will do. Experience with a structured higher-level language is indeed valuable in the process of learning to program in C.

This book has ambitious objectives. We assume you have little if any experience or knowledge of C and were alarmed at your first sight of C source code. However, if you have the desire to generate code that isn't tedious to write and achieve compact, transportable, fast running, powerful programs this book is for you. We show you how to write useful, complex, multi-function applications programs as well as simple and valuable utilities.

Another objective of this book is to provide instructors with a tutorial textbook for a full course in C that moves progressively from the fundamental to the very advanced levels in a series of logical steps.

Throughout this book, you will learn by doing—by writing bits and pieces of code that can be compiled, linked and executed as short programs. You will also work with large, complex programs. The book is abundant with examples, both simple and complex. In this way you will gain a strong familiarity with the concepts that are involved in C.

This book is not intended for ''night-table reading.'' It is pragmatic. The best way to read this book is at your terminal's keyboard. By practicing each of the numerous examples included, the learning process will be dramatically enhanced. And, of course, you will be able to see results instantly. With Chapter One, you will begin to taste the satisfying fruits of C.

Each chapter guides you comfortably and securely along the path toward more advanced knowledge and practical programming. You will learn how to direct programs to your computer's console, to your printer, and to other physical devices; how to read other files; how to create, write to, and modify other files. There are chapters that include explanations, applications, and examples of pointers, arrays, do, while, for, if, else, arguments, constants, variables, declarations, arithmetic, logical, and relational operators, type conversions, conditional expressions, error handling, I/O, and more.

The mysteries of the ''shorthand'' code constructions which account in part for C's compactness are exposed so that you will understand and know how to use them to maximum advantage. This book closely follows the language, syntax, and precedents already established by Kernighan and Ritchie, whose valuable work has rightfully become the classic reference in its field and as close as possible to a standard, de facto or otherwise.

There is every reason to believe that, by faithfully following and practicing the instructions and guides provided by this book, you can become remarkably, satisfyingly proficient in the use of the C programming language. It is designed to be used either as a self-teaching text for the soloist, or as a workbook for small and large groups, classrooms, seminars, and workshops.

The program-codes for the many examples in this book were compiled and tested under **CP/M-80**, **CP/M-86**, **MS-DOS**, and **UNIX**. The programs are intended to compile and run on systems that have a compiler supporting the full **C** programming language as defined by Kernighan and Ritchie.

If the mysteries of **C** have taken on some of the aspects of a highly disturbing enigma, if you don't like being kept in the dark, we think this book will help you turn on the lights brightly. There's a whole new world of programming excitement about to unfold for you.

Trademarks

WordStar is a trademark of MicroPro International Corporation.

CP/M is a trademark of Digital Research, Inc.

MS-DOS is a trademark of Microsoft Corporation.

UNIX is a trademark of Western Electric Company.

VEDIT is a trademark of CompuView Products, Inc.

C86 is a trademark of Computer Innovations, Inc.

LATTICE C is a trademark of Lattice, Inc.

Microsoft C is a trademark of Microsoft Corporation.

Mark Williams C is a trademark of the Mark Williams Company.

BDS C is a trademark of BD Software, Inc.

C80 is a trademark of Software Toolworks, Inc.

AZTEC C is a trademark of Manx Software Systems.

DRC is a trademark of Digital Research, Inc.

Limits of Liability and Disclaimer of Warranty

Special Note

Throughout this book we have tried to be consistent in our use of the male pronouns: he, him, his. This is done solely to eliminate the awkwardness of having to write and read expressions like "he/she," "him/her," and "his/hers." We hope you will not think our use of the male pronoun or the exclusion of the female pronoun is sexism or discrimination. As have so many other authors, we have unsuccessfully struggled with this modern language difficulty. We have often taken a neutral ground offered by the words "you" and "we." It is our observation and conviction that effectiveness as a person has nothing whatsoever to do with gender. This fact is demonstrated convincingly in the computer industry.

Leon A. Wortman
Thomas O. Sidebottom

Note to Authors

Do you have a manuscript or software program related to personal computers? Do you have an idea for developing such a project? If so, we would like to hear from you. The Brady Company produces a complete range of books and applications software for the personal computer market. We invite you to write to David Culverwell, Editor-in-Chief, Robert J. Brady Co., Bowie, MD 20715.

About the Authors

Dr. Leon A. Wortman is president of Success Analysis Corporation, management consultants, Palo Alto, California. He has written numerous books on management, technology, and computers. His books *Business Problem Solving with the IBM PC & XT* and *Business Solutions with the Texas Instruments Professional Computer* were also published by the Robert J. Brady Company. He has written business software in many languages, but prefers C.

Thomas O. Sidebottom has been a professional programmer for a major communications equipment company and microprocessor designers and manufacturers in Silicon Valley. Fluent in many computer languages, he has been an independent custom-software programmer for a number of companies. Many of his programs are being marketed nationally to the serious computer user. All his programs have been written in C.

Part One

The Tutorial

The first part of this book is a tutorial that guides you step-by-step through an understanding of the **C** programming language. The objectives are to enable you to learn to write your own programs in **C**, and to read and comprehend **C** code written by others. While reading this book, you should be at the terminal of a computer system that lets you write, compile, and run interactive **C** programs. You should have access to a text editor with which you will enter and edit the large number of examples of **C** code contained in this book. You should have ready access to the programmer's guide, the documentation for the **C** compiler you intend to use.

1

Getting Started

About Compilers and Linkers

When you write a program, you express your ideas in a format called a programming language. The **C** programming language has strict rules of grammar and meaning much like the natural languages people speak. A program written in **C** cannot be understood directly by the computer system. It must be translated before it can be run. The translator is called the *compiler*. The compiler for **C** is a complex program that converts source code into an intermediate form called an *object module*.

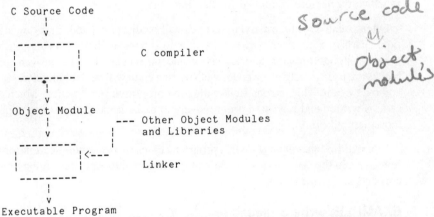

An object module cannot be run any more than can original source code written in the **C** programming language. The program must first be combined or linked with support utilities provided by a part of the compiler known as the **C library**. Linking the object module produces the final program you can run. *Linking* programs may be unfamiliar to you if you have worked in languages such as **Pascal** and **BASIC**, which may not need linking to produce executable programs. Linking, although an additional step, gives **C** much of its power because **C** relies heavily on support utilities that the **C library** provides, and which may be called from the source code of the **C** programs. These support utilities provide additional resources to help you rapidly create executable programs. We will spend much useful time describing and using the standard **C library** which adheres essentially to the **UNIX library**.

A Bit Of Philosophy

This book is not just about **C**, but about programming in **C**. You program when you use a programming language and a computer to solve a problem or create an effect. The skills involved in programming in **C** are not based merely on learning the peculiarities of **C**, but learning how to express a problem or an objective clearly in the language.

The most important step in writing a program is understanding the problem in need of a solution, and in defining the objective that must be reached. The better you understand the problem and the objective, the better your solution will be.

We never work on isolated programs, problems or objectives in this book. Instead, in every case, a problem or an objective is posed, then an achievable solution is provided. The process of clearly defining the goal is a critical programming skill you can expect to learn from this book.

You learn by examples given in clean, tested programs you should be able to duplicate on your computer system. As each language feature is presented, it is explained in a section called **ANATOMY** which follows each of the groups of code in which the feature is applied for the first time.

Often, related problems and objectives will be discussed and, in following sections, parts of a program may be rewritten to show specific effects and actions in a simple, straightforward, logical, easy to understand way. Because proven building blocks are used to help write code, well-written code will be deliberately used over and over again. This is consistent with good programming practice. Much of the code is written and rewritten progressively to make it more clear or to express it more naturally in **C**.

You will find that good style in a program comes by reworking sections of it, by revising it in the same way you edit and refine a manuscript; improving upon the concepts and expressions.

EXAMPLE: write a message

The first example is a simple program:

Write a message to the user's display.
Make the message simple.
Say something specific.

Here is one way to write it with **C** program code:

```
#include "stdio.h"

main()
{          /* main */
    printf("This is the start of something wonderful!") ;
}          /* main */
```

function - performs a single action

When this program is run (after compiling and linking, of course), one line of information is displayed on the screen:

```
This is the start of something wonderful!
```

Let's examine the anatomy of the example.

ANATOMY: C program files

A C *program file* is a text file you create with your text editor. All C program files have these sections:

```
--------------
Headers and definitions

Variable declarations

Function1
Function2
Function3
     .
     .
     .
-----------
```

Some of these sections can be reordered, but the above is a representation of the usual arrangement.

The short C example that displayed **This is the start of something wonderful!** is one of the simplest possible constructions that can be created and still be called a program. This is because it has nothing more than a header and one function:

```
Header      #include "stdio.h"

Function    main()
            {            /* main */
               printf("This is the start of something wonderful!") ;
            }            /* main */
```

ANATOMY: headers and directives

The majority of C programs refer to special names that the programmer does not define. These names are defined in *header files* that are made part of the program as it is compiled. Most headers contain system-related information. A header file is brought into a program with this instruction:

```
#include "name"
```

special name — program does not define

The expression used in the header of the above program is:

```
#include "stdio.h"
```

⟹ *header*

Therefore, "**stdio.h**" is the name of the "header file." Some C compilers use this form:

```
#include <stdio.h>
```

The angle brackets, instead of the double quotes, indicate that the header file, **stdio.h**, may not be in the same disk directory in which the program appears and, therefore, the compiler must search another directory for it. Compilers and operating systems differ in how they handle angle brackets in **#include** (pronounced "pound-sign include") directives. We will distinguish system header files by using angle brackets. But we will use double quotes for header files which we create specifically for use in this book.

Write each **#include** directive on a line that contains no other statement. Start the line in the first column with **#include** followed by the name of the header file in either double quote marks or angle brackets as are appropriate to the requirement. No blanks should precede the pound sign; enter each one flush with the left margin.

Most programs use **stdio.h** as a required header. Some programs need additional header files. We will meet other header files shortly.

Note that **#include** is a compiler directive, not a statement. *Compiler directives* are special instructions to the compiler to help it compile a program. Compiler directives do not end with a semicolon.

ANATOMY: functions, comments, and statements

C programs are made of functions. A *function* is a unit of a program that performs a single action. Think of a function as a paragraph of text; a related group of **C** statements which serve a specific purpose. A function begins running when its name is used in the program. This is known as *calling* a function. Every function has a name in **C**. Any name may be used in a program if it:

- begins with a letter (Note: in **C**, the underscore character (__) is considered a letter),
- uses only letters and digits in the name (Note: punctuation is not allowed), and
- is unambiguously named in the program within its first eight characters. (Note: Some **C** compilers allow up to thirty-one unambiguous characters in a function name. See your compiler's documentation and Appendix A.)

All **C** programs need a **main** function. The programs in this book begin with the **main** function. Re-examine the first example:

```
Function Name    main()
Start            {              /* main */
Body             printf("This is the start of something wonderful") ;
End              }              /* main */
```

The name of this function is **main**. The function name is followed immediately by a set of parentheses.

Everything inside a **C** function is enclosed in left and right curly brackets: **{** and **}**. The closing right parenthesis after the function's name (**main**) is followed by a left curly bracket to signal "this function begins here." The body of the function is followed by a right curly bracket to signal "this function ends here."

C programs can have almost any layout you find pleasing. **C**'s only restrictions on program layout are:

- All words in a program line must be separated from each other by either one space, a tab, or a punctuation mark.

- Pound signs must appear in the first column of the line for all compiler directives, such as **#include**.   *a text for humans reading.*

In the example, comments are inserted to the right of the curly brackets. A comment is text for human reading only. It is completely ignored by the C compiler. Each comment is preceded by a slash-star **/*** and is ended with a star-slash ***/**. Above, the beginning and end of the **main** function is marked with comments:

```
{    /* main */      comment - for humans
     . . . lines of code .  . .        only.
}    /* main */
```

A comment can be inserted almost anywhere that a space can appear in a **C** program (but never in the middle of a word).

A function's *body* is a series of **C** statements that describe what the function is to do. A *statement* is an action that is to be performed. All **C** statements end with a semicolon, simply the **;** punctuation mark.

In the example, the function **main** contains a single statement that begins with **printf**. **printf** is a function that causes everything between the starting and ending quote marks to be displayed on the screen of the video terminal. **printf** is called by using its name, then enclosing in parentheses the text to be displayed. Double quotes must be used in addition to the set of parentheses that follows the function **printf**.

ANATOMY: C program layout

Unlike some programming languages, **C** programs may be written without regard to the spacing of the source code. The **C** compiler accepts programs with virtually any layout.

This can be a license for disaster if not used properly. While the **C** compiler may not look at the layout of the program, we humans certainly do when we read the program. We may be in trouble should it be necessary to quickly make changes in a program with a poor layout if, at some later time, we cannot read and understand our own code. It can happen! All examples and programs in this book have a definite style of layout. If you don't like the one used in this book, that's okay, but establish one of your own. Then use it with total consistency.

Display Two Messages on the Screen

After one message has been written, it may be desirable to say still more.

Let's make this an objective:

> Write two messages to the screen.
> Say anything at all.
> But make the messages appear on
> two separate lines.

ending. Quote marks to be displayed.

This is the structure:

```
#include <stdio.h>

main()
{           /* main */
    printf("This is the start of something wonderful!") ;
    printf("And now we can say even more!") ;
}           /* main */
```

This function, **main**, has two statements in its body. You may have as many statements inside a function as you want. However, remember every statement must end with a semicolon.

When this program is compiled, linked, and run, the following is displayed on the screen:

This is the start of something wonderful!And now we can say even more!

Not exactly what was wanted. Apparently a new **printf** call does not automatically start a new line. But how are two separate lines displayed? There is a way, of course.

ANATOMY: newlines

C permits a new line to be started at any point in text that is displayed with **printf**. To begin a new line of output, type a backslash \ and a lowercase letter **n**. Do not enter any spaces between the backslash \ and the letter **n**. This combination of characters is the symbol called *newline*.

Therefore, to start a new line at the end of the word "wonderful," the program's code becomes:

```
#include <stdio.h>

main()
{           /* main */
    printf("This is the start of something wonderful!\n") ;
    printf("And now we can say even more!") ;
}           /* main */
```

And now the program displays two sentences, each on a separate line:

```
This is the start of something wonderful!
And now we can say even more!
```

The program can be written in another way and still produce the same effect:

```
#include <stdio.h>

main()
{           /* main */
    printf("This is the start of something ") ;
    printf("wonderful! \nAnd now we can say even more!") ;
}           /* main */
```

In the above example, the second **printf** starts displaying the word **wonderful** on the same line as **This is the start of something**. The newline symbol, **\n**, after the exclamation point starts the second line. However, here the **C** program becomes more difficult for human reading than it should be. The first usage of the **\n** is preferable simply because it is more readable to the human eye.

EXAMPLE: add two numbers and display the result

The objective is:

> Add any two constant numbers and display the
> result. Then display another message on a
> separate line.

Here is the program structure:

```
#include <stdio.h>

main()
{         /* main */
    int    Result ;

    Result = 5 + 10 ;
    printf("Result is: %d\n",Result) ;
    printf("All Done!") ;
}         /* main */
```

ANATOMY: variables

The word **Result**, as used here, is a *variable*, a place to store information. Information can be stored in a variable and recalled later in the program by using the name of the variable. Any name can be given to a variable, provided the name:

- begins with a letter (remember, underscores are letters),
- uses only letters and digits in the name, (no punctuation allowed), and
- is unambiguous within its first eight characters (with some exceptions as noted earlier and below).

These are the same rules as for naming functions. Be aware that some **C** compilers allow names to be unambiguous within the first 31 characters of the name. Other compilers require uniqueness within the first seven characters. (See your compiler's documentation and Appendix A.)

The example programs in this book use long identifier names, many times longer than eight characters. The names are chosen to retain uniqueness within the first eight characters.

ANATOMY: declaration and type

The **C** compiler must be instructed that we want to use a variable in the program. The variable is *declared* before it is used. Declaring a variable tells the compiler that information in the program will be referenced by the declared name.

For example, **Result** is declared with this instruction:

```
int Result ;
```

This means **Result** is a variable that can hold an **integer**; **Result** can store any number that has no fractional part. Beware: an **int** has a *maximum* value that can be stored in it. This varies from compiler to compiler. (See your compiler's documentation and Appendix A.) The declaration follows the first left curly bracket. Declarations should be the first characters to appear after the start of a function.

As many variables can be declared as are needed in the function **main** by giving their names. For instance, the phrases **Result** and **AnotherResult** can be declared to be variables with these instructions:

```
int   AnotherResult ;
int   Result ;
```

Declarations for variables can be combined if they store the same *type* of information. **Result** and **AnotherResult** are the same type because they are both **int**egers. Therefore, this is valid:

```
int   AnotherResult,Result ;
```

We will not often combine declarations for variables in this book. Until one becomes accustomed to the form, it can make programs harder for people to read.

ANATOMY: assignment

Information is stored in a variable by *assigning* a value to it. The variable is referred to by name on the left hand side of the statement, and the value to be given to the variable is placed on the right hand side of the statement. The two sides of the statement are connected with a single equal sign:

```
        Result = 5 + 10 ;
        ------ - ------ -
           !    !   !    !
           !    !   !    !
           !    !   !    ----> (end of statement)
           !    !   !
 (target) <----  !         ----> (new value)
                 !
                 ----> (assignment)
```

Result is the *target variable*; its value is changed to a new value by the assignment statement. In the above, the new value is calculated by adding the numbers five and ten. We evaluate the right hand side of the statement between the equal sign and the semicolon to get the new value to give to **Result**.

Assignment does not work the same way an equal sign works in algebra. The statement above says **Result** is given the new value **5 + 10**. First the side of the statement to the right of the equal sign is evaluated to arrive at the new value. This value is then stored in the variable on the left side of the equal sign.

ANATOMY: displaying numbers

An **int**eger is displayed with **printf**. A special symbol, **%d**, is placed inside the double quotes:

```
     printf("Result is: %d\n",Result) ;
                        --   ------
        (Place an       !      !
          integer       !      ---> (The value to display)
           here) <---
```

The symbol **%d** means an **int**eger is to appear at this point in the display of the program. After the closing double quote mark, a comma is inserted, followed by the name of the variable whose value is to be displayed. In this example, right after the **int**eger is displayed, a new line is inserted with the symbol **\n**.

EXAMPLE: total the number of two groups of students

This program is a simple but important extension of the previous one. Digits are used to represent the numbers to be added. This is not usually a good idea for two reasons: (1) Digits may mean something specific when you first write the program, but you may forget what a certain number meant when you reread the program some months later. (2) You may also need to change a number to a new value. Changing five hundred occurrences of a number where five are to be left alone and the other four hundred ninety-five are to be changed can be a nasty experience.

The objective is:

Add together the number of students in
two groups and display the result.

The program code is:

```
#include <stdio.h>
#define    GROUP1NUM    5
#define    GROUP2NUM    10

main()
{          /* main */
     int    Result ;

     Result = GROUP1NUM + GROUP2NUM ;
     printf("Total number of students is: %d\n",Result) ;
     printf("All Done!") ;
}          /* main */
```

ANATOMY: define

Often we want a name for a constant in a program. We never want to change its value, but we don't want a bare number in the program. A constant can be referred to by a special name by defining it as in this example:

```
#define    GROUP1NUM    5
#define    GROUP2NUM    10
```

The two **#define** (pronounced "pound-sign define") instructions define values for the two names **GROUP1NUM** and **GROUP2NUM**. The program simply refers to these two names. The **C** compiler substitutes the constant values automatically. To change a value, simply change the definition.

To define a constant, start at the beginning of a line with the instruction **#define**, enter the name of the constant, and then enter the value of the constant. Most **C** programmers use all upper case letters in naming a **#define** constant to distinguish easily between variables and defined constants. **#define** instructions are usually placed at the beginning of the program, either before or after the **#include** instructions.

#define and **#include** are compiler directives. They are not statements. Therefore they should not end with a semicolon. If a **;** mark is used after the value, the compiler will literally incorporate the semicolon into the value of the defined constant.

Note: Defined constants are not **variables**. You may not change their values within the program by using an assignment statement. For example, this statement is illegal:

```
GROUP1NUM = 25 ;
```

If this were to be done as shown, the compiler would see it as:

```
5 = 25 ;
```

And this is clearly not what was intended.

2

Interactive Programming

An interactive program is a program that directly involves the user as the program is running. When writing a program, you must keep in mind the interaction between the user and your program. A program that helps the user with prompts that clearly explain what is happening is popularly known as "friendly." Many programs have "unfriendly" characteristics. Either they do not involve the user—there is little or no interaction as they are being run—or they do interact but assume too much prior knowledge on the user's part.

This chapter is about the steps essential to writing interactive programs. Our work will center on two friendly programs that do the following useful tasks:

1. Ask the user a question and read a single letter that represents the user's response, then take appropriate action.
2. Validate the response. You cannot depend on the user of the program to enter proper responses. Therefore, the program must check the correctness of the user's entry.

Ask a Question and Read a Response

The objective is to:

Ask the user a Yes/No question.
Read a single letter that the user
types at the keyboard in response
to the question. Display one message
if the user presses a *Y* and another
if the user presses an *N*.

This program is used as an example:

```
#include <stdio.h>

main()
{        /* main */
    int  RawResponse ;
    char Response ;

    printf("Do you like programming? (Y or N): ") ;
```

```
RawResponse = getchar() ;
Response = RawResponse ;
if (Response == 'Y') {
    printf("Just wait until you see what you can do!") ;
}
if (Response == 'N') {
    printf("Keep trying! I bet you'll change your mind.\n") ;
    printf("Programming can be a blast!") ;
}
}        /* main */
```

The first **printf** displays a prompt for the user. No newline is used in the text to be printed so that the prompt and the user's response appear on the same line.

ANATOMY: character variables

Response, in our program, is a variable that stores a **char**acter (pronounced **char** as in the name "Charlie," not as in the word "car"). We declare **Response** to be a **char**acter variable with this instruction:

```
char  Response ;
```

As in the above example, we may identify a character variable by any valid **C** name.

A **char** variable can store exactly one character. The character may be any ASCII character representing either a letter or a digit. A **char** variable can also store a **control character**, a non-printing character that has meaning in some context. We will revisit **control characters** later.

ANATOMY: Reading a character with getchar

A new **char**acter entered at the keyboard by the user is read by calling the **C** function **getchar**. As with **printf**, **getchar** is called by using its name. But, look at something new:

```
RawResponse = getchar() ;
```

When **printf** was used, it was used as the only element in the statement. Now **getchar** is being used on the right hand side of an assignment statement. Recall, from Chapter One, to make an assignment we must determine the value of the right side of the sign, and then place or store this value in the variable on the left hand side of the equal sign. What value does **getchar** have?

getchar causes the computer to wait until the user presses a key. **getchar**'s value becomes this character. The above statement then assigns this new character as the value of **RawResponse**.

The **C** language requires a set of parentheses after **getchar**. This means **getchar** is a function, not a variable. Whenever we use a function we must use parentheses to show that it is a function.

What's the Funny Business With int's?

This program has an unusual feature. A **char**acter is read using **getchar** and it is assigned to **RawResponse** which is an **int**eger, not a **char**acter variable. Why?

getchar can return special codes that show a failure to successfully read a character. These error codes cannot be represented by a **char**acter **variable**. To see these codes, **getchar**'s value must be assigned to an **int**eger **variable**, not a **char**acter.

Some programs will check for these error codes because correct operation must be verified as the program procedes. Here, **RawResponse** is immediately reassigned to **Response** and the error code is dropped in the process.

The result of **getchar** could have been assigned directly to **Response** without any problems for this program. Though it may be clumsy, this construction makes plain what is happening.

Assigning **RawResponse** to **Response** changes the value of the variable from an **int**eger to a **char**acter. **C** usually enables movement back and forth freely between **int**egers and **char**acters: **C** converts the type of the value of **RawResponse** to that of **Response**. This is a harmless case of type conversion; sometimes type conversion plays havoc with programs. Chapter 3 discusses a way of making these conversions explicit in the code.

ANATOMY: decision making with if

C enables a test of the truth of a hypothesis, then acts upon a group of statements to be performed if the hypothesis is true. The anatomy of **if** is:

```
if ( hypothesis ) {
    first statement to be done if the hypothesis is true ;
    second statement to be done if the hypothesis is true ;
    . . .
}
```

The statement begins with **if**, a keyword in **C**. You may not use **if** to name a variable within a program. This isn't a severe restriction, but it must be observed without exception. Think how confusing it could be should you mean the keyword **if** at certain points in a program and the variable **if** at others.

After **if**, a pair of parentheses is opened. The hypothesis is placed entirely between these parentheses. **C** does not use the keyword **then** as do, for example, **Pascal** and **BASIC**. Instead, parentheses are used to set the hypothesis off from the rest of the program.

If the hypothesis is **TRUE**, we want to execute some statements. Surround these statements with curly brackets. Notice the indenting and the relative locations of the code's elements, such as the brackets and the statements. The **C** compiler does not care whether or not indentions are used. However, the indentations do improve the clarity and human comprehension when a program is reexamined at some later time. Good **C** programming practice calls for consistent use of indentations.

ANATOMY: posing is-equal hypotheses

Examine this query in **C**: Is one thing equal to another?

To ask "is the value of Response equal to the uppercase letter Y?" we write:

```
Response == 'Y'
```

The double equal signs mean "is equal to." To ask is equal, two equal signs must be used, not one. Remember that one equal sign means assignment, and two equal signs mean one thing is equal to another. (Be sure to learn this well. The incorrect use of = and == is among the most common of all errors in C programming.)

Note the uppercase letter Y is in single quotes to mean "**Response** is equal to the uppercase letter Y." The C compiler removes the single quotes. Single quotes must be used to show this is a **literal letter** (a **char**acter constant), not a **variable** whose name is the letter Y.

Revising the Program

The program can benefit from a simple revision, one that makes it more clear:

```
#include <stdio.h>
#define YES     'Y'
#define NO      'N'

main()
{       /* main */
    int         RawResponse ;
    char        Response ;

    printf("Do you like programming? (Y or N): ") ;
    RawResponse = getchar() ;
    Response = RawResponse ;
    if (Response == YES)
        printf("Just wait until you see what you can do!") ;
    if (Response == NO) {
        printf("Keep trying! I bet you'll change your mind.\n") ;
        printf("Programming can be a blast!") ;
    }
}       /* main */
```

ANATOMY: character constants

character constants can be defined with the **#define** instruction, as was done for number constants. Note the single letters Y and N are kept in single quotes as they were in the body of the first draft of the program.

The use of defined constants here is a matter of personal choice. Some programmers feel this is more readable than our original program; others feel the extra names are confusing.

ANATOMY: eliminating extra curly brackets

When executing only one statement in an **if** statement, the set of curly brackets can be eliminated. This is a matter of style. In the example program, the first **if** has only one statement, so the curly brackets can be eliminated as superfluous code. The second **if** has two **printf** statements to be executed, so the curly brackets must be kept. Extra curly brackets, properly placed within the program, do not cause a problem.

Another Approach

We can improve upon this. The second test or condition determines whether **Response** is equal to *N*. If, in the example, the user were to type something other than a *Y* or an *N* in response to the question "Do you like programming?" the program would display nothing—not even the character that was typed. Let's revise the definition:

Ask the user a Yes/No question. Read
a single letter the user types in response
to the question. Display one message if the
user presses a *Y*. Display another message
if the user presses any other key.

This assures the user will see a message displayed on the screen of the video terminal regardless of the character entered. Here is the code that fulfills the new specification:

```
#include <stdio.h>
#define YES     'Y'

main()
{       /* main */
    int         RawResponse ;
    char        Response ;
    printf("Do you like programming? (Y or N): ") ;
    RawResponse = getchar() ;
    Response = RawResponse ;
    if (Response == YES)
        printf("Just wait until you see what you can do!") ;
    if (Response != YES) {
        printf("Keep trying! I bet you'll change your mind.\n") ;
        printf("Programming can be a blast!") ;
    }
}       /* main */
```

ANATOMY: testing the not-equal status

The **double equal** signs are used to test **is equal to**. The C programming language permits tests for a status that is **not equal to** with the symbols:

!=

Therefore, the second **if** can be rewritten as:

if (Response != YES)

This means (and is pronounced as):

if the value of **Response** is not equal to **YES**

A Revision Using else

Another improvement can be made. Instead of doing a second test to see **if Response is not equal to YES**, write:

```
#include <stdio.h>
#define YES    'Y'

main()
{      /* main */
    int         RawResponse ;
    char        Response ;
    printf("Do you like programming? (Y or N) ") ;
    RawResponse = getchar() ;
    Response = RawResponse ;
    if (Response == YES)
        printf("Just wait until you see what you can do!") ;
    else {
        printf("Keep trying! I bet you'll change your mind.\n") ;
        printf("Programming can be a blast!") ;
    }
}      /* main */
```

ANATOMY: the else clause

Instead of having a second not equal test after an is equal test has been done, an optional second clause in the **if** statement can be used. It begins with the keyword **else**. Note that following the **else** are a left curly bracket and a set of statements. This construction is required because there are two statements which, in this example, begin with **printf** and follow the **else** clause.

The statements following the **else** are only executed if the question evaluated in the preceding **if** test is **false**, the character *Y* is not typed at the keyboard.

A Fly in the Ointment

Experimenting with the program, as it is now written, we find the program runs correctly if the upper-case *Y* is entered from the keyboard. It fails if the equivalent lower-case letter *y* is entered. One can hardly expect the user to keep the shift key locked when running an interactive program. This problem must be eliminated.

Thus, the program specification changes to:

Ask the user a Yes/No question. Read a
single letter the user presses in
response to the question. Display one
message if the user presses a *Y* or a *y*,
and another if the user presses any other key.

The program's code for this revised specification becomes:

```
#include <stdio.h>

main()
{      /* main */
    int         RawResponse ;
    char        Response ;

    printf("Do you like programming? (Y or N): ") ;
    RawResponse = getchar() ;
    Response = RawResponse ;
```

```
      if (Response == 'Y' || Response == 'y')
         printf("Just wait until you see what you can do!") ;
      else {
         printf("Keep trying! I bet you'll change your mind.\n") ;
         printf("Programming can be a blast!") ;
      }
   }      /* main */
```

ANATOMY: or

With **C** more complex conditions can be presented than in the previous example. (The correct term for "question" is *condition*.) We want to display "Just wait until you see what you can do!", if **Response** is equal to *Y* or **Response** is equal to *y*. This is written in **C** as:

```
      if (Response == 'Y' || Response == 'y')
```

The two conditions are:

```
      Response == 'Y'    /*  Response is equal to 'Y' */
      Response == 'y'    /*  Response is equal to 'y' */
```

Either condition, *Y* or *y*, is acceptable. The two vertical bars (called "sticks") represent the **or** conjunction.

Note that since **Response** is used twice in this test, **getchar** cannot be used in the condition directly; two **getchar** calls will read two characters. A variable must be used to hold the character so it can be tested twice.

A Revision For Conciseness

The program's code can be made still more concise. While this notation may be confusing at first, it is commonly used in writing compact, efficient **C** programs. There are occasions when it is especially useful. For example:

```
      #include <stdio.h>

      main()
      {      /* main */
         int        Response ;

         printf("Do you like programming? (Y or N): ") ;
         if ((Response = getchar()) == 'Y' || Response == 'y')
            printf("Just wait until you see what you can do!") ;
         else {
            printf("Keep trying! I bet you'll change your mind.\n") ;
            printf("Programming can be a blast!") ;
         }
      }      /* main */
```

ANATOMY: embedded assignments

An assignment may be embedded in the middle of a **C** statement:

```
      if ((Response = getchar()) == 'Y' || Response == 'y')
```

This statement is deciphered by reading the innermost set of parentheses first:

```
      Response = getchar()
```

The character the user next types is put in **Response** which, as a result of the typed entry, now has a value. Remember that **Response** is an **int**eger to store error codes, but it now stores a **char**acter. Thus, we read:

```
if (Response == 'Y' || Response == 'y')
```

The net effect is that the assignment of **getchar**'s value to **Response** has been embedded in the condition itself. The second subcondition (**Response** == **'y'**) uses the value of **Response** assigned in the embedded assignment because the assignment is evaluated first. Note integers and characters can be freely mixed in conditions. **Response** is an integer, but is compared with two literal characters.

Multiple conditions in a single **if** connected by || are evaluated left to right. In the previous example, the assignment is evaluated first because it is in the left hand condition. In the next example:

```
if (Response == 'Y' || (Response = getchar()) == 'y')
```

Response is not assigned a value until after the first test is evaluated.

Using System Functions

One of the wonders of **C** is in the fact that program code can be simplified by using a function which makes the job easier.

HAZARD: ctype.h

The following programs use special functions some **C** compilers define in a special header file called "ctype.h." Many compilers, including UNIX, put the definitions for character testing functions inside **ctype.h**. If you use these compilers and you reference these functions inside your programs, you must put a **#include <ctype.h>** instruction in your code. Other compilers, especially microcomputer **C** compilers, have no **ctype.h** file and put the definitions for these functions in the system library that is referenced at link time. Unfortunately, some compilers do not support these functions at all. (See Appendices A, B, and C for details.)

```
#include <stdio.h>
#include <ctype.h>

main()
{       /* main */
    int       Response ;
    char      Transformed ;

    printf("Do you like programming? (Y or N): ") ;
    Response = getchar() ;
    Transformed = tolower(Response) ;
    if (Transformed == 'y')
       printf("Just wait until you see what you can do!") ;
    else {
       printf("Keep trying! I bet you'll change your mind.\n") ;
       printf("Programming can be a blast!") ;
    }
}       /* main */
```

ANATOMY: case conversion with tolower and toupper

C provides a way to automatically convert an upper-case character to lower case with the function **tolower**. If the original character is a letter, **tolower** takes the character and returns a new character guaranteed to be lower case. If the original character is not a letter, it is returned unchanged. Note **tolower** takes either a character to be converted, or an **int**eger that represents a character, as we've used in this program. (Remember **getchar**'s result is assigned to an **int**eger to let us see special error codes.)

The flow of the code resembles a corridor with a way in and a way out:

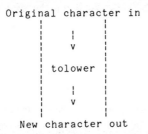

```
Original character in
    ¦           ¦
    ¦     ¦     ¦
    ¦     v     ¦
    ¦           ¦
    ¦ tolower   ¦
    ¦           ¦
    ¦     ¦     ¦
    ¦     v     ¦
    ¦           ¦
  New  character  out
```

A character is put in and a new character comes out. **tolower** transforms the original character so that, assuming the character is a letter, we will always get back a lower-case character.

tolower is used this way:

```
NewCharacterOut = tolower(OriginalCharacterIn) ;
```

The original character is given to **tolower** by putting it in parentheses after the name **tolower**. The new character comes from **tolower** just as we get characters from **getchar**. The character is assigned to a variable. Usage in the above program is:

```
Transformed = tolower(Response) ;
```

This statement takes the character in **Response**, transforms it to lower case if it is upper case, and assigns the result to **Transformed**.

To shift the original letter to upper case, **toupper** can be used exactly as **tolower** is used. The program changes to:

```
Transformed = toupper(Response) ;
if (Transformed == 'Y')
```

The program now tests the character and transforms it, if necessary, to an upper-case *Y*. Use of **toupper** or **tolower** is one's own choice. Both work equally well in this example.

ANATOMY: assignments revisited

The previous program example introduces the variable: **Transformed**. It stores the result of **tolower**. Its use makes the program clearer. But **Transformed** is really an unnecessary variable. Therefore, the program can be revised:

```
#include <stdio.h>
#include <ctype.h>

main()
{       /* main */
    int         Response ;

    printf("Do you like programming? (Y or N): ") ;
    Response = getchar() ;
    Response = tolower(Response) ;
    if (Response == 'y')
        printf("Just wait until you see what you can do!") ;
    else {
        printf("Keep trying! I bet you'll change your mind.\n") ;
        printf("Programming can be a blast!") ;
    }
}       /* main */
```

The statement **Response = tolower(Response) ;** may be confusing. Consider the assignment process again. The original value of **Response** is given to **tolower** which returns a new **char**acter, replacing the original value of **Response** with the new value. Take note of this construction; it will be used often.

The result of **tolower** can be assigned to an **int**eger as well as to a **char**acter. This **int**eger can be tested in the **if** statement with a character constant. This moving back-and-forth between types can be confusing, but it is harmless here.

What Kind of Character Is It?

When the user enters a character, it may be necessary to know what kind of character has been entered. **C** enables code to be written that tests to determine what class or kind of character entered: letter, digit, punctuation, or some other sort.

The objective is:

Prompt the user to enter a character.
Display a unique response that tells
whether the character is a letter, a
digit, a punctuation mark, or any other
character.

The first solution is:

```
#include <stdio.h>
#include <ctype.h>
#define  FALSE     0

main()
{       /* main */
    int     Response ;
```

```
        printf("Enter a character: ") ;
        Response = getchar() ;
        if (isalpha(Response) != FALSE)
            printf("You entered a letter.") ;
        else if (isdigit(Response) != FALSE)
            printf("You entered a digit.") ;
        else if (ispunct(Response) != FALSE)
            printf("You entered a punctuation mark.") ;
        else
            printf("You entered a character I can't identify") ;
}       /* main */
```

ANATOMY: character class tests

To determine if a character is a letter, another **C** facility now comes to our attention, **isalpha**:

```
    isalpha(Response) != FALSE
```

Response is the character the user enters. It is given to the function **isalpha** by enclosing it in parentheses after the **function** name, exactly as a character was given to **tolower** in the last program. Giving a **value** to a **function** is called "passing the value to the function."

```
        Response
            |
            |
            v
    -------------
    |  isalpha  |
    -------------
            |
            |
            v
    TRUE or FALSE
```

isalpha does not give or return a character as **tolower** does. It returns the value **TRUE** or **FALSE**. **isalpha** returns **TRUE** if the character given to it is a letter; it returns **FALSE** if the character is not a letter.

C provides additional functions such as **ispunct** (which returns **TRUE** if the character is a punctuation mark) and **isdigit** (which returns **TRUE** if the character is a digit). Your **C** compiler may provide additional functions. Consult the documentation for your specific **C** compiler to determine which functions, sometimes colloquially referred to as "is functions" or "is library functions," are available.

It is safer to test to see if the function returns **FALSE** rather than **TRUE**. **C** actually allows any non-zero number to represent **TRUE**, while only zero represents **FALSE**. While initially confusing, this allows more concise programs to be written as later chapters will show.

Again, many compilers define these character class (**is**) functions in the header file called **ctype.h**.

ANATOMY: else-if

Character-class test functions can be done with **if** alone:

```
if (isalpha(Response) != FALSE)      /* first test  */
    printf("You entered a letter.") ;
if (isdigit(Response) != FALSE)      /* second test */
    printf("You entered a digit.") ;
if (ispunct(Response) != FALSE)      /* third test  */
    printf("You entered a punctuation mark.") ;
```

The first **if** tests to determine whether or not the character is a letter. If it is, the response is displayed, and the program continues with all the following tests. This does much unnecessary work. The following construction is simpler:

```
if (isalpha(Response) != TRUE)       /* first test  */
    printf("You entered a letter.") ;
else if (isdigit(Response) != TRUE)  /* second test */
    printf("You entered a digit.") ;
else if (ispunct(Response) != TRUE)  /* third test  */
    printf("You entered a punctuation mark.") ;
else                                 /* otherwise   */
    printf("You entered a character I can't identify!") ;
```

If the first **if** test fails, the next **else** action becomes, in effect, a new **if**; and the second test is made. If the second test fails, the next test is performed; and so on. Each test is made in turn and, if each fails, the test is continued until the final **else** test is reached and, as a result, the **printf** argument **You entered a character I can't identify!** is displayed. **C** lets us continue this chaining process as many times as we want.

ANATOMY: TRUE and FALSE
and the value of conditions

FALSE is defined in the program as the number **0**. If any of the character tests is **FALSE**, the number **0** is returned. Although it has not been used yet, **TRUE** is defined in **C** programs to be any non-zero number.

If the character test functions return any non-zero number, they effectively return **TRUE**. If they return the number **0**, they effectively return **FALSE**. This means they can be used alone as a condition in an **if** statement. The code can be rewritten:

```
#include <stdio.h>
#include <ctype.h>

main()
{       /* main */
    int    Response ;

    printf("Enter a character: ") ;
    Response = getchar() ;
    if (isalpha(Response))
        printf("You entered a letter.") ;
    else if (isdigit(Response))
        printf("You entered a digit.") ;
    else if (ispunct(Response))
        printf("You entered a punctuation mark.") ;
    else
        printf("You entered a character I can't identify!") ;
}       /* main */
```

In general, any function that returns a number can be used as an **if** condition. In **C** programming practice, if the function returns a zero, the condition is **FALSE**. If the function returns a non-zero number—not just the number one—the condition is true.

Write Your Own Functions

What if your compiler does not have one of these functions in its library? With **C**, new functions can be defined when needed. If the functions are well written, they can be reused at any time in writing programs. Thus, the functions created extend the utility of the language to meet a variety of needs.

Let's hypothesize the function **isdigit** is missing from our **C** compiler's library of functions. An appropriate function can be written for this specification:

> Write a function that receives a single
> character. If the character is a digit
> between zero and nine, return TRUE.
> Otherwise, return FALSE.

This is the program:

```
#include <stdio.h>
#define TRUE    1
#define FALSE   0

main()
{       /* main */
     char    Response ;

     printf("Enter a character: ") ;
     Response = getchar() ;
     if (isdigit(Response))
          printf("You entered a digit.") ;
     else
          printf("You entered a non-digit.") ;
}       /* main */

int isdigit(CharIn)
char        CharIn ;
{       /* isdigit */
     int    Result ;

     if (CharIn >= '0' && CharIn <= '9')
          Result = TRUE ;
     else
          Result = FALSE ;
     return (Result) ;
}       /* isdigit */
```

ANATOMY: functions revisited

isdigit works as it did in our previous diagram:

```
        CharIn                   int isdigit(CharIn)
          |                      char        CharIn ;
          |                      {    /* isdigit */
          v                      int     Result ;
    -----------
   |  isdigit  |                 if (CharIn >= '0' && CharIn <= '9')
    -----------                      Result  = TRUE ;
          |                      else
          |                          Result  = FALSE ;
          v
        Result                   return (Result) ;
                                 }    /* isdigit */
```

isdigit is a function that returns an integer. Immediately following the name **isdigit** is a set of parentheses. Inside the parentheses is **CharIn**, the name of a variable that contains the value coming into the function. On the next line is a declaration for **CharIn**; it is a character.

The start of the function follows the declaration and is indicated by a left curly bracket. The function continues until the matching right curly bracket is found.

Within this particular function, **CharIn** represents the character that **isdigit** receives from outside the function.

Functions return values to their callers. A value is returned inside a function by putting it in a **return** statement. This statement takes the value of **Result** inside **isdigit** and gives it back to the calling function which, in this case, is the **main** function. The value **isdigit** gives back is an integer because it was declared to be **int isdigit(CharIn)**.

Information is passed into a function with a variable called a *parameter*. **Response** is an *actual parameter*, the value to be processed by the function. It is given to **isdigit**. **CharIn** is a *formal parameter*: the formal parameter is the variable name used within the function. **CharIn** (and all formal parameters) gets its value from the *actual* parameter which it is given. In this example, **CharIn** receives the value of the variable **Response**. If in our main program we have:

```
Temp2 = isdigit(AnotherResponse) ;
```

AnotherResponse is the actual parameter. When **isdigit** is called with **Another-Response**, its value is assigned to **CharIn**, the formal parameter for **isdigit** used inside the **function**.

This separation of *formal* and *actual* parameters enables the use of the functions in many ways. The variables used in the outside program are separated from those inside the function. This means the same function can be used with different variables simply by using them by name inside the function parameter list.

Notes:
- Functions may have as many parameters as needed. However, functions return only one value.
- If a function returns an integer, the **int** may be dropped. It is always good style, though, to declare the values returned.

We may write either:

```
return (Result) ;
```

or

```
return Result ;
```

The parentheses surrounding **Result** are optional.

ANATOMY: complex conditions

A complex condition with double sticks, ||, is used to mean **OR**. In **isdigit**, the double ampersand **&&** is used to mean **AND**:

```
if (CharIn >= '0' && CharIn <= '9')
```

Read this as:

> If CharIn is greater-than-or-equal-to
> a character representing zero **AND**
> CharIn is less-than-or-equal-to a character
> representing nine

The two simple conditions are connected by the operator **&&**. This is now a complex condition which is **TRUE** only if both simple conditions are **TRUE**.

ANATOMY: more operators for testing

C makes use of several condition-testing operators:

```
==      is equal to
!=      is not equal to
>       greater than
<       less than
>=      greater than or equal to
<=      less than or equal to
```

Some illustrations of operators and test results:

```
C Code:          Read as:               Is it TRUE?
============================================================

5 == 3 + 2       five is equal to       Yes
                 three plus two

'A' != 'B'       letter 'A' is not      Yes
                 equal to letter 'B'

3 >= 0           three is greater than  Yes
                 or equal to zero
```

In applying **if** to test a condition, the above simple operators can be used alone or combined into more complex conditions with **&&** (AND), and with || (OR).

A Revision Using the Ternary Operator

The previous use of **isdigit** can now be revised:

```
int isdigit(CharIn)
char      CharIn ;
{     /* isdigit */
    int      Result ;

    Result = (CharIn >= '0' && CharIn <= '9') ? TRUE : FALSE ;
    return (Result) ;
}     /* isdigit */
```

We depend on the file to contain the same definitions for **TRUE** and **FALSE**.

A New Construction for if-else Tests

Often it is necessary to set a variable equal to one thing if a condition is **TRUE**, and to another if the condition is **FALSE**. The first attempt at isdigit used a straightforward, long approach. C enables the use of a special construction to set a variable to two values that depend on a condition:

```
Result = (CharIn >= '0' && CharIn <= '9') ? TRUE : FALSE ;
  ^                                                ^      ^
  |                        |                       |      |
  -----                    |                       |      |
  |       if (CharIn >= '0' && CharIn <= '9')      |      |
  |------< Result = TRUE ; >------------------------      |
  |                                                       |
  |       else                                            |
  ------< Result = FALSE ; >-------------------------------
```

The variable to be changed is placed on the left-hand side of the assignment statement. On the right-hand side is the condition, surrounded by parentheses. A question mark **?** follows the right parenthesis. Following the question mark is the value to be assigned if the condition is **TRUE**. This is followed by a colon **:** and the value to be assigned if the value is **FALSE**. This pattern is called the **ternary** operator.

Using the **ternary** operator, **isdigit** can be compactly written:

```
int isdigit(CharIn)
char      CharIn ;
{    /* isdigit */
   return((CharIn >= '0' && CharIn <= '9') ? TRUE : FALSE);
}    /* isdigit */
```

To return the value directly, the entire **ternary** operator is placed inside the parentheses of the **return** statement.

Test for A Correct Response

The user's responses must be checked to ensure they are as expected. If the user has made an incorrect entry, he must be prompted again for the correct answer. Define the objective:

> Write a prompt for the user to enter either
> the letter *Y* or the letter *N*. Continue
> prompting and accepting characters until a
> correct letter is read.

The logic in this program is more complex than in previous efforts. It is prudent to analyze the problem before proceeding to a solution. A good way to analyze a problem is to describe the solution step-by-step in simple English phrases:

> keep repeating
>   display prompt for user
>   get user's response
> while the response is wrong.

This technique for designing a section of code, using plain English phrases, is called "pseudocode." While it is not really code, it is easy to convert directly to code.

The program is:

```
#include <stdio.h>
#include <ctype.h>

main()
{        /* main */
    int         Response ;

    do {
        printf(
            "Are you feeling better about programming? (Y/N): ") ;
        Response = getchar() ;
        Response = tolower(Response) ;
        if (Response != 'y' && Response != 'n') {
            printf("Please enter either 'Y' or 'N'.\n") ;
            /* Extra newline left over when user presses ENTER.
             * Read and discard this extra character.
             */
            Response = getchar() ;
        }
    } while (Response != 'y' && Response != 'n') ;

    if (Response == 'y')
        printf("I'm glad.") ;
    else
        printf("Keep trying!") ;
}        /* main */
```

The new **if** statement handles a problem that often happens when reading responses directly from a user. When the user types a response, the ENTER or RETURN key is typed to end the response. If a single character is read with **getchar**, only the first character typed is read. The ENTER or RETURN is also considered a character, and is still waiting to be read. An extra **getchar** within the **if** statement reads and discards this second character.

ANATOMY: do/while loops

It is often necessary to continue doing an action while a condition is **TRUE**. C provides the powerful **do/while** construction to perform this continuous action, shown here in pseudo-code:

```
do {                        /* keep repeating */
    action1 ;               /* display prompt for the user */
    action2 ...             /* get the user's response */
} while (condition) ;       /* while the condition is TRUE */
```

The C keyword **do** and a left curly bracket **{** are placed before the list of actions. The list of action statements may be as long as necessary, and can include any C statement (including more **do/while**s). A right curly bracket **}**, the C keyword **while**, and a condition in parentheses are placed at the end of the list of actions.

The program will continue to act on the list of actions, starting with the first action and continuing until the **while** is reached, as long as the condition being tested is **TRUE**. As soon as the condition being tested is **FALSE**, the loop is exited and the program passes to the next statement after the **while**. The program will run every action in a **do/while** loop at least once. (We only check to see if we should continue after the last action is passed.)

Another Kind of Prompting

This is another strategy in prompting the user:

> Write a prompt for the user to enter a
> letter *Y* or a letter *N*. Read the
> response. If the response is valid, accept
> it and continue. If it is invalid, print
> an error message and read a new response
> until the response is valid.

The analysis in pseudocode is:

> prompt the user the first time
> get the first response
> as long as the response is invalid
>   display an error message
>   get a new response

The **C** program is:

```
#include <stdio.h>
#include <ctype.h>

main()
{       /* main */
    int         Response ;

    printf(
        "Are you feeling better about programming? (Y/N): ") ;
    Response = getchar() ;
    Response = tolower(Response) ;
    while (Response != 'y' && Response != 'n') {
        /* Throw away extra character left when user
         * typed ENTER.
         */
        Response = getchar() ;
        printf("\nYou entered an incorrect letter.\n") ;
        printf("Enter only 'Y' or 'N': ") ;
        Response = getchar() ;
        Response = tolower(Response) ;
    }
    if (Response == 'y')
        printf("I'm glad.") ;
    else
        printf("Keep trying.") ;
}       /* main */
```

ANATOMY: while loops

A **while** loop has this form:

```
while (Condition) {
    action1
    action2
. . .
}
```

The **C** keyword **while** begins the construction. After the word **while**, a condition is placed in parentheses. This condition follows the same format as the **if** and **do/while** constructions. After the parenthesis, a list of action statements is written, all enclosed in curly brackets. (Note: If there is only one action statement, the curly brackets may be dropped, just as in the **if** statement.)

A **while** loop does its test before the first action inside the loop is run. If the test fails, none of the actions is performed. It is important to know the crucial difference between **while** and **do/while** loops:

1. A **do/while** loop always does the actions at least once.
2. A **while** loop may never run at all if the condition fails the first time.

while loops are more frequently used in **C** programs than are **do/while loops**. It is usually important not to do an action the first time if a condition is **FALSE**.

3

Working With Numbers

We saw in Chapter 1 how **C** provides the capability for doing simple arithmetic.
C lets us do arithmetic much the same way we would when using a calculator; enter
the names of the constants or numeric variables and use numeric operators to do
the work:

```
+       Addition
-       Subtraction
*       Multiplication (prounounced star)
/       Division (prounounced slash)
```

Then, assign the results to a variable, or display the results directly.

This short program illustrates how numbers are handled in the **C** programming
language:

```
main()
{       /* main */
    int    Q,R,S ;

    Q = 15 ;
    R = 30 ;
    S = Q + R ;
    printf("The answer is: %d\n",S) ;
}       /* main */
```

The value of **S** is displayed as **45**.

More complex numeric operations can be performed. Such as:

```
Q = 15 ;
R = 30 ;
S = -3 ;
T = Q + R + S ;
```

S is valued at minus three. This is an example of the **unary minus** operator: take
the value and change the sign. **T** is equal to **42**, of course. Several addition operations are combined on one line; **C** permits arbitrarily complicated arithmetic
expressions.

This example presents a new problem:

```
Q = 15 ;
R = 30 ;
S = 3 ;
T = Q + R * S ;
```

Are Q and R added, then multiplied by S? Or, are R and S multiplied first, then Q added to the product? Each course of action produces a different result. The C programming language defines strict rules of *precedence* for the ordering of operators. They determine which operator precedes another in the order of execution.

Multiplication and division are performed first, moving from left to right in an expression. Addition and subtraction are next. After all these operators are evaluated, C recognizes the comparison operators such as $==$ and $>$. Next in order of precedence are the complex **&&** (AND) and the **||** (OR) operators. Only after all these are executed does C do **=** (assignment).

This means that, in the above example, R and S are multiplied first and Q is added to the product. Take this example:

```
if (A == 5 + 8 && B > 19)
```

The precedence rules say the **addition** operator is executed first; five and eight are added together. This is equivalent to:

```
if (A == 13 && B > 19)
```

It is then determined whether A is equal to thirteen and B is greater than nineteen. Assume A is thirteen and B is equal to twenty-five. Therefore:

```
if (TRUE && TRUE)
```

Both simple conditions are **TRUE**, so the complex condition is **TRUE**.

In C programming, always remember and refer to the order of precedence:

```
* and /              before
+ and -              before
== != > < >= <=      before
&& and ||            before
= (assignment)
```

An operation can be done out of the normal sequence by placing the desired operation inside a set of parentheses. In the previous example Q and R are added and then the result is multiplied by S. The correct form is:

```
T = (Q + R) * S ;
```

As many parentheses as are needed may be used to properly group the operators. Extra sets of parentheses are acceptable if they are matched in left and right pairs.

C provides several additional kinds of arithmetic operators that we will describe soon. Let's create a new program.

A Simple Calculator

Ask the user to select addition, subtraction, multiplication, or

division. Then read two numbers
from the keyboard and do the operation.
Display the results. Repeat the steps
until the user says to stop.

Pseudocode for this program specification is:

keep repeating
    ask the user for an operation
    ask the user for two numbers
    Do the operation and display the result
while the user waits to continue.

To ask the user whether we should continue
    read the response
    if a "y", return TRUE, otherwise return FALSE

A separate function will be written to ask the user whether or not to continue.

The program is:

```
#include <stdio.h>
#include <ctype.h>
#define TRUE   1
#define FALSE  0

main()
{    /* main */
    int     BadOperator ;
    int     Dummy ;
    int     FirstNumber ;
    int     Operation ;
    int     Result ;
    int     SecondNumber ;

    do {
        BadOperator = FALSE ;
        printf("Pick an operation: +, -, *, / ") ;
        Operation = getchar() ;
        printf("Enter your first number: ") ;
        scanf("%d",&FirstNumber) ;
        printf("Enter your second number: ") ;
        scanf("%d",&SecondNumber) ;
        switch (Operation) {
            case '+':   Result = FirstNumber + SecondNumber ;
                        break ;

            case '-':   Result = FirstNumber - SecondNumber ;
                        break ;

            case '*':   Result = FirstNumber * SecondNumber ;
                        break ;

            case '/':   Result = FirstNumber / SecondNumber ;
                        break ;

            default:    printf("You entered a bad operator.\n") ;
                        BadOperator = TRUE ;
                        break ;
        }
```

```
          /* Throw away extra character.
           */
          Dummy = getchar() ;
          if (BadOperator == FALSE)
               printf("The result is: %d\n",Result) ;
     } while (ContinueWorking()) ;
}        /* main */

int ContinueWorking()
/* ContinueWorking returns TRUE if the user presses a 'y'
 * in response to our prompt, and FALSE if the user presses
 * 'n' otherwise.
 */
{        /* ContinueWorking */
     int     Dummy ;
     int     Response ;

     printf("Would you like to do another problem? (Y/N): ") ;
     do {
          Response = getchar() ;
          Response = tolower(Response) ;
          if (Response != 'y' && Response != 'n') {
               printf("Enter only 'Y' or 'N': ") ;
               /* Throw away extra character.
                */
               Response = getchar() ;
          }
     } while (Response != 'y' && Response != 'n') ;
     /* Throw away extra character before returning.
      */
     Dummy = getchar() ;
     return((Response == 'y') ? TRUE : FALSE) ;
}        /* ContinueWorking */
```

This is our first major program, and deserves considerable explanation. Let's work downward.

The user is instructed to enter an **Operation**. The value entered is received into **Operation**. Note the validity of the entry is not yet checked. This is done in a later step.

Next, the user is instructed to enter two numbers. Numeric values entered by the user are read with the function **scanf** which has special properties.

The operation the user requests is performed. The **C switch** statement selects which operation to do. The result is displayed and the function **ContinueWorking** is called to ask the user the ''do another problem?'' question. **ContinueWorking** returns **TRUE** or **FALSE**, and is used directly in the condition. If **ContinueWorking** returns **TRUE**, the program loops back to the **do** and begins the statement list again. Note the **do/while** loop lets us do the loop once in any condition; the obvious assumption is the user will not run the program unless at least one problem is to be done.

ANATOMY: scanf and reading numbers

printf has a companion function for reading information: **scanf**. Compare the two functions:

```
printf("The result is: %d\n",Result) ;
scanf(                 "%d"  ,&FirstNumber) ;
```

The spacing has been exaggerated to emphasize the common components. As with **printf**, the first **scanf** argument is surrounded by double quotes. It defines what type of input to expect, just as the first **printf** argument describes what sort of output to display. **%d** is used as a parameter which means "read an integer." A comma is placed after the closing double quote, then the name of the **variable** to be read.

Notice the **C** operator **&** (prounounced "ampersand"). **&** means that **scanf** has permission to change the value of **FirstNumber**. Normally, the actual parameters given to a function are never changed by the function. To enable a function to change the value of a **variable**, you must prefix its name with **&**.

scanf changes the value of **FirstNumber**, so the **&** operator must be used. Leaving out **&** is one of the most common causes of problems in dealing with **scanf**. Unfortunately, the **C** compiler will not tell you if the **&** has been omitted. You must observe the rule without depending on the compiler to signal an error when the **&** has been omitted.

Several numbers can be read at once using **scanf**. To read both **FirstNumber** and **SecondNumber**, write:

```
scanf("%d %d",&FirstNumber,&SecondNumber) ;
```

Two **%d** symbols are used to show we want to read two integers. List in sequence the names of the two integers to be read, prefixing each with **&**, and separating each from the other with a comma.

scanf requires that an ENTER or RETURN end the input line. This extra character is not processed by **scanf**, and is read by the next input statement. An extra **getchar** reads and discards this character. This code is not bullet-proof: if the user enters extra spaces after the number these spaces must also be read and discarded. There is another function we will meet that solves this problem.

ANATOMY: switch

Different actions depend on the value of **Operation**. A series of **if-else** statements could be written:

```
if (Operation == '+')
   Result = FirstNumber + SecondNumber ;
else if (Operation == '-')
   Result = FirstNumber - SecondNumber ;
else if (Operation == '*')
   Result = FirstNumber * SecondNumber ;
else if (Operation == '/')
   Result = FirstNumber / SecondNumber ;
else {
   printf("You entered a bad operator.\n")
   BadOperator = TRUE ;
}
```

C provides the **switch** construction to simplify this code. The code is rewritten to show this construction:

```
switch (Operation) {        /* start switch */
   case '+':    Result = FirstNumber + SecondNumber ;
                break ;
   case '-':    Result = FirstNumber - SecondNumber ;
                break ;
```

```
case '*':      Result = FirstNumber * SecondNumber ;
               break ;
case '/':      Result = FirstNumber / SecondNumber ;
               break ;
default :      printf("You entered a bad operator.\n") ;
               BadOperator = TRUE ;
               break ;
}          /* end switch */
```

The format begins with the **C** keyword **switch**. This keyword is followed by a single value inside a set of parentheses; here it is **Operation**. This value can also be an arithmetic expression of any complexity. A left curly bracket starts the **switch** body.

Operation is matched against several constants: the characters '+', '−', '*', and '/'. Recall that character constants are enclosed in a set of single quotes. The constants to match are entered starting with the **C** keyword **case**, the constant itself, and then a colon. This is called a *case selector*. The spacing of each of the characters, constants, and keywords in our example is done purely to aid people reading the code.

If the character entered matches a case selector, an action is performed. This action is a set of statements that follows the colon and continues until either the keyword **break** or the closing right curly bracket that encloses all **case**s is found. For example, if the **Operation** entered is '+', the first selector is matched. Then:

```
Result = FirstNumber + SecondNumber ;
break ;
```

FirstNumber is added to **SecondNumber** and the value that results is assigned to **Result**. The keyword **break** stops the switch action and steers the program to the statement immediately following the closing right curly bracket. In this program example, when a character is matched, the program does the indicated action and then continues with **printf**.

What happens if **Operation** does not match any of the selectors? Normally, the program continues with the first statement following the closing right curly bracket. However, to trap all these exceptions, the keyword **default**, a colon, and an action are used. If the user accidently enters a # instead of a valid operator, the program goes to:

```
printf("You entered a bad operator.\n") ;
BadOperator = TRUE ;
```

Then the program continues. Displaying the result is conditional on **BadOperator** being **FALSE**. This test could be avoided by validating the **Operation** the user enters before continuing. In that case a **default** selector would not be needed because a valid **Operation** would have been ensured. This is done in the next example.

More About Functions

The function **ContinueWorking** prompts the user and determines whether the program should continue in the loop. Using this function in the **while** condition simplifies

the main program and makes the function clearer. A small piece of code fills in part
of the pseudocode analysis "while the user wants to continue":

```
int ContinueWorking()
/* ContinueWorking returns TRUE if the user presses a 'y'
 * in response to our prompt, and FALSE if the user presses
 * 'n' otherwise.
 */
{       /* ContinueWorking */
    int     Dummy ;
    int     Response ;

    printf("Would you like to do another problem? (Y/N): ") ;
    do {
        Response = getchar() ;
        Response = tolower(Response) ;
        if (Response != 'y' && Response != 'n') {
            printf("Enter only 'Y' or 'N': ") ;
            /* Throw away extra character.
             */
            Response = getchar() ;
        }
    } while (Response != 'y' && Response != 'n') ;
    /* Throw away extra character before returning.
     */
    Dummy = getchar() ;
    return((Response == 'y') ? TRUE : FALSE) ;
}       /* ContinueWorking */
```

ContinueWorking takes no parameters because the user supplies all the responses
directly; thus we have a set of parentheses containing nothing in our function definition. Note that, when using **ContinueWorking**, the empty parentheses must be used
to show **ContinueWorking** is a function, not a variable.

Inside the function, **Response** is defined to hold the user's *Y* or *N* response to the
question. The program prompts for an answer, then continues looping until either
a *Y* or a *N* is entered. (An upper-case or a lower-case letter, *Y* or *y*, or *N* or *n*, may
be entered.) Again the **do/while** loop lets us do the action once, then continue the action
until the conditions are met.

After a valid response is received, the **ternary operator** returns **TRUE** or **FALSE**
in a simple way. If **Response** is a y (notice **Response** was shifted to lower case with
tolower), **TRUE** is returned; otherwise **FALSE** is returned.

Note the extra **getchar** calls to discard unwanted characters left over when the user
presses RETURN or ENTER.

A Revision Using continue and break

Let's revise the specification slightly:

> Ask the user to select addition, subtraction,
> multiplication, or division. Then read two
> numbers from the keyboard and do the operation.
> Display the results. Repeat the steps until
> the user says to stop. If the user enters an
> unknown operator, reprompt and continue. If
> the user enters a negative number for either
> number, stop the program.

Pseudocode for this program specification is:

keep repeating
>   ask the user for an operation
>   if (the operation is unknown)
>>   start the loop over
>   ask the user for two numbers
>   if (either number is negative)
>>   stop the program
>   Do the operation and display the result
while the user wants to continue.

The revised program is:

```c
#include <stdio.h>
#include <ctype.h>
#define TRUE    1
#define FALSE   0

main()
{       /* main */
    int     Dummy ;
    int     FirstNumber ;
    int     Operation ;
    int     Result ;
    int     SecondNumber ;

    do {
        printf("Pick an operation: +, -, *, / ") ;
        Operation = getchar() ;
        /* Check Operation for validity.  Return immediately
         * to the beginning of the loop if Operator is
         * unknown.
         */
        if (Operation != '+' && Operation != '-' &&
                    Operation != '*' && Operation != '/') {
            printf("You entered a bad operation.\n") ;
            /* Discard unwanted character.
             */
            Dummy = getchar() ;
            continue ;
        }
        printf("Enter your first number: ") ;
        scanf("%d",&FirstNumber) ;
        printf("Enter your second number: ") ;
        scanf("%d",&SecondNumber) ;
        /* If either number is negative, stop immediately.
         */
        if (FirstNumber < 0 || SecondNumber < 0)
            break ;
        switch (Operation) {
            case '+':   Result = FirstNumber + SecondNumber ;
                        break ;

            case '-':   Result = FirstNumber - SecondNumber ;
                        break ;

            case '*':   Result = FirstNumber * SecondNumber ;
                        break ;

            case '/':   Result = FirstNumber / SecondNumber ;
```

```
                        break ;
            }
        printf("The result is: %d\n",Result) ;
        /* Discard the unwanted character remaining.
         */
        Dummy = getchar() ;
    } while (ContinueWorking()) ;
}       /* main */
```

ContinueWorking is the same as in the first version of the program. The program is considerably simplified by using two **C** statements, **break** and **continue**.

ANATOMY: continue

If the user enters an unknown operation, we want to stop running through the loop and start the loop all over again. This is easily done with the **continue** statement:

```
do {

    beginning of loop . . .

    /* Check Operation for validity.  Return
     * immediately to the beginning of the loop
     * if Operator is unknown.
     */
    if (Operation != '+' && Operation != '-' &&
            Operation != '*' && Operation != '/') {

            . . .

            continue ;
    }

        rest of loop . . .
} while ( . . . ) ;
```

If **Operation** is not an allowed operator, an error message is displayed and the loop is executed from the beginning again. A diagram makes this clearer:

```
|      do {
|
|          beginning of loop . . .
|
 -----> if (. . .) {

                . . .

            continue ;
        }

        rest of loop . . .
    } while ( . . . ) ;
```

The error-test succeeds, and the error message is displayed, and the program continues (**continue**):

```
            do {

                    beginning of loop . . .

                    if (. . .) {
                          . . .
-- go to end <-- continue ;
¦              }
¦
¦                   rest of loop . . .
¦
-----> } while ( . . . ) ;
```

continue causes the program to jump to the end of the loop. In this case, the **while** test is made. If the condition succeeds, the loop begins again:

```
            do {

--------->    beginning of loop . . .
¦
¦             if (. . .) {
¦
¦                   . . .
¦
¦                   continue ;
¦             }
¦
¦             rest of loop . . .
¦
------ } while ( . . . ) ;
```

continue enables an escape from an error state before entering the **switch**. The **default** clause is not needed in **switch** because **Operation** is validated before use.

ANATOMY: break

It has been shown how **break** works in **switch** statements to skip all the remaining statements in the **switch**. **break** also takes the program immediately out of any loop:

```
do {

        beginning of loop . . .

        read FirstNumber and SecondNumber . . .
      /* If either number is negative, stop immediately.
       */
      if (FirstNumber < 0 ¦¦ SecondNumber < 0)
         break ;
         remainder of loop . . .

} while (ContinueWorking()) ;
```

Assume that **FirstNumber** is less than zero. The loop execution starts with the **do**:

```
¦   do {
¦
¦          beginning of loop . . .
¦
¦          read FirstNumber and SecondNumber . . .
¦        /* If either number is negative, stop immediately.
¦         */
¦        if (FirstNumber < 0 ¦¦ SecondNumber < 0)
---->      break ;

           remainder of loop . . .

      } while (ContinueWorking()) ;
```

When **break** is executed, the program immediately leaves the loop and moves to the statement following the **while**:

```
do {
        beginning of loop . . .

        read FirstNumber and SecondNumber . . .
     /* If either number is negative, stop immediately.
      */
     if (FirstNumber < 0 || SecondNumber < 0)
----<   break ;

        remainder of loop . . .

    } while (ContinueWorking()) ;

----> remainder of program
```

A Table Of Squares

Suppose a table of squares of integers is needed. The requirements are:

Print a table with the square of all
numbers between one and one hundred.

The program is short and simple:

```
#include <stdio.h>

main()
{       /* main */
    int     Count ;

    printf("Table of Squares:\n\n") ;
    for (Count = 1 ; Count <= 100 ; Count = Count + 1)
        printf("Number: %d   Square: %d\n",Count,Count * Count) ;
}       /* main */
```

ANATOMY: for

for is the most powerful **C** looping statement because it defines the loop starting state, the **while** condition, and the increment condition in a single statement. Using **while**, the program is formed as follows:

```
Count = 1 ;
while (Count <= 100) {
    printf("Number: %d   Square: %d\n",Count,Count * Count) ;
    Count = Count + 1 ;
}
```

for makes it possible to express this more clearly and simply as shown in the next diagram. The initialization statement is placed after the left parenthesis. This sets up the variables to start the loop. The **while** condition is put after the first semicolon; while this condition is **TRUE**, continue looping. The increment statement is placed after the second semicolon; every time the program goes through the loop, this statement is done after every other action has been performed.

```
-- Count = 1 ;
|
| while (Count <= 100) { -
|     printf( . . . ) ;      |
|     Count = Count + 1 ; --------------
| }                        |           |
|                          |           |
 -----------               |           |
           |               |           |
           v               v           v
     for (Count = 1 ; Count <= 100 ; Count = Count + 1)
          printf( . . . ) ;
```

This loop starts **Count** at one and displays **Count** and its square. This is the only action statement in the loop. Then one is added to the old value of **Count**, which sets **Count** equal to one plus its old value. On the second trip through the loop, **Count** (now equal to two) and its square are displayed. We continue taking trips until **Count** equals one hundred. When one is added to it, we get one hundred one and the **while** condition fails; it is no longer **TRUE**. Exit the loop and go on with the next statement in the program. In this short program, we stop.

A Revision for Conciseness

The program can be written more concisely with another **C** numeric operator:

```
#include <stdio.h>

main()
{       /* main */
    int     Count ;

    printf("Table of Squares\n\n") ;
    for (Count = 1 ; Count <= 100 ; Count++)
        printf("Number: %d    Square: %d\n",Count,Count * Count) ;
}       /* main */
```

ANATOMY: the autoincrement and
autodecrement operators

It is often necessary to take the old or original value of a variable and add one to it, incrementing the variable's value. C has an operator that simplifies and makes the code compact. The construction:

```
Count = Count + 1 ;
```

can be replaced by:

```
Count++ ;
```

The double-plus signs **++** mean "increment the value of this variable."

In the sequence of statements:

```
I = 5 ;
J = I ;
I = I + 1 ;
```

I is five and J is six.

These statements can be rewritten as:

```
I = 5 ;
J = I++ ;
```

First the value of I (which is five) is assigned to J. Then the value of I is incremented by one, setting I to six. The autoincrement operator can be combined into other statements, eliminating separate increment statements in the process.

The form **I++** is called the *autopostincrement* operator. The old value of I is assigned to J. I is incremented only after the statement is performed.

C provides another form, called the *autopreincrement* operator. It increments the value of its variable before it is used. Replace:

```
I = 5 ;
I = I + 1 ;
J = I ;
```

with

```
I = 5 ;
J = ++I ;
```

In C there are also two operators to decrement the value of a variable. They are the *autopredecrement* and *autopostdecrement* operators. To assign J the value of I and then subtract one from I, write:

```
J = I-- ;
```

To subtract one before it is assigned, write:

```
J = --I ;
```

Order Of Evaluation

The autoincrement and autodecrement operators can be used in complex statements. They apply only to the variable immediately preceding them (for the post-operators) or following them (for the pre-operators).

```
J = I++ - K + 3 ;
```

Take the old value of I, subtract K, and add three. Assign this value to J, and then increment I. The autopostincrement operator applies only to I.

More Problems

Hypothesize that the table of squares must be longer. Squares of numbers through two hundred are required. Rewrite the program using a temporary variable assigned the value of the square:

```
#include <stdio.h>
#define STARTNUM    1
#define ENDNUM      200
```

```
main()
{      /* main */
    int    Count ;
    int    Square ;

    printf("Table of Squares\n\n") ;
    for (Count = STARTNUM ; Count <= ENDNUM ; Count++) {
        Square = Count * Count ;
        printf("Number: %d   Square: %d\n",Count,Square) ;
    }
}      /* main */
```

A problem may be found on many, but not all microcomputers when the square of 182 is written:

```
Number: 182   Square: -32412
```

What happened? Negative numbers have not been used at all. How can the square of a positive number be negative?

The problem is that the largest number C can store in an **int**eger has been exceeded. Many microcomputers have a limit of 32,767 as the largest positive integer they can store in an **int**eger. When that limit is passed, the machine *overflows* and the number is transformed into something unexpected! Some machines have a larger limit on **int**egers; consult your C compiler documentation for more information.

ANATOMY: longs

C gets around all these limitations with a data type for integers that need more storage space. Whenever large integers are needed, the variable is declared **long**. On many machines, a **long** stores numbers that can range up to two billion. Again, see your C compiler documentation for details and limitations.

The program now becomes:

```
#include <stdio.h>
#define STARTNUM   1
#define ENDNUM     200

main()
{      /* main */
    int    Count ;
    long   Square ;

    printf("Table of Squares\n\n") ;
    for (Count = STARTNUM ; Count <= ENDNUM ; Count++) {
        Square = Count * Count ;
        printf("Number: %d    Square: %ld\n",Count,Square) ;
    }
}      /* main */
```

Square is now a **long**. Is the wraparound problem into negative numbers solved? We shall see.

ANATOMY: printing longs

Something must be added to the **printf** statement:

```
printf("Number: %d    Square: %ld\n",Count,Square) ;
                                ^
                                !
                          print a long
```

To display a **long**, the letter l (lowercase L) must be placed between the percent sign and the **d**. This means the integer to be displayed is really a **long**.

But It Still Doesn't Work!

If you tried the last solution, you found the problem still is there. What happened?

C looks at the statement:

```
Square = Count * Count ;
```

This statement is interpreted to mean:

"Take the **int**eger **Count** and multiply it by
Count. Both these numbers are **int**egers,
and so we get an **int**eger back. Assign this
number to the **long** number **Square**."

The problem is that **int**eger is still being used in the calculation. When the multiplication is performed, **C** gives an *integer*, not a *long* as the result. The wraparound occurs until the calculation uses **longs**.

Two choices are available. (1) Change the declaration for **Count** to **long**; now the calculation involves two **longs**. (2) Or this can be done:

```
#include <stdio.h>
#define STARTNUM    1
#define ENDNUM     200

main()
{      /* main */
    int    Count ;
    long   Square ;

    printf("Table of Squares\n\n") ;
    for (Count = STARTNUM ; Count <= ENDNUM ; Count++) {
        Square = (long)Count * (long)Count ;
        printf("Number: %d    Square: %ld\n",Count,Square) ;
    }
}      /* main */
```

ANATOMY: casts

C enables the conversion of one data type to another in the middle of a statement. This is done with a new construction, called a *cast*. The multiplication reads:

```
Square = (long)Count * (long)Count ;
            ^              ^
            !              !
            ---------------- convert to a long
```

The variable name is prefixed with the name of the desired data type in parentheses. **C** converts the old type into the new data type before doing the calculation. Casts have a higher precedence than any other operator we have used. Therefore, it is guaranteed the type conversion happens before the multiplication.

long can be converted to **int**, **char** to **int**. Almost any data type can be converted to any other.

ANATOMY: mixed type arithmetic

With **C**, types can be mixed in an expression. The multiplication can be rewritten as:

```
Square = (long)Count * Count ;
```

Because one of the two numbers in the multiplication is **long**, the calculation is done using **long** arithmetic. Before doing the calculation, **C** converts all other numbers automatically to this data type. **C** automatically:

1. converts **char** to **int** in all expressions;
2. converts **int** or **char** to **long** whenever one part of the expression is **long**.

Use casts to do explicitly the type conversion whenever your program depends on the conversion being done correctly. Depending on automatic conversion is dangerous.

4

Numbers with Fractions

Preview

C provides comprehensive mathematical facilities, and we begin to look at them closely in this chapter. All the numbers used so far are **int**egers. They are whole numbers with zero values to the right of the decimal point. Problems we want to solve may deal with fractions; numbers with greater-than-zero values to the right of the decimal point.

C has two data types to handle numbers with fractions: **float** and **double**. Numbers with fractional parts or decimal points are often called "floating point" numbers. Hence we have the short-form reference, the declaration **float**.

float and **double** numbers must be declared, just as **int**egers must be declared:

```
float      A ;
double     B ;
```

A is a **float**, and **B** is a **double**.

float and **double** differ only in the number of fractional digits the computer will store. If the requirement is for great precision in calculation, declare **double**; otherwise use the **float** declaration. Internally, **C** performs all calculations using **double** so precision is not lost and roundoff errors are not incurred. Floating point arithemetic can defy the rules of mathematics. All floating point calculations are subject to errors in calculation. Take this equation as an example:

```
Q = 5.0
R = 4.0
S = 5.0 / 4.0 ;
```

Here, the value of S may equal 1.24999—not exactly 1.25. The computer rounds off floating point calculations.

Writing Floating Point Constants

Floating point constants are written in two ways.

49

1. The most straightforward is as a number with a decimal point:

```
 1.3
111.7
-15.0
```

Each number has an integer part, a decimal point, and a fractional part. Note that, even if the number has no fractional part, a zero may be explicitly written as the fraction.

2. Floating point can be written to represent numbers larger or smaller than those we would normally write in a simple decimal notation. For example:

```
 0.00000345    becomes    3.45E-6
1234000000.0   becomes    1.234E9
```

The decimal number is followed by the letter **E** and an exponent value:

```
10exponent
```

The decimal number is multiplied by this power. This provides an easy way to write numbers with great variation in magnitude.

Different **C** implementations have different degrees of precision for **float**s and **double**s. (See your compiler's documentation for specific details.)

Round-off errors can be a problem in floating point calculations. Although this is the most serious problem, there are others to be aware of. Floating point operations take longer to do than **int**egers. **float** and **double** take much more memory to store than do **int**egers. In the interest of efficiency, floating point arithmetic should be used only when actually needed.

A Useful Exercise: Temperature Conversion

A table can be created for converting temperatures from Fahrenheit to Celsius. The objective is:

Display a table of degrees in Fahrenheit from zero to three hundred. Display an entry for every fifth-degree Fahrenheit.

The program is:

```
#include <stdio.h>
#define   ENDINGDEG     300
#define   INCREMENT     5
#define   STARTINGDEG   0

main()
{     /* main */
    float      DegCel ;
    int        DegFahr ;

    for (DegFahr = STARTINGDEG ; DegFahr < ENDINGDEG ;
            DegFahr = DegFahr + INCREMENT) {
        DegCel = (5.0 / 9.0) * ((float)DegFahr - 32.0) ;
        printf("Fahrenheit: %5d Celsius: %6.2f\n",
            DegFahr,DegCel) ;
    }
}     /* main */
```

DegFahr is declared as **integer**. **DegCel** is declared as **float**. The starting degree, the ending degree, and the increment are defined as integer constants. This shift from integers to floats is intentional. Round-off errors occur in floating point arithmetic. It is always best to use integer values as loop variables and test against integer constants. In particular, do not test for equality against a floating point constant; because of round-off, things that should be equal very often are not!

The **for** loop operates on **DegFahr** from **STARTINGDEG** while it is less than **ENDINGDEG**. Each time the program passes through the loop, the value of **DegFahr** is incremented by 5.

Words and operators have been spaced in the **for** statement and in **printf** for cosmetic reasons, to visually clarify the program; this is not done for the sake of the compilation process, as has been pointed out before. Within certain limitations, you can lay out **C** programs as you see fit without changing their meaning.

The cast **(float)** is used in the calculation to explicitly convert the integer **DegFahr** to a float before doing the calculation.

ANATOMY: printing floating point numbers

Floating point numbers are displayed using **printf**. The formatting specification (the value between the double quotes) uses a new notation for floating point numbers:

```
printf("Fahrenheit:  %5d Celsius:  %6.2f\n",DegFahr,DegCel) ;
                                      ^
                                      ¦
                            print a float
```

A **float** is specified by the symbols **%f**. This means "display a **float** in the usual format without an exponent;" that is, 15.5.

printf provides special controls we have not yet used. The specification **%6.2f** means "display a **float** value in a minimum of six print positions, including one position for the decimal point, and allow for two digits to the right of the decimal point." Thus we have:

```
-----------------
¦                ¦
¦          %6.2f
¦             ¦
¦             ---- two digits to the right of the
¦                ¦  decimal point.
¦              . v
¦    ¦__¦__¦__¦__¦__¦
¦     1  2  3  4  5  6
¦
--------> total width is six
```

If the number is 15, the specification **%6.2f** will display:

```
      1  5  .  0  0
 ¦__¦__¦__¦__¦__¦__¦
  1  2  3  4  5  6
```

A leading space is displayed in the above example. However, if the number is greater than one thousand, the entire number is displayed; it appears to be more space than the **%6.2f** format specifies. Remember: the specification is the *minimum* space used for formatting. **C** prefers the right answer rather than a consistent format.

If the numbers are quite large or very small, you may want to display them with an exponent. For such situations, rewrite the above statement as:

```
printf("Fahrenheit: %5d Celsius: %6.2e\n",DegFahr,DegCel) ;
```

The **%e** means "display a **float** in exponential notation." The specification **%6.2** means "display the number in a *minimum* of six print positions and allow for two digits to the right of the decimal point." When the **e** format is used, space must be reserved for the exponent in the field width. When 15 is displayed in a **%6.2e** format, it appears as:

```
   1 .  5   E   0   0
|__|__|__|__|__|__|
   1   2   3   4   5   6
```

A **double** is displayed by adding a lower-case L to the printing format in the same way as for a **long**. If **A** is a **double**, it is displayed as:

```
printf("The value of A is: %10.5lf\n",A) ;
                               ^
                               |
                          print a double
```

The **l** symbol (lower-case L) establishes the value of **A** as a **double**.

C provides a third format. The **printf** statement can be written as:

```
printf("Fahrenheit: %5d Celsius: %6.2g\n",DegFahr,DegCel) ;
```

The **%g** symbol instructs the program to use either **%f** or, **%e**, whichever is shorter. Some **C** compilers do not implement **%g**. (See your compiler's documentation for details.)

Rewrite The Program

The program can be more concisely written by using the arithmetic operator **+ =**

```
#include <stdio.h>
#define   ENDINGDEG     300
#define   INCREMENT     5
#define   STARTINGDEG   0

main()
{      /* main */
    float       DegCel ;
    int         DegFahr ;

    for (DegFahr = STARTINGDEG ; DegFahr < ENDINGDEG ;
            DegFahr += INCREMENT) {
        DegCel = (5.0 / 9.0) * ((float)DegFahr - 32.0) ;
        printf("Fahrenheit: %5d Celsius: %6.2f\n",
                DegFahr,DegCel) ;
    }
}      /* main */
```

ANATOMY: combined arithmetic-assignment operators

The autoincrement and autodecrement operators can replace statements such as:

```
I = I + 1 ;
```

with

```
I++ ;
```

In the original program, five was added to **DegFahr** to get the next value to display. C has a set of operators to handle this sort of expression. Rewrite:

```
DegFahr = DegFahr + 5 ;



DegFahr += 5 ;
```

Take the **variable** name from the right hand side of the assignment operator and replace the assignment operator = with the add-and-assign operator **+ =**. This operator means "add the right hand side of the statement to the old value of the variable on the left hand side of the statement, then reassign this new value to the same variable."

C provides a full range of these operators:

```
+=    means add and assign
-=    means subtract and assign
*=    means multiply and assign
/=    means divide and assign
```

A Table of Squares and Square Roots

Square roots can be added to the table-of-squares program. The new definition of the objective is:

Print all square roots and squares for
whole numbers between zero and one hundred.

HAZARD: math.h

Many C's, including UNIX's, require the additional header file **math.h** whenever a special mathematical function is used. Other compilers have no such **#include** file. (Consult Appendixes A and D, and your compiler's documentation for details.)

The program's code is:

```
#include <stdio.h>
#include <math.h>
#define STARTNUM    1
#define ENDNUM      200
```

```
extern double  sqrt() ;

main()
{       /* main */
    int     Count ;
    double Root ;
    long    Square ;

    printf("Table of Squares and Square Roots\n\n") ;
    for (Count = STARTNUM ; Count <= ENDNUM ; Count++) {
        Square = (long)Count * (long)Count ;
        Root = sqrt((double)Count) ;
        printf("Number: %d Square: %ld Root: %10.5lf\n",
                Count,Square,Root) ;
    }
}       /* main */
```

ANATOMY: Math Functions

C provides a rich set of mathematical functions. Check the documentation for your compiler. Most compilers minimally provide:

```
sqrt()    square root
sin()     sine of a radian value
cos()     cosine of a radian value
exp()     exponential function
log()     natural logarithm
```

These math **functions** take a single parameter which must be a **double**. They return a **double** to the caller. Whenever one of these **functions** is used in a program, it must be specifically declared. We will learn more about declaring functions later. For the moment, do remember, before any of them is used, the **functions** must be declared as:

```
extern double sqrt() ;
extern double sin()  ;
```

The C compiler will not warn of incorrect use or display a relevant error message. A C program checker like **lint** may find these problems. Sometimes the **math.h** header file includes these definitions. (Check the content of your compiler's **math.h** file.)

Casts Again

Unlike most of the functions discussed so far, these math functions require a double as their parameter. In all our previous uses of functions, either **char**acters or **int**egers have been passed. If a function requires a parameter to be a particular type, your system's documentation will say:

```
double sqrt(val) ;
double val ;
```

This means that **sqrt** (square root) is a function that returns a **double** and takes a single parameter. The parameter (in the documentation, the formal parameter **val**) is a **double**. (Always check the documentation for the specific compiler to determine its requirements, before using a new function.)

When a parameter of a particular type is to be passed and there is any doubt of the type of the parameter, use a **cast**:

```
Root = sqrt( (double)Count ) ;
```

Count is declared an **int**eger. It must be converted to a **double** before giving it to **sqrt**. A **cast**, **(double)**, converts the type to a **double** before it is used.

Mixed Type Calculations

In dealing with **int** and **long**, an **int** is promoted automatically to a **long** before calculation. In floating point calculations, **int**, **long**, and **float** are converted to **double**. However, if the right-hand expression contains only **int**egers, the arithmetic is calculated in the **int**eger mode:

```
double    A ;

A = (5 + 6) / 12 ;
```

Because of the parentheses surrounding them, 5 and 6 are added first to give 11. Eleven is divided by 12. This produces A as 0, not as a fraction. Eleven divided by 12 is 0 plus a fraction. Since the only **double** is on the left-hand side of the assignment operator, the arithmetic is done in **int**eger mode, and then the result is converted to **double**. We can write either:

```
A = (5.0 + 6.0) / 12.0 ;
```

or

```
A = ((double)5 + (double)6) / (double)12 ;
```

Each produces the same result.

5

Arrays and Input/Output to Strange Places

A Series of Instructive Histogram Programs

In business and science, one often has the need to display data graphically in histograms or bar charts. A program to generate histograms can be written easily from what we've learned so far.

The objective is:

Ask the user to state the number of
values to graph in the histogram.
Read the values in and print a bar
graph made of stars to the display.

This is the strategy:

Prompt the user to enter the number of values to plot.
for this number of values {.
Get the value to graph from the user.
Print the number at the beginning of the line,
followed by the correct number of stars.
}

Here's the first solution, HISTOGRAM-1:

```
#include <stdio.h>

main()
{       /* main */

    int     EntryCount ; /* looping variable--the entry number */
    int     NumEntries ; /* total number of entries */
    int     StarCount ;  /* counter of the current number of stars */
    int     Value ;      /* value of the specific entry */
    printf("How Many Entries Will You Make? ") ;
    scanf("%d",&NumEntries) ;
```

```
for (EntryCount = 0 ; EntryCount < NumEntries ; EntryCount++) {
    printf("\nFor Entry %d, Type a Value Between 0 and 100: ",
                    EntryCount + 1) ;
    scanf("%d",&Value) ;

    /* First, display the Value, then a bar to
     * represent the base of the graph.
     */
    printf("%d | ",Value) ;

    /* To fit up to 100 stars on a single line, display
     * half-the number of stars according to Value.
     */
    for (StarCount = 0 ; StarCount < Value / 2 ; StarCount++)
        printf("*") ;
    printf("\n") ;
  }
}       /* main */
```

The first **for** loop repeats for the number of entries the user has requested. The program prompts the user to enter a number. Note that one is added to **EntryCount** in the **printf** statement so the count begins with one, not zero. The inner **for** loop repeats for the number of stars to be displayed, represented by the user's entry. The value entered is divided by two so that fifty stars can be displayed on one line to represent a number of one hundred. This value-modification is called *scaling*.

Using Floating Point Numbers

It's unreasonable to expect the user to enter only integers. Floating point numbers can easily be added to the program. And, to dress things up a bit, the program is revised to clear the screen before displaying new information. Here, therefore, is the revised histogram program HISTOGRAM-2:

```
#include <stdio.h>
#define NUMTOCLEAR   25

main()
{       /* main */
    int     EntryCount ; /* looping variable--the entry number */
int     LineCount ;
int     NumEntries ; /* total number of entries */
int     StarCount ;   /* counter of the current number of stars */
float   Value ;       /* value of the specific entry */

/* Clear the screen with NUMTOCLEAR newlines.
 */
for (LineCount = 0 ; LineCount < NUMTOCLEAR ; LineCount++)
    printf("\n") ;

printf("How Many Entries Will You Make? ") ;
scanf("%d",&NumEntries) ;

for (EntryCount = 0 ; EntryCount < NumEntries ;
                EntryCount++) {
    printf("\nFor entry %d, type a value between 0 and 100: ",
                EntryCount + 1) ;
    scanf("%f",&Value) ;
```

```
/* Display the floating-point Value, then a bar
 * to represent the base of the graph.
 */
printf("%5.1f | ",Value) ;

/* To fit a value up to 100 on a single line, display
 * half the number of stars according to "Value" by
 * dividing Value by 2.
 */
for (StarCount = 0 ; StarCount < (int)Value / 2 ;
            StarCount++)
    printf("*") ;
printf("\n") ;
    }
}      /* main */
```

The screen is cleared by sending **NUMTOCLEAR** newlines to the screen. **NUMTOCLEAR** is defined as the quantity 25.

The first arguments have been changed in **scanf** and **printf** to read and write floating point numbers. Note a cast is used to convert **Value** from a float to an integer in the **for** loop comparison because **Value** is divided by an integer (the number two) and compares the result with an integer (**Count**). The cast isn't necessary, but it is good programming style to explicitly show the type conversion.

How to Save the Result

HISTOGRAM-2 is a useful program, but it only displays its results on the screen. However, **C** does enable the output of a program to be saved in a file by using redirection. Let's see how this works.

Redirection of Input and Output

C programs often behave like a machine with one way in and one way out:

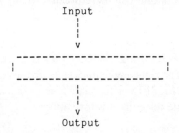

```
Input
    |
    |
    v
-----------------------
|                       |
-----------------------
    |
    |
    v
Output
```

Input data comes from one place; output data goes to another. Our example programs so far have depended on information taken from the user's keyboard as the input source. Then, each of the example programs has written or displayed the output on the terminal's screen.

Suppose we prefer to route the output of a program to a new, separate file on a disk instead of to the screen. Let's say the last histogram program is named **HISTOGRM**. Without any change to the program itself, enter the following on the command line when calling up the program:

```
histogrm >outfile
```

The program will run, and its output will be written directly to the file which, on the command line, is named **OUTFILE**. This is an example of *redirection* of output.

C has two keywords associated with programs; one is **stdin** (standard input) and the other is **stdout** (standard output). If we say all input normally is read from **stdin** (the keyboard), and all output is written to **stdout** (the display), the diagram becomes:

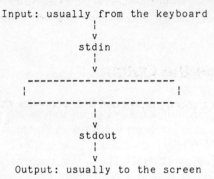

```
Input: usually from the keyboard
                    ¦
                    v
                 stdin
                    ¦
                    v
       ------------------------
       ¦                      ¦
       ------------------------
                    ¦
                    v
                 stdout
                    ¦
                    v
      Output: usually to the screen
```

All calls to **scanf** are read from **stdin**. All calls to **printf** are written to **stdout**. When a **C** program that uses these functions to read and write with **stdin** and **stdout** is run, the input can be made to come from any file by placing a left angle bracket < on the command line after the program name and immediately before the input file name:

```
progname <inputfile
```

The program named **PROGNAME** redirects **stdin** to come from **INPUTFILE** rather than from the keyboard.

Likewise, with a right angle bracket > all output can be redirected to any file by writing:

```
progname >outputfile
```

Thus, the program redirects all output from *PROGNAME* to **OUTPUTFILE** which otherwise would go to the terminal's screen. The right angle bracket > on the command line means ''redirect output to the named file.'' The left and right angle brackets may be freely combined on the command line to redirect information:

```
progname <inputfile >outputfile
```

Problems With Redirection: stderr

When running the histogram program with redirection, you will note all output which would have otherwise gone to the screen passed instead, to the redirected file. This means all prompts the user normally sees are also redirected. Therefore, redirection does not work satisfactorily with *interactive* programs.

Non-interactive programs may print error messages to **stdout**, the screen. Obviously, you will not see these messages if you use redirection. **C** deals with this problem by providing a third file, **stderr** (pronounced ''standard error''), where serious error messages the user should see are displayed. **stderr** is not usually redirected.

Strictly speaking, **stdin**, **stdout**, and **stderr** are not part of the **C** language itself. Rather, they are defined in the header file **stdio.h**. Whenever reference is made to these names, or to functions that require these names, **stdio.h** must be included in the program.

Explicit Files Neatly Save the Output

As an introduction to files in **C**, let's specify a program that meets this simple objective:

Write a program that displays a message
on the screen and, at the same time, writes
one to a new file that you create.

Here is the solution demonstrated in HISTOGRAM-3:

```
#include <stdio.h>

main()
{        /* main */
    FILE   *OutFile ;

    OutFile = fopen("OUT","w") ;
    printf("This line is going to the screen.\n") ;
    fprintf(OutFile,"But this one is going to the file OUT.\n") ;
    fclose(OutFile) ;
}        /* main */
```

ANATOMY: files

C enables reading and writing information to many files. When it is necessary to read and write to a file and redirection is not desirable, explicit file input and output routines are used. **stdin**, **stdout**, and **stderr** are files that are usually predefined in **C** programs. If **stdio.h** is included, these names are reserved. To use a new file, declare it this way:

```
FILE   *OutFile ;   /* This means OutFile is a
                     * pointer to FILE.
                     */
```

This declaration is read: ''**OutFile** is a pointer to a **FILE**.'' **FILE** is a type defined in **stdio.h**. We will explain later what the ''star'' (asterisk) adjacent to **OutFile** means; but remember that the * must be used in front of the variable name when a **FILE** is declared.

The operating system you use refers to information as being stored in files. These files are named when they are created. For example, a file is named and created when you use a text editor. This is *file creation*. A file is opened and updated when a pre-existing file is edited with a text editor; this is *file updating*. Four kinds of files are defined:

1. Files for input: read-only from these files.
2. Files for output: write-only to these files.
3. Files for appending: write-only to these files, but start at the end of an existing file.
4. Files for update: modify an existing file.

C enables control over the class of file used in the programs.

Before the variable **OutFile** is used in the program, it must be given a value. The following statement uses **fopen** to create a file named **OUT**.

```
OutFile = fopen("OUT","w") ;
```

A file with a name of your choice can be created merely by replacing **OUT** with a different name.

fopen is a system function that takes two arguments inside a set of parentheses. The first is the name the operating system uses to refer to the file to be operated on. The second argument is the mode in which the file is to be opened:

```
      OutFile = fopen("OUT","w") ;
         ^              ^    ^
         !              !    !
  the new file          !    --- open for writing
     variable           !
                        --- open the file named OUT
```

When the program ends, the new file **OUT** is written (''w'') to the disk. Outside the program, the operating system knows the file by the name enclosed in the first pair of double quotes. Inside the program, the file variable **OutFile** is used to refer to the same file. The **C** file variable and the operating system name are associated by **fopen**.

As shown above, a file is opened for writing by passing a lowercase **w** in double quotes as the second parameter to **fopen**.

A file is opened for reading by passing a lowercase **r** in double quotes as the second parameter:

```
InFile = fopen("INPUT","r") ;
```

The above statement opens the existing file named ''INPUT'' for reading. Again, all **C** file variables must be opened before use.

C assumes all files opened for reading already exist. If the program cannot find the requested file, **fopen** returns a zero. Correct file opening can be checked with this statement:

```
if ((InFile = fopen("INPUT","r")) == 0)
   display an error message
```

The embedded assignment attempts to open the file, then tests to determine whether **fopen** was successful.

C assumes all files opened for writing DO NOT exist. If they DO exist under the same name, the previous content is destroyed and we start afresh. To append information to an already existing file, open the file for appending:

```
OutFile = fopen("OUT","a") ;
```

The lowercase **a** in double quotes means "append."

If the program cannot open a file for writing or appending, **fopen** again returns zero. This is usually a symptom of a serious operating system problem.

ANATOMY: closing files

Before a program finishes, all opened files must be closed. Usually the program closes all files automatically before it ends. It is good practice, however, to explicitly close files opened by the program. The function **fclose** closes a file:

```
fclose(OutFile) ;
```

fclose takes a single parameter, a pointer to a file returned by a call to **fopen**.

ANATOMY: file handling functions

C provides a full set of functions for reading from and writing to files. To read a character at a time, use **getc**:

```
InputChar = getc(InFile) ;
```

where **InFile** is a file opened for reading. Remember that **C** predefines a file for reading called **stdin**. **getchar** is a special case of **getc** that does not require an explicit **stdin**:

```
InputChar = getc(stdin) ;
InputChar = getchar() ;
```

getchar can be replaced with **getc(stdin)** at any time.

To read input with a desired format, use **fscanf**:

```
int     Q,R ;
FILE    *InFile ;

InFile = fopen("NAME","r") ;
fscanf(InFile,"%d %d",&Q,&R) ;
```

Use **fscanf** in the same way as **scanf**; the opened file variable is the first parameter to the function, followed by the parameters normally used for **scanf**. **scanf** is a special case of **fscanf**; it can be written:

```
fscanf(stdin,"%d",&Q) ;
```

or

```
scanf("%d",&Q) ;
```

Either **printf** or **fprintf** is used to print text. **printf** does not require an explicit **stdout**. Notice the differences in this example:

```
printf("Result is: %d\n",Result) ;
```

or

```
fprintf(stdout,"Result is: %d\n",Result) ;
```

Again, **printf** is a special case of **fprintf**:

```
printf("Result is: %d\n",Result) ;
```

or

```
fprintf(OutFile,"Result is: %d\n",Result) :
```

A More Advanced Histogram Program

The objective is:

Prompt the user to enter the number of
values to process.
Prompt the user to type entries between
one and fifty.
Write each entry and create a bar graph whose
length is proportional to the number entered.
Send the data to the display and to a second file.

Pseudocode for the program is:

get the number of entries to process
for (this number of entries) {
    get a value from the user
    write a bar to the display
    write a bar to the second file
}

"Write a bar" can be used in the pseudocode as a basic operation. A function specifically called "Write a bar" can be created. Here is pseudocode for this function, detailing how it must work:

write a bar(where to write it,what size bar) {
    for (the number of stars in the bar)
        write a star to the correct file
    write a new line
}

Here is the program, HISTOGRAM-4:

```
#include <stdio.h>
#define MAXVALUE 100.0
#define NUMTOCLEAR 25
#define VOID      int
```

```
main()
{       /* main */
    int     EntryCount ;      /* looping variable--
                               * the current entry number
                               */
    int     NumEntries ;      /* total number of entries */
    FILE    *OutFile ;        /* where we're writing information */
    float   Value ;           /* value for this entry */

    if ((OutFile = fopen("histgrm4","w")) == 0) {
        fprintf(stderr,"Can't open output file.\n") ;
        exit(0) ;
    }
    ClearScreen() ;
    printf("How Many Entries Will You Make? ") ;
    scanf("%d",&NumEntries) ;

    for (EntryCount = 0 ; EntryCount < NumEntries ; EntryCount++) {
        printf("\nFor Entry %d, Type a Value Between 0 and 100: ",
                EntryCount + 1) ;
        scanf("%f",&Value) ;

        /* Trap all illegal values here.
         */
        while (Value > MAXVALUE) {
            printf("\n\tMAXIMUM VALUE YOU MAY ENTER IS 100!") ;
            printf("\n\tPLEASE RE-ENTER THE VALUE: ") ;
            scanf("%f",&Value) ;
        }
        WriteBar(stdout,Value) ;
        WriteBar(OutFile,Value) ;
    }
    PrintRuler(stdout) ;
    PrintRuler(OutFile) ;
}       /* main */

VOID ClearScreen()
/* ClearScreen writes NUMTOCLEAR newlines to the screen.
 */
{       /* ClearScreen */
    int  Counter ;

    for (Counter = 0 ; Counter < NUMTOCLEAR ; Counter++)
        putchar('\n') ;       /* note the single quotes */
}       /* ClearScreen */

VOID PrintRuler(TargetFile)
FILE    *TargetFile ;
/* PrintRuler writes a ruler line to TargetFile.
 */
{       /* PrintRuler */
    fprintf(TargetFile,"        | ----+----+----+----+----+") ;
    fprintf(TargetFile,"----+----+----+----+----|\n") ;
}       /* PrintRuler */

VOID WriteBar(TargetFile,NumToWrite)
float   NumToWrite ;
FILE    *TargetFile ;
{       /* WriteBar */
    int  Count ;

    /* First print the number to write on the line, then a bar
     * to signal the start of the graph.
     */
    fprintf(TargetFile,"%5.1f | ",NumToWrite) ;
```

```
        for (Count = 0 ; Count < (int)NumToWrite / 2 ; Count++)
            putc('*',TargetFile) ;
        fprintf(TargetFile,"\n") ;
    }       /* WriteBar */
```

Note the changes made to the earlier program. The code writing the bars of stars was moved to a function called **WriteBar**. **WriteBar**'s first parameter is the file where we want to print; this allows the same code to be used to print to the screen and to the explicit file. The clear-screen code was moved to the function **ClearScreen**. A ruler line was added with another function called **PrintRuler** to clearly mark every five spaces in the listing.

ANATOMY: the tab character

Several **printf** statements in this example use the tab character. To print a tab, use the sequence **\t**. Just as with the newline, no white space may appear between the backslash and the lower case letter **t**.

ANATOMY: writing characters

We have written entire lines using **printf** and **fprintf**. This time, however, we want to write a single character. **putc** (pronounced ''put-see'') writes a single character to a specified file:

```
    putc('*',OutFile) ;
```

This statement writes a star to **OutFile**, which has been opened for *writing*. Characters can be written to **stdout** (the display) either with

```
    putc('*',stdout) ;
```

or

```
    putchar('*') ;
```

putchar is a shorthand way of writing characters to **stdout**.

Note that all characters are enclosed in single quotes when written with **putc**. Single quotes mean the single character is treated as a raw character. Double quotes have a very different meaning that will be discussed in the next chapter.

ANATOMY: functions that return nothing

WriteBar is a function that returns no value to the caller. All functions in **C** return values; zero is returned if no value is explicitly returned. **WriteBar** returns a value that is ignored. **VOID** is defined as **int** in the program.

In declaring

```
    VOID WriteBar()
```

the **C** compiler interprets it as

```
    int WriteBar()
```

When the program is read, **VOID** is the reminder ''this is a function that returns nothing.''

Using **VOID** (and similar **#define**s), the code can be commented more effectively.

Hazard: some compilers predeclare void

Some compilers, especially on large computers, predeclare **void** (in lower case) as an additional keyword. You may freely substitute the keyword **void** for **VOID** in all programs in the book—if you do so, remove the **#define** directive defining **VOID**.

ANATOMY: stopping the program

C programs normally stop when they finish the last statement in the **main** function. The **C** system function **exit** ends the program prematurely if an error occurs. For example:

```
if ((OutFile = fopen("OUT","w")) == 0) {
    fprintf(stderr,"Can't open output file.\n") ;
    exit(0) ;
}
```

The program stops if the output file can't be opened. **exit** takes an integer value as its parameter. Depending on the operating system, this value is either ignored or used to determine if the program finished normally or was stopped with an error. The specific compiler's documentation must be referenced for actual usage.

Saving Information

It may be desirable to read all values from the user before anything is displayed on the screen. This would provide a clean display for the viewer, free of visible clutter from any intervening prompts.

Unique variable-names could be invented to store all the responses. But, this becomes a problem if, for example, it becomes necessary to invent fifty unique names. A way of storing many things by one simple name is needed. And **C** has the array construction to solve this problem.

PREVIEW: arrays

An *array* is a place where many values can be stored under a single name, and from which they can be easily recalled.

An **array variable** is declared in this example:

```
int     Value [5] ;
```

Value is an array that stores five integers. The stored data is type **int**; this is the *base type* of the array. The number of elements in the array is placed inside the square brackets. An array can have any base type and any size, depending on the computer's limitations. An array must have a declared fixed size to correctly compile the program.

To refer to the third integer inside **Value**, write:

```
A = Value[2] ;
```

CPT-F

This means:

```
!__!__!__!__!__!   Value
 0  1  2  3  4
       ^
       !
       !
       ---> A = Value[2] ;
```

This time, the number inside square brackets is the number of the element to reference. C goes to the named array, counts up to this element, and uses it just as it would any other variable. Array elements can be used anywhere regular variables are used. For example, the first element to the value of an expression can be set with:

```
Value[0] = A + Q * (int)R ;
```

Notice C numbers elements in an array from ZERO, not ONE. This is different from many other computer languages. It may be confusing initially, but C programs can often be simpler than equivalent programs in many other languages.

A warning about arrays is in order. C gives no help with this type of problem:

```
Value[5] = 12 ;
```

Value has been declared to be **int Value[5]** but, because C numbers arrays from zero and not from one, these elements number from zero through four. The element **Value[5]** doesn't really exist; the last value is actually **Value[4]**. Unfortunately, C will not tell us if an attempt is made to use information that isn't there. This type of error can be a major cause of insidious bugs that appear when the program is run. Some C program-checkers (such as *lint* on **UNIX** systems) flag this error.

Rewriting the Histogram Program with Arrays

The program, HISTOGRAM-5, demonstrates arrays:

```
#include <stdio.h>
#define MAXNUMENTRIES    50
#define MAXVALUE         100.0
#define NUMTOCLEAR       25
#define VOID             int

main()
{      /* main */
    int    EntryCount ;     /* looping variable--
                             * the current entry number
                             */
    FILE   *OutFile ;       /* where we're writing information */
    int    NumEntries ;     /* total number of entries */
    float  Value [MAXNUMENTRIES] ; /* all values the user enters */

    if ((OutFile = fopen("histgrm5","w")) == 0) {
        fprintf(stderr,"Can't open output file.\n") ;
        exit(0) ;
    }
    ClearScreen() ;
    printf("How Many Entries Will You Make? ") ;
    scanf("%d",&NumEntries) ;
    while (NumEntries > MAXNUMENTRIES || NumEntries < 1) {
```

```
        printf("\n\tI Can Only Accept a Number Between 1 and %d!\n",
                MAXNUMENTRIES) ;
        printf("\nHow Many Entries Will You Make? ") ;
        scanf("%d",&NumEntries) ;


 /  Get the entries.
 /
   or (EntryCount = 0 ; EntryCount < NumEntries ; EntryCount++) {
        printf("\nFor Entry %d, Type a Value Between 0 and 100: ",
                EntryCount + 1) ;
        scanf("%f",&Value[EntryCount]) ;
        /* Trap all illegal values here.
         */
        while (Value[EntryCount] > MAXVALUE) {
            printf("\n\tMaximum value you may enter is 100.") ;
            printf("\n\tPlease re-enter the value: ") ;
            scanf("%f",&Value[EntryCount]) ;
        }


 /* Write the histogram.
  */
   or (EntryCount = 0 ; EntryCount < NumEntries ; EntryCount++) {
            WriteBar(stdout,Value[EntryCount]) ;
            WriteBar(OutFile,Value[EntryCount]) ;
        }
        PrintRuler(stdout) ;
        PrintRuler(OutFile) ;
        fclose(OutFile) ;
            /* main */

   OID ClearScreen()
 /* ClearScreen writes NUMTOCLEAR newlines to the screen.
  */
 {          /* ClearScreen */
        int   Counter ;

        for (Counter = 0 ; Counter < NUMTOCLEAR ; Counter++)
            putchar('\n') ;
            /* ClearScreen */

 VOID PrintRuler(TargetFile)
 FILE    *TargetFile ;
 /* PrintRuler writes a ruler line to TargetFile.
  */
 {          /* PrintRuler */
        fprintf(TargetFile,"       | ----+----+----+----+----+") ;
        fprintf(TargetFile,"----+----+----+----+----|\n") ;
 }          /* PrintRuler */

 VOID WriteBar(TargetFile,NumToWrite)
 float   NumToWrite ;
 FILE    *TargetFile ;
 {          /* WriteBar */
        int   Count ;

        /* First print the number to write on the line, then a bar
         * to signal the start of the graph.
         */
        fprintf(TargetFile,"%5.1f | ",NumToWrite) ;

        for (Count = 0 ; Count < (int)NumToWrite / 2 ; Count++)
            putc('*',TargetFile) ;
        fprintf(TargetFile,"\n") ;
 }          /* WriteBar */
```

ANATOMY: arrays and for loops

for loops let us look at every element in an array one-by-one. The following loop prompts the user for values and stores each value received in an element of **Value**:

```
for (EntryCount = 0 ; EntryCount < NumEntries ;
            EntryCount++) {
    printf("For Entry %d, Type a Value Between 0 and 100: ",
            EntryCount + 1) ;
    scanf("%d",&Value[EntryCount]) ;
}
```

For this example, assume that **MAXNUMENTRIES** is five. When **Value** is declared as **int Value[MAXNUMENTRIES]**, five spaces are reserved:

```
!__!__!__!__!__!    Value
 0  1  2  3  4
```

When the **for** loop starts, **EntryCount** is set to zero. Assume that **NumEntries** is three in this example. On the first pass through the loop the zeroth element in **Value** is filled:

```
 1
!__!__!__!__!__!    Value
 0  1  2  3  4
 ^

 !
 ^
```

```
scanf("%d",&Value[EntryCount]) ;
                    EntryCount is 0
```

EntryCount is then incremented and checked to determine if it is less than **NumEntries**. It is, so the program continues with **EntryCount** equal to one:

```
 1  15
!__!__!__!__!__!    Value
 0  1  2  3  4
    ^

 !
 ^
```

```
scanf("%d",&Value[EntryCount]) ;
                    EntryCount is 1
```

Again, **EntryCount** is incremented and checked against **NumEntries**. The test succeeds, and the program continues with **EntryCount** equal to two:

```
 1  15 30
!__!__!__!__!__!    Value
 0  1  2  3  4
       ^

 !
 ^
```

```
scanf("%d",&Value[EntryCount]) ;
                    EntryCount is 2
```

Again, increment and test. Now, **EntryCount** is equal to three, which is no longer less than **NumEntries**. The loop stops here.

In summary, when the loop starts, **EntryCount** is zero. **scanf** fills **Value[0]**. Each successive trip through the loop fills the next entry in **Value** because **EntryCount** is incremented by one each time. When the test in the **for** loop fails, the program stops. Exactly the same construction is used to print the entire array element-by-element at the end of the program. The **for** loop prints each element in turn.

Note the initialization and testing conditions. Always:

- Start the control variable (in this example, **EntryCount**) at zero to reference the zero-th element of arrays.
- Add one for each trip through the loop (**EntryCount++**) to access each element in the array in turn.
- Do the continuance test as a less-than test. (Remember that arrays run from zero to one less than the array's declared size.)

Scaling the Histogram

It is unrealistic to expect that data a user enters will only have values between one and one hundred. Most sets of information programs generally encounter have widely varying ranges. The numbers must be scaled after the entire set is read. Remember, values have been scaled by dividing them by two before printing. Now, to determine the largest value to print, all values must be checked after they are read. The scaling number is determined from that largest value.

This is a specification for scaling a set of numbers:

First, find the largest number in the set.
Then, find a fraction which, when multiplied
by this largest number, gets the maximum
number of stars we want to print. This is
the scaling fraction. Every element in the
array is multiplied by this scaling fraction
to determine the number of stars to be printed.

Pseudocode for this specification:

FindScalingFraction(InputArray,NumElements,MaxSize) {
   go through each element in InputArray and find the
   largest element. Assign this value to MaxElement.
   ScalingResult = MaxSize / MaxElement ;
}

The new program is HISTOGRAM-6:

```
#include <stdio.h>
#define MAXNUMSTARS      50
#define MAXNUMENTRIES    50
#define NUMTOCLEAR       25
#define VOID             int

extern double FindScalingFraction() ;

main()
{       /* main */
   int    EntryCount ;      /* looping variable--
                             * the current entry number
                             */
   FILE   *OutFile ;        /* where we're writing information */
```

```
    int    NumEntries ;     /* total number of entries */
    double ScalingMultiplier ; /* the scaling value */
    double Value[MAXNUMENTRIES] ; /* all values the user enters */

    if ((OutFile = fopen("histgrm6","w")) == 0) {
        fprintf(stderr,"Can't open output file.\n") ;
        exit(0) ;
    }
    ClearScreen() ;
    printf("How Many Entries Will You Make? ") ;
    scanf("%d",&NumEntries) ;
    while (NumEntries > MAXNUMENTRIES || NumEntries < 1) {
        printf("\n\tI Can Only Accept a Number Between 1 and %d!\n",
                MAXNUMENTRIES) ;
        printf("\nHow Many Entries Will You Make? ") ;
        scanf("%d",&NumEntries) ;
    }

    /* Get the entries.
     */
    for (EntryCount = 0 ; EntryCount < NumEntries ; EntryCount++) {
        printf("\nFor Entry %d, Type a Value: ",
                EntryCount + 1) ;
        scanf("%lf",&Value[EntryCount]) ;
    }

    ScalingMultiplier = FindScalingFraction(Value,NumEntries,
                            MAXNUMSTARS) ;
    WriteHistogram(stdout,Value,NumEntries,ScalingMultiplier) ;
    WriteHistogram(OutFile,Value,NumEntries,ScalingMultiplier) ;
    fclose(OutFile) ;
}     /* main */

VOID ClearScreen()
/* ClearScreen writes NUMTOCLEAR newlines to the screen.
 */
{      /* ClearScreen */
    int  Counter ;

    for (Counter = 0 ; Counter < NUMTOCLEAR ; Counter++)
        putchar('\n') ;
}      /* ClearScreen */
double FindScalingFraction(InputArray,NumElements,MaxSize)
double InputArray[] ;
int    MaxSize ;
int    NumElements ;

/* FindScalingFraction returns the multiplier which scales
 * every element of InputArray to be no larger than MaxSize.
 */
{      /* FindScalingFraction */
    int       CurElement ;
    double    MaxElement ;

    /* Find the largest element in InputArray by looking at each
     * element in turn and, if the element under examination is larger
     * than the old value of MaxElement (initially set to zero), make
     * MaxElement equal to that value.
     */
    for (CurElement = 0,MaxElement = 0.0 ; CurElement < NumElements ;
                    CurElement++)
        MaxElement = (InputArray[CurElement] > MaxElement) ?
                    InputArray[CurElement] : MaxElement ;
```

```
      /* The scaling multiplier is the maximum number divided
       * by the MaxElement, the largest element in the array.
       */
      return((double)MaxSize / MaxElement) ;
}       /* FindScalingFraction */

VOID PrintRuler(TargetFile)
FILE     *TargetFile ;
/* PrintRuler writes a ruler line to TargetFile.
 */
{        /* PrintRuler */
     int     Ruler ;
     fprintf(TargetFile,"\nSCALE | ") ;
     for (Ruler = 0 ; Ruler < 10 ; Ruler++)
         fprintf(TargetFile,"----+") ;
}        /* PrintRuler */

VOID WriteHistogram(TargetFile,InputArray,NumElements,ScalingFactor)
double   InputArray[] ;
int      NumElements ;
double   ScalingFactor ;
FILE     *TargetFile ;
{        /* WriteHistogram */
     int   ElementCount ;
     int   NumStarsToWrite ;
     int   StarCount ;

     /* Cycle through each element,
      * printing each on a separate line.
      */
     for (ElementCount = 0 ; ElementCount < NumElements ;
                    ElementCount++) {

         /* First, print the number to write on the line, then
          * a bar to signal the start of the graph.
          */
         fprintf(TargetFile,"%5.1f | ",InputArray[ElementCount]) ;

         /* Calculate the number of stars to write by multiplying the
          * value by the ScalingFactor.  Note that the multiplication is
          * done with floating point arithmetic, but the final answer is
          * converted to an integer with a cast.
          */
         NumStarsToWrite =
                 (int)(InputArray[ElementCount] * ScalingFactor) ;

         /* Now write the stars and a newline.
          */
         for (StarCount = 0 ; StarCount < NumStarsToWrite ;
                     StarCount++)
            putc('*',TargetFile) ;
         fprintf(TargetFile,"\n") ;
     }
     /* Print the ruler line at the end of every histogram.
      */
     PrintRuler(TargetFile) ;
}        /* WriteHistogram */
```

The program has been revised to use **double**s for each **Value** element. **WriteBar** was changed to **WriteHistogram**, which takes a whole array and scaling factor as parameters.

ANATOMY: commas in for clauses

Sometimes the initialization or termination sections in a **for** loop comprise more than one **C** statement. In the loop above, two variables must be initialized and incremented:

```
for (CurElement = 0,MaxElement = 0.0 ; CurElement < NumElements ;
                    CurElement++)
```

With **C**, multiple statements separated by a comma can be put into any expression. In the **for** loop, the initialization clause sets the values of **CurElement** and **MaxElement**.

ANATOMY: passing arrays as parameters

Single numbers and characters have been passed as parameters to functions many times. Also, an entire array can be passed to a function. We work with the array within the function just as we would normally. One way to pass an array to a function is to declare it as a parameter array with fixed length:

```
double FindScalingFraction(InputArray,NumElements,MaxSize)
double InputArray[MAXNUMENTRIES] ;
int    MaxSize ;
int    NumElements ;
```

InputArray is now an array parameter with **MAXNUMENTRIES** elements. Inside **FindScalingFraction**, we work with **InputArray** just as with any other array. Every element of the array passed to **FindScalingFraction** is associated automatically with the corresponding element of **InputArray**. In this example, the two bare integers **NumElements** and **MaxSize** are passed along with the array, **InputArray**. Arrays can be combined with other arrays, bare numbers, or characters as needed. If the definition of **MAXNUMENTRIES** is changed, both the declaration of the array in **main** and in **FindScalingFraction** will be updated when the code is recompiled.

But, let's say it is necessary to scale several arrays in our program. Thus, these arrays:

```
double    Array1[100] ;
double    Array2[10] ;
double    Array3[500] ;
```

The sizes of these three arrays vary widely. How can the size of **InputArray** be declared in a function that is supposed to receive all three arrays as parameters?

C enables an array parameter to be declared as an array of a variable length to be determined at run time. Write:

```
double FindScalingFraction(InputArray,NumElements,MaxSize)
double InputArray[] ;
int    MaxSize ;
int    NumElements ;
```

The empty square brackets mean **InputArray** is an array of **double**s. The length of the array is not known when the program is written, but the length of the array is passed in **NumElements**. This allows **FindScalingFraction** to determine how many elements to consider.

Let's look at some examples. In **main**, the statement marked with an arrow in the left column is executed first:

```
 main:
    double Array1[100] ;
    double Array2[10] ;
    double Array3[500] ;
    double Result1,Result2,Result3 ;

------> Result1 = FindScalingFraction(Array1,100,25) ;
                                          |      |  |
                                          v      v  v

         Result2 = FindScalingFraction(Array2,10,50) ;
         Result3 = FindScalingFraction(Array3,500,50) ;



                                     |        |       |
                                     v        v       v
          FindScalingFraction(InputArray,NumElements,MaxSize)
                              Array1      100         25
```

Here, **InputArray** is linked to **Array1**, an array of one hundred **doubles**. Remember that **C** doesn't know the size of **InputArray** even now; the number of elements to use must be passed explicitly in **NumElements**.

Let's go on to the next use of **FindScalingFraction**.

```
 main:
    double Array1[100] ;
    double Array2[10] ;
    double Array3[500] ;
    double Result1,Result2,Result3 ;

    Result1 = FindScalingFraction(Array1,100,25) ;
------> Result2 = FindScalingFraction(Array2,10,50) ;
                                         |     |  |
                                         v     v  v

         Result3 = FindScalingFraction(Array3,500,50) ;



                                     |        |       |
                                     v        v       v
          FindScalingFraction(InputArray,NumElements,MaxSize)
                              Array2      10          50
```

Now **InputArray** is linked to **Array2**. Again the length of **Array2** is passed explicitly so that **FindScalingFraction** knows how many elements there are.

Finally the last statement in **main** is executed:

```
 ------------------------------------------------------------
| main:                                                       |
|   double Array1[100] ;                                      |
|   double Array2[10] ;                                       |
|   double Array3[500] ;                                      |
|   double Result1,Result2,Result3 ;                          |
|                                                             |
|   Result1 = FindScalingFraction(Array1,100,25) ;            |
|   Result2 = FindScalingFraction(Array2,10,50) ;             |
  ------> Result3 = FindScalingFraction(Array3,500,50) ;      |
|                                          ¦    ¦ ¦           |
|                                          v    v v           |
 -- ----------------------------------------------------------|
|                                                             |
 ------------------------------------------------------------
     ------------------------------------------------------
                       ¦           ¦           ¦
                       v           v           v
          FindScalingFraction(InputArray,NumElements,MaxSize)
                       Array3        500          50
```

Here **InputArray** is linked to the largest array, **Array3**. The same function is used for all arrays. The variable length array parameter in **C** simplifies this.

Remember, only parameters to functions can be declared in this way. Regular arrays must be declared with some fixed array size. Also remember, the number of elements to consider must be passed to the function. The function uses this number to know how large the array is when the program is running.

Producing Hard Copies of the Histograms

There are other places to send the completed histogram; to a printer instead of to a disk file, for example. The methods which can be used depend on the computer's operating system and the requirements of the C compiler. Specific details should be found in the compiler's documentation. However, some of this information has been extracted and made part of Appendix A, which discusses the specifics of several commercially available compilers for microcomputers. The following are suggestions which may enable you to immediately generate hard copies of the histograms produced by the programs in this chapter.

If your computer operates under CP/M or MS-DOS, you can use the Control-P function to direct the output of the computer to the printer as well as, or instead of, to the screen. The procedure is:

1. Create the histogram using an example-program in this chapter that saves the information automatically as a disk file. These programs are HISTOGRAM-3 through HISTOGRAM-6.
2. Having completed the run of the program, type the name of the file that has been saved. For example, HISTOGRAM-5 creates a file called HISTGRM5 that contains the output to be printed.
3. While pressing and holding the CONTROL key (CTRL), press the P key; then release both.

4. Press the RETURN or ENTER key and, if your printer is turned on and ready, the content of the HISTGRM5 file will be printed.
5. When the printout has been completed and the system prompt is displayed again on the screen, repeat action #3 above to cancel the CTRL-P command. (Note: some microcomputers use CTRL-N to cancel CTRL-P.)

Revising the Code to Print Instead of Save

Each of the programs HISTOGRAM-3 through HISTOGRAM-6, uses the **fopen** instruction to save or write the output of the histogram program to the disk under a predefined name. This is the typical instruction, as used in HISTOGRAM-3, for accomplishing the naming/saving action automatically:

```
OutFile = fopen("OUT","w") ;
```

The word "OUT" is the name of the file saved on disk.

Depending, once again, on your particular computer's operating system and your C compiler, the word "OUT", or whatever name has been used in the specific program, can be changed to one of the following to represent the printer:

```
"PRN"
"PRN:"
"LST"
"LST:"
```

If your operating system and compiler recognize the use of the appropriate word, surrounded by double quote marks, followed by a comma and the "w" expression, the hard copy will be made. The output will not be saved as a disk file.

Things Called Strings

Preview: What Are Strings?

Strings are arrays of characters. Think of strings as more than a collection of characters. Groups of characters can form words, phrases, and sentences. Strings are different from other kinds of arrays because they have meaning as a collective entity, not just as a group of characters.

Consider these seven individual characters:

'T' 'h' 'i' 's' ' ' 'i' 's'

Each character by itself means little. But when grouped together in a character string, they take on meaning:

```
T  h  i  s     i  s  \0
|_|_|_|_|_|_|_|_|
0  1  2  3  4  5  6  7
```

This is a seven-character array that spells the words **This is**.

Read and Write a Line

Let's read a line typed at the keyboard and display it on the screen. The objective is:

Prompt the user to enter a line of characters and end it with a carriage return. Read this line as a string and echo it back to the screen.

The program is:

```
#include <stdio.h>
#define   STRINGLENGTH   255

main()
{      /* main */
    char   InString[STRINGLENGTH] ;

    printf("Enter a line of text and press RETURN.\n") ;
    fgets(InString,STRINGLENGTH,stdin) ;
```

```
        printf("Your string is: %s\n",InString) ;
        printf("Again, your string is:") ;
        fputs(InString,stdout) ;
}       /* main */
```

ANATOMY: declaring character strings

Declare a character string as an *array* of characters:

```
    char      InString[STRINGLENGTH] ;
```

InString is a *character array* with a length equal to the constant value **STRINGLENGTH**.

ANATOMY: reading and writing strings

To read a line of text from a file and store it in a string, use **fgets** (pronounced "eff-get-ess"):

```
    fgets(InString,STRINGLENGTH,stdin) ;
          ^           ^           ^
          |           |           |
          |           |           --- file pointer
          |           |               to read from
    string ---        |
    to fill           --- maximum number of
                          characters to read
```

fgets's first argument is the name of the string to fill. Simply enter the name of the string. This is contrary to the rule requiring an ampersand in front of a variable you want a function to modify. Unlike filling numeric values using **scanf**, do not prefix the name of the string to be filled with an ampersand. The difference between these cases is explained in the next chapter; remember not to use an ampersand here.

fgets's second argument is the maximum number of characters minus one to be read from the file. Normally, the length of the string is entered for this parameter. The significance of subtracting one from the string's length is made clear below.

fgets reads from any file opened for reading. The third parameter to **fgets** must be a pointer to a currently open file that **fopen** returns to you. Do not try to read from a file opened for writing or appending.

fgets reads characters from the input file until it finds an end of line mark, usually a newline, or it reads the maximum number of characters.

HAZARD: when is a newline not a newline?

Most **C** compilers view a carriage return entered from the keyboard as a newline. Newlines read from disk files are viewed differently than those read from the keyboard by some microcomputer **C** compilers. Be cautious whenever writing code that depends on the interpretation of newlines in a particular way. (See Appendix A and your compiler's documentation for details.)

ANATOMY: writing strings with fputs and (f)printf

C has two functions for writing strings. To write a string to a file, use **fputs** (pronounce "eff-put-ess").

```
fputs(InString,stdout) ;
       ^           ^
       |           |
       |           |  --- file pointer opened for
       |               writing, or appending
       |
       --- name of character array
           to write as a string
```

fputs takes the name of the character array to be written, and the name of a pointer to a currently opened file. This file pointer is returned by a call to **fopen**; the file must be opened for writing or appending. In this example, **fputs** then writes all the characters in **InString** to **stdout**.

Although **fprintf** is used in the following example, if it is necessary to write a string as part of other text or with other variables, use either **printf** or **fprintf**.

```
fprintf(OutFile,"This is the string: %s\n",InString) ;
        ^                              ^      ^
        |                              |      |
    file pointer opened for        print a   string to
    writing or appending           string    print
```

%s in the above format means print a string at this location. **fprintf** (or **printf**) writes all the characters in **InString** to **OutFile** after having printed "This is the string: ". Note that **OutFile** is a file pointer for writing or appending which **fopen** returns. Single characters from a string can be printed using either **putc** or **fprintf** (or **printf**). The fourth character in the string **InString** can be printed (remember **C** arrays start with zero):

```
putc(InString[3],OutFile) ;
```

fprintf (or **printf**) prints characters with the **%c** directive:

```
fprintf(OutFile,"Here's the character: %c\n",InString[3]) ;
                                        ^
                                        |
                         print a single character
```

ANATOMY: all C strings are variable in length

A question: How do **fputs** and **fprintf** or **printf** know how many characters to write in a string? If the string is shorter than the maximum size of the string, something unexpected might be printed. All strings in **C** are variable in length. They will accommodate fewer characters than declared and will cause no problem. Strings in **C** always end with the *null character*—a character whose value is zero. Don't confuse this with the ASCII '0' character, which is a printable character. The **null character** (also known as "ASCII NUL") is really ZERO, a non-printable character. Thus:

```
char    Label[10] ;

T h i s   i s \0
|_|_|_|_|_|_|_|_|_|_|
0 1 2 3 4 5 6 7 8 9
                ^ -----> undefined -- past the
                |                end of the string
                |
          string terminator:
          zero, the null character
```

Note the end of the string is marked with the null character. The null character is written as: **\0**.

All **C** strings end with a zero, expressed as "all **C** strings are zero-terminated." The length of a string in **C** can always be found by looking for this zero character. All **C** string functions work in this way.

When declaring a string, always count the zero terminator as part of the maximum length of a string. Thus, to store a maximum of fifteen characters in **Label**, declare:

```
char    Label[16] ;
```

Reading a string with **fgets** ensures the string is automatically zero-terminated; thus, you can begin working immediately with the strings you read. Again, count the zero terminator both in the declared string length and in the length passed to **fgets**.

Extra Newlines

Enter, compile, and run the previous example program. Enter the word **Hi!** when prompted. You see this unusual line spacing:

```
Your string is: Hi!

Again your string is: Hi!
```

There is an extra blank line between the two lines! Why?

The problem is **fgets** includes the newline read from the keyboard in the string it returns. When the string is displayed with **fputs**, **fprintf**, or **printf**, this extra newline is also displayed. Obviously, extra newlines must be stripped from the ends of the strings. This can be done with a short function whose objective is:

Write a function that removes newlines from the ends of strings. Assume that the string contains only one newline at its end. Make the function apply to strings of any length.

STRATEGY: StripNewLines

Pseudocode for **StripNewLines** follows:

```
StripNewLines(StringToProcess)
char    StringToProcess[] ;
{           /* StripNewLines */
    Advance a character at a time until the
    end of the string is found   {
        Examine the current character.  If it's a newline
        replace it with a '\0' and exit the loop.
    }
}           /* StripNewLines */
```

Let's diagram the strategy, starting with this string:

```
T  e  s  t  i  n  g  \n \0
|_|_|_|_|_|_|_|_|_|
0  1  2  3  4  5  6  7  8
```

StripNewLines receives this string as its parameter, but does not know its length. If we advance a character at a time, we will eventually run into the zero terminator. When we arrive at the zero we must stop.

On the first pass, we look at **StringToProcess[0]**:

```
T e s t i n g \n\0
|_|_|_|_|_|_|_|_|_|
0 1 2 3 4 5 6 7 8
^
|
--- is this character a newline?
```

Test to see if this is a newline. If it isn't, go on to the next character.

Eventually, we come to **StringToProcess[7]**:

```
T e s t i n g \n\0
|_|_|_|_|_|_|_|_|_|
0 1 2 3 4 5 6 7 8
          ^
          |
--- is this character a newline?
```

This character is a newline. Therefore, it is converted to a null character. This terminates the string earlier than it did before and adjusts the length while it removes the newline. The extra null character left over at the end can be ignored. (Characters after the terminating null-character are ignored.)

Convert the pseudocode directly into **C** code:

```
VOID StripNewLines(StringToProcess)
char    StringToProcess[] ;
{       /* StripNewLines */
    int         I ;

    /* Advance a character at a time until
     * the zero terminator is found.
     */
    for (I = 0 ; StringToProcess[I] != '\0' ; I++)
        /* If the character being examined is a
         * newline, replace it with a null character
         * and stop looping.
         */
        if (StringToProcess[I] == '\n') {
            StringToProcess[I] = '\0' ;
            break ;
        }
}       /* StripNewLines */
```

The **for** loop examines each character in the string. The loop counter **I** is incremented until the terminator is found. If a newline is found, it is changed to a zero terminator and we **break** out of the loop.

In **C**, a non-zero value is **TRUE**. The **for** loop continues when the character is non-zero. The routine can be rewritten as follows:

```
VOID StripNewLines(StringToProcess)
char    StringToProcess[] ;
{       /* StripNewLines */
    int         I ;
```

```
/* Advance a character at a time until
 * the zero terminator is found.
 */
for (I = 0 ; StringToProcess[I] ; I++) {

    /* If the character being examined is a
    newline, replace it with a null and
    stop looping. */
    if (StringToProcess[I] == '\n') {
        StringToProcess[I] = '\0' ;
        break ;
    }
}
}       /* StripNewLines */
```

The continuation condition in the **for** loop is now simply a check that
StringToProcess[I] is non-zero. The two routines are equivalent. Choose whichever
you find more clear.

Using The Function

Here is how **StripNewLines** is used in the program:

```
#include <stdio.h>
#define STRINGLENGTH   255
#define VOID     int

main()
{       /* main */
    char   InString[STRINGLENGTH] ;

    printf("Enter a line of text and press RETURN.\n") ;
    fgets(InString,STRINGLENGTH,stdin) ;
    StripNewLines(InString) ;
    printf("Your string is: %s\n",InString) ;
    printf("Again, your string is:") ;
    fputs(InString,stdout) ;
}       /* main */

VOID StripNewLines(StringToProcess)
char    StringToProcess[] ;
{       /* StripNewLines */
    int        I ;

    /* Advance a character at a time until
     * the zero terminator is found.
     */
    for (I = 0 ; StringToProcess[I] ; I++) {

        /* If the character being examined is
           a newline, stop. */
        if (StringToProcess[I] == '\n') {
            StringToProcess[I] = '\0' ;
            break ;
        }
    }
}       /* StripNewLines */
```

Using **fgets**, **StripNewLines** is called immediately after the string is read. When
the program is run again, the display is:

```
Your string is: Hi!
Again your string is: Hi!
```

Much better! The extra blank line has been eliminated.

Printing the Length of a Line

It is often necessary to know the length of a line in number of characters. The objective here is:

Read a line from the user and display its length.

The main program is:

```
#include <stdio.h>
#define MAXBUFSIZE        255

main()
{       /* main */
    char        InBuffer[MAXBUFSIZE] ;

    printf("Enter a line of text: ") ;
    fgets(InBuffer,MAXBUFSIZE,stdin) ;
    printf("Your string has %d characters\n",strlen(InBuffer)) ;
}       /* main */
```

ANATOMY: strlen

The program uses a **C** system function, **strlen**, to find the length of a string. **strlen** (pronounced 'stirlen,'' meaning ''string length'') takes the name of a string, and returns its length.

Writing strlen

strlen is easily written. Here's the design:

```
strlen(String)
{
    count until the zero terminator in String is found
    return the count
}
```

The function's code is:

```
int strlen(String)
char    String[] ;
{       /* strlen */
    int         Counter ;

    for (Counter = 0 ; String[Counter] ; Counter++)
    /* NULL loop */ ;
    /* The loop only counts -- nothing else.
     * The bare semicolon shows a loop body with
     * nothing in it.
     */
    return (Counter) ;
}        /* strlen */
```

The continuation condition says ''continue while **String[Counter]** is non-zero. Stop when the terminator is found.''

Note a couple of details. Take the string:

```
T e s t i n g\0
|_|_|_|_|_|_|_|_|
0 1 2 3 4 5 6 7
```

It begins with **Counter** equal to zero. The loop continues until **Counter** is seven, then examines **String[7]** and finds a zero. The length is then 7, not 8. **strlen**'s length does not include the zero terminator.

In the above program, the newline is not stripped from the end of the string before getting its length. **strlen** counts newlines in the length it returns. If you want just the length of the printing characters, you must strip newlines by calling the function **StripNewLines** before calling **strlen**.

Putting Strings Together

Strings can be put together and taken apart in **C**. This provides much power in transforming textual data. Let's say we want to put two strings together. Our objective is:

> Read three words from the user and
> stick them together to form one
> long phrase. Print both the original
> words and the new phrase.

The program is:

```
#include <stdio.h>
#define MAXSTRLEN   255
#define VOID        int

main()
{       /* main */
     char      First[MAXSTRLEN] ;
     char      Result[MAXSTRLEN] ;
     char      Second[MAXSTRLEN] ;
     char      Third[MAXSTRLEN] ;

     printf("Enter a word: ") ;
     fgets(First,MAXSTRLEN,stdin) ;
     StripNewLines(First) ;
     printf("Enter another word: ") ;
     fgets(Second,MAXSTRLEN,stdin) ;
     StripNewLines(Second) ;
     printf("Enter yet a third word: ") ;
     fgets(Third,MAXSTRLEN,stdin) ;
     StripNewLines(Third) ;
     printf("\n\n") ;             /* just for a little space */

     strcpy(Result,First) ;      /* copy the first string */
     strcat(Result,Second) ;     /* append the second string */
     strcat(Result,Third) ;      /* append the third string */

     printf("Your first string is: %s\n",First) ;
     printf("Your second string is: %s\n",Second) ;
     printf("Your third string is: %s\n",Third) ;
     printf("After joining the strings I have: %s\n",Result) ;
}      /* main */

VOID StripNewLines(StringToProcess)
char     StringToProcess[] ;
{    /* StripNewLines */
     int        I ;
```

```
/* Advance a character at a time until
 * the zero terminator is found.
 */
for (I = 0 ; StringToProcess[I] ; I++)
    if (StringToProcess[I] == '\n') {
            StringToProcess[I] = '\0' ;
            break ;
        }
}    /* StripNewLines */
```

When the program is compiled and run, the following interaction occurs:

```
Enter a word: Hi
Enter another word: there
Enter yet a third word: !!!
```

The results are displayed as:

```
Your first string is: Hi
Your second string is: there
Your third string is: !!!
After joining the strings I have: Hithere!!!
```

Not exactly what was wanted. But, let's keep going!

ANATOMY: copying strings

The intent is to join the three strings the user enters to form one string and preserve the original strings at the same time. The joining process starts by copying the first string into **Result**, the final product of the joining.

Strings are arrays of characters. A string cannot be copied by assigning one string to another; rather, each character must be copied from one string to the new one. This happens so often that **C** provides a system function **strcpy** (pronounced "stircopy"):

```
strcpy(Result,First) ;
       ^      ^
       |      |
       |      |      --- string we're copying from
       |
       --- string we're copying to
```

strcpy copies each character from the second string argument to the first string argument. **strcpy** doesn't destroy any of the values in the string being copied from, but it does completely destroy any previous value of the string being copied to.

Writing strcpy

strcpy is as easy to write as **strlen**. Here's the code:

```
int strcpy(ToString,FromString)
char    FromString[] ;
char    ToString[] ;
{      /* strcpy */
    int             Counter ;
```

```
            Counter = 0 ;
            do {
                ToString[Counter] = FromString[Counter] ;
            } while (FromString[Counter++]) ;
        }        /* strcpy */
```

Start copying with the zero-th element in both strings; so, set **Counter** to zero initially. In a **do/while** loop, characters are copied from **FromString** into **ToString** while non-zero **FromString** elements continue to be found. Why use the unusual combination of a **do/while** loop and an autoincrement at the end of the loop? Let's take an example. Say that **FromString** is:

```
T  e  s  t  i  n  g\0
|_|_|_|_|_|_|_|_|
0  1  2  3  4  5  6  7        FromString
```

Begin copying with element zero:

```
T
|_|_|_|_|_|_|_|_|            ToString
0  1  2  3  4  5  6  7
^
|
^
```

```
T  e  s  t  i  n  g\0
|_|_|_|_|_|_|_|_|            FromString
0  1  2  3  4  5  6  7
                             Counter is 0
```

Continue assigning character by character until the **g** (**FromString[6]**) is reached.

```
T  e  s  t  i  n  g
|_|_|_|_|_|_|_|_|            ToString
0  1  2  3  4  5  6  7
                  ^
                  |
                  ^
```

```
T  e  s  t  i  n  g\0
|_|_|_|_|_|_|_|_|            FromString
0  1  2  3  4  5  6  7
                             Counter is 6
```

Check to see if **FromString[6]** is zero. It isn't. So, increment **Counter** and continue. This time assign and test **FromString[7]**:

```
T  e  s  t  i  n  g\0
|_|_|_|_|_|_|_|_|            ToString
0  1  2  3  4  5  6  7
                     ^
                     |
                     ^
```

```
T  e  s  t  i  n  g\0
|_|_|_|_|_|_|_|_|            FromString
0  1  2  3  4  5  6  7
                             Counter is 7
```

Now, check **FromString[7]**. It is equal to the null character. Stop.

Why use this strategy? When working with strings, the zero terminator must be preserved. **strcpy** must be aware of this property of strings, because an old string is being copied into a new one. It cannot be guaranteed that the string being copied into will have zeros conveniently located for our use. The zero must be copied explicitly. The strategy here is to test for zero termination and increment the loop counter after assigning the terminating zero to **ToString**. The **do/while** loop is used to test after the assignment statment. **Counter** is incremented after testing. This sequence of operations is crucial.

HAZARD: running out of space

strcpy continues copying from the starting string into the result string until it finds a zero terminator in the starting string. If it doesn't find a terminator, it continues copying forever. Remember, all **C** string functions require strings to be properly terminated.

   strcpy continues copying until it finds a terminator in the starting string; the length of the result string is never checked. Indeed, **strcpy** never knows how long either string is. You must give **strcpy** a large enough result string to completely accommodate the copied string. **C** won't offer help in solving either of these problems, so be aware!

ANATOMY: joining strings

Now, to join strings together. Technically, joining two strings together to make one string is called *concatenation*. **C** provides a system function **strcat** (pronounced ''stir-cat,'' meaning ''string-concatenate'') that does the work:

```
strcat(Result,First) ;
       ^         ^
       |         |
       |         --- copying-from string
       |
       --- adding-to string
```

strcat adds each character from the second string argument to the end of first string argument. The old value of the string being added to is unchanged; characters are added at the end.

HAZARD: bad joins

strcat expects both strings to be zero terminated. Do not use **strcat** this way:

```
strcat(Result,First) ;    /* copy the first string */
strcat(Result,Second) ;   /* append the second string */
strcat(Result,Third) ;    /* append the third string */
```

In the above program the value of Result is not known at the start. We don't know it is zero terminated. Using **strcat** here can cause disastrous run-time errors. Always set the value of a string first (for example, with **strcpy**) before adding to it with **strcat**.

   Just like **strcpy**, **strcat** never knows the length of its strings. Because we're adding to the length of the first string, it is easy to ''run off'' the declared length of the string. Make sure the strings are declared large enough before using **strcat**.

Writing strcat

strcat looks much like **strcpy**. Here's the design:

```
strcat(ToString,FromString)
{
    Advance to the end of ToString.
    Copy all the characters from FromString to
    the end of ToString, including the zero terminator
}
```

The function code is:

```
int strcat(ToString,FromString)
char    FromString[] ;
char    ToString[] ;
{       /* strcat */

    int         FromCounter ;
    int         ToCounter ;

    /* Advance to the end of ToString in this loop.
     * Continue counting while we have nonzero elements.
     */
    for (ToCounter = 0 ; ToString[ToCounter] ; ToCounter++)
        ;

    /* ToCounter is now ToString's zero terminator.
     * Start copying.
     */
    FromCounter = 0 ;
    do {
        ToString[ToCounter++] = FromString[FromCounter] ;
    } while (FromString[FromCounter++]) ;
}       /* strcat */
```

Let's use an example. Say that **FromString** and **ToString** are:

```
T e s t i n g\0
|_|_|_|_|_|_|_|_|_|_|_|_|_|_|_|_|_|_|    ToString
 0 1 2 3 4 5 6 7 8 9 10 12   14   16
```

```
A g a i n\0
|_|_|_|_|_|_|    FromString
 0 1 2 3 4 5
```

First, move down **ToString** until the zero terminator is found:

```
T e s t i n g\0
|_|_|_|_|_|_|_|_|_|_|_|_|_|_|_|_|_|_|    ToString
 0 1 2 3 4 5 6 7 8 9 10 12   14   16
 ^
 |
 --- is it zero?

    ToCounter is 0
```

Finally, it is found:

```
T e s t i n g\0
|_|_|_|_|_|_|_|_|_|_|_|_|_|_|_|_|_|_|    ToString
 0 1 2 3 4 5 6 7 8 9 10 12   14   16
             ^
             |
             --- is it zero?

        ToCounter is 7
```

Starting with the zero-th element of **FromString** and the seventh element of **ToString**, we begin joining the strings by copying **FromString** into **ToString**:

```
T  e  s  t  i  n  g  A
|_|_|_|_|_|_|_|_|_|_|_|_|_|_|_|_|_|_|_|
 0  1  2  3  4  5  6  7  8  9 10  12    14    16          ToString
                      ^
                      |
                      ^

A  g  a  i  n\0
|_|_|_|_|_|_|_|
 0  1  2  3  4  5                                         FromString

ToCounter is 7
FromCounter is 0
```

We continue assigning, character by character, until the character **n** (**FromString[4]**) is reached. Note that **ToCounter** is autoincremented after every assignment, but autoincrementing of **FromCounter** is delayed until after the test:

```
T  e  s  t  i  n  g  A  g  a  i  n
|_|_|_|_|_|_|_|_|_|_|_|_|_|_|_|_|_|_|_|
 0  1  2  3  4  5  6  7  8  9 10  12    14    16          ToString
                                  ^
                                  |
                                  ^

A  g  a  i  n\0
|_|_|_|_|_|_|_|
 0  1  2  3  4  5                                         FromString

ToCounter is 11
FromCounter is 4
```

Check to see if **FromString[4]** is zero. It isn't. So, **FromCounter** is incremented and the program continues.

Finally, assign and test **FromString[5]**:

```
T  e  s  t  i  n  g  A  g  a  i  n\0
|_|_|_|_|_|_|_|_|_|_|_|_|_|_|_|_|_|_|_|
 0  1  2  3  4  5  6  7  8  9 10  12    14    16          ToString
                                     ^
                                     |
                                     ^

A  g  a  i  n\0
|_|_|_|_|_|_|_|
 0  1  2  3  4  5                                         FromString

ToCounter is 12
FromCounter is 5
```

Now, check **FromString[5]**. It is equal to zero.

strcat uses the same copying strategy as **strcpy**. To copy the zero terminator into **ToString** we use the same combination of **do/while** loop to test after the assignment, and the autoincrement of **ToCounter** after the test.

More Phrase Building

Our example builds a string out of words the user enters. But there's a problem: spaces between words are needed. We may also want to add additional phrases to the result string. Therefore, revise the program:

```
#include <stdio.h>
#define MAXSTRLEN    255
#define VOID        int

main()
{      /* main */
    char        First[MAXSTRLEN] ;
    char        Result[MAXSTRLEN] ;
    char        Second[MAXSTRLEN] ;
    char        Third[MAXSTRLEN] ;
    printf("Enter a word: ") ;
    fgets(First,MAXSTRLEN,stdin) ;
    StripNewLines(First) ;
    printf("Enter another word: ") ;
    fgets(Second,MAXSTRLEN,stdin) ;
    StripNewLines(Second) ;
    printf("Enter yet a third word: ") ;
    fgets(Third,MAXSTRLEN,stdin) ;
    StripNewLines(Third) ;
    printf("\n\n") ;                    /* just for a little space */

    strcpy(Result,"all stuck together: ") ;
    strcat(Result,First) ;     /* add the first string */
    strcat(Result," ") ;       /* add space */
    strcat(Result,Second) ;    /* add the second string */
    strcat(Result," ") ;       /* add space */
    strcat(Result,Third) ;     /* add the third string */

    printf("Your first string is: %s\n",First) ;
    printf("Your second string is: %s\n",Second) ;
    printf("Your third string is: %s\n",Third) ;
    printf("After joining the strings, %s\n",Result) ;
}       /* main */

VOID StripNewLines(StringToProcess)
char    StringToProcess[] ;
{      /* StripNewLines */
    int         I ;

    /* Advance a character at a time until
     * the zero terminator is found.
     */
    for (I = 0 ; StringToProcess[I] ; I++)
        if (StringToProcess[I] == '\n') {
            StringToProcess[I] = '\0' ;
            break ;
        }
}       /* StripNewLines */
```

When the code is entered, compiled, and the program is run, this is the interaction:

```
Enter a word: Hi
Enter another word: there
Enter yet a third word: !!!
Your first string is: Hi
Your second string is: there
Your third string is: !!!
After joining the strings, all stuck together: Hi there !!!
```

Much better!

ANATOMY: constant strings

A constant string can be put in the program by surrounding text with double quotes:

```
"All stuck together: "
```

C stores these characters in a reserved area. C automatically zero-terminates these constant strings. Constant strings can be used anywhere an explicitly declared character array would be used—with one exception: the constant string's value must not be altered during the program. A constant string cannot be used as the first argument to **strcpy** or **strcat**, although the length of a constant can be taken with **strlen**.

The string " " means one *literal space*. When it is passed to **strcat** or **strcpy**, the *space* must be enclosed in double quotes, not single quotes. Again: a letter in single quotes is a single letter; a letter in double quotes is a string:

- 'a' is just the letter **a**. It is not zero-terminated.
- "a" is a string, length of one, with value **a**. It is zero-terminated.

Using Variable Strings to Hold Filenames

Constant strings have been used to hold the names of files opened with **fopen**:

```
if ((OutFile = fopen("histgrm6","w")) == 0) {
    fprintf(stderr,"Can't open output file.\n") ;
    exit(0) ;
}
```

fopen takes two arguments: the first is a string containing the name of the file to be opened; the second is a string containing the file opening option to use. So far, in this book, we've always used constant strings as arguments to **fopen**.

But string variables can be used as well as string constants with any of the **C** functions that expect strings (and vice versa). This means the **main** function from the last histogram program in Chapter 5 can be rewritten:

```
#include <stdio.h>
#define MAXNUMSTARS     50
#define MAXNUMENTRIES   50
#define MAXSTRLEN       255
#define NUMTOCLEAR      25
#define VOID            int

extern double FindScalingFraction() ;

main()
{       /* main */
    int     EntryCount ;    /* looping variable--
                            * the current entry number
                            */
    char    FileName[MAXSTRLEN] ;
    FILE    *OutFile ;      /* where we're writing information */
    int     NumEntries ;    /* total number of entries */
    double  ScalingMultiplier ; /* the scaling value */
    double  Value[MAXNUMENTRIES] ; /* all values the user enters */

    printf("Enter the name of the file to write to: ") ;
    fgets(FileName,MAXSTRLEN,stdin) ;
    StripNewLines(FileName) ;

    if ((OutFile = fopen(FileName,"w")) == 0) {
        fprintf(stderr,"Can't open %s for output.\n",FileName) ;
        exit(0) ;
    }
```

```
        ClearScreen() ;
        printf("How Many Entries Will You Make? ") ;
        scanf("%d",&NumEntries) ;
        while (NumEntries > MAXNUMENTRIES || NumEntries < 1) {
            printf("\n\tI Can Only Accept a Number Between 1 and %d!\n",
                MAXNUMENTRIES) ;
            printf("\nHow Many Entries Will You Make? ") ;
            scanf("%d",&NumEntries) ;
        }

        /* Get the entries.
        */
        for (EntryCount = 0 ; EntryCount < NumEntries ; EntryCount++) {
            printf("\nFor Entry %d, Type a Value: ",
                    ·    EntryCount + 1) ;
            scanf("%lf",&Value[EntryCount]) ;
        }

        ScalingMultiplier = FindScalingFraction(Value,NumEntries,
                        MAXNUMSTARS) ;
        WriteHistogram(stdout,Value,NumEntries,ScalingMultiplier) ;
        WriteHistogram(OutFile,Value,NumEntries,ScalingMultiplier) ;
        fclose(OutFile) ;
}       /* main */
```

All the other functions are the same as in Chapter 5. Note that the code requires **StripNewLines**.

FileName is declared as a string of length **MAXSTRLEN**:

```
    char    FileName[MAXSTRLEN] ;
```

The user is prompted to enter the name of a file to create for the output and the string containing the filename is read using **fgets**:

```
    fgets(FileName,MAXSTRLEN,stdin) ;
```

Newlines must be removed before the string is passed to **fopen**:

```
    StripNewLines(FileName) ;
    if ((OutFile = fopen(FileName,"w")) == 0) {
        fprintf(stderr,"Can't open %s for output.\n",FileName) ;
        exit(0) ;
    }
```

Note the test for successful opening of the file remains the same. This makes the program much more flexible and easier to use.

Word Scrambling: An Encryption Program

C also allows work with the individual characters in a string. This program takes a password a user enters and then unscrambles it. The objective is:

Prompt the user to enter a password.
Unscramble the word and compare the
result against a known, internal password.
If the password entered is not valid,
display a message to the user and exit
the program.

The encryption algorithm is a simple one: reverse all the characters in the string:

```
#include <stdio.h>  iostream.h
#include <ctype.h>
#define EQUALS      0
#define MAXSTRLEN   255
#define PASSWORD    "havefun"   PPP
#define VOID        int

main()
{       /* main */
    int         I ;
    int         PassWordLength ;
    char        Temp ;
    char        UserPassWord[MAXSTRLEN] ;

    /* Get the password from the user.
     */
    cout <<  printf("Enter the password, then press RETURN: \n") ;
    fgets(UserPassWord,MAXSTRLEN,stdin) ;

    /* Strip newlines and shift to lower case.
     */
    StripNewLines(UserPassWord) ;
    LowerString(UserPassWord) ;

    /* Determine the length of the user's string.
     * This is required for the word scrambling.
     */
    PassWordLength = strlen(UserPassWord) ;
    for (I = 0 ; I < PassWordLength / 2 ; I++) {
        /* Do the scrambling by exchanging the I-th character
         * with the PassWordLength - I-th character.
         */
        Temp = UserPassWord[I] ;
        UserPassWord[I] = UserPassWord[PassWordLength - I - 1] ;
        UserPassWord[PassWordLength - I - 1] = Temp ;
    }

    if (strcmp(UserPassWord,PASSWORD) != EQUALS) {
        printf("Your password is incorrect.\n") ;
        exit(0) ;
    }
    else
        printf("Your password is correct.\n") ;

    /* Now that the user has successfully entered the password,
     * the program continues as needed.
     */
}       /* main */

VOID LowerString(StringToProcess)
char        StringToProcess[] ;
{   /* LowerString */
    int         I ;
    /* Advance a character at a time, shifting each to
     * lower case until the terminator is found.
     */

    for (I = 0 ; StringToProcess[I] ; I++)
        StringToProcess[I] = tolower(StringToProcess[I]) ;
}   /* LowerString */
```

```
VOID StripNewLines(StringToProcess)
char    StringToProcess[] ;
{       /* StripNewLines */
    int         I ;

    /* Advance a character at a time until
     * the zero terminator is found.
     */
    for (I = 0 ; StringToProcess[I] ; I++)

        if (StringToProcess[I] == '\n') {
            StringToProcess[I] = '\0' ;
            break ;
        }
}           /* StripNewLines */
```

Converting strings to contain only lower case letters works just like stripping new lines. The strategy is to look at one character at a time. Each character is passed through **tolower** to convert it to lower case, then placed back in the string.

main inverts the letters in **UserPassWord**, the string the user enters. Examine the process in detail. Suppose the user enters the word 'nUfeVAH' in response to the prompt. **fgets** reads the string and inserts it in **UserPassWord** with a newline and a null character at the end. **StripNewLines** removes the newline, and **LowerString** converts all the letters to lower case. After this preliminary processing, **User-PassWord** is:

```
n u f e v a h\0
|_|_|_|_|_|_|_|_|_|_|...       UserPassWord
0 1 2 3 4 5 6 7 8 9
```

strlen gets the length of the string: seven. When the **for** loop starts, the variables are:

```
n u f e v a h\0
|_|_|_|_|_|_|_|_|_|_|...       UserPassWord
0 1 2 3 4 5 6 7 8 9

        PassWordLength is 7
```

The loop variable **I** starts at zero. The **for** loop continues while **I** is less than **PassWordLength / 2**. Because integer division is being used which *throws away* any remainder, the quotient is *3*.

On the first trip through the loop, the first and last letters in **UserPassWord** are exchanged. This means:

```
n u f e v a h\0
|_|_|_|_|_|_|_|_|_|_|...       UserPassWord
0 1 2 3 4 5 6 7 8 9
v           v
|           |
--         --
  |-- --|
--         --
|           |
v           v
h u f e v a n\0
|_|_|_|_|_|_|_|_|_|_|...       UserPassWord
0 1 2 3 4 5 6 7 8 9
```

UserPassWord[0] and **UserPassWord[6]** are exchanged.

The problem is it is not known how long a word the user will enter until the program is running. Instead of exchanging the zero-th and sixth elements in **UserPassWord**, the exchange is based on the length of the string. This is the approach:

```
I is 0
PassWordLength is 7
PassWordLength - I - 1 is 6
```

```
        n  u  f  e  v  a  h\0
       |_|_|_|_|_|_|_|_|_|_|...          UserPassWord
        0  1  2  3  4  5  6  7  8  9
        v           v
        |           |
        --          --
        |--       --|
        --          --
        |           |
        v           v
        h  u  f  e  v  a  n\0
       |_|_|_|_|_|_|_|_|_|_|...          UserPassWord
        0  1  2  3  4  5  6  7  8  9
```

Exchange the **I**-th element, here the zero-th element, with the **PassWordLength - [I] - 1**th element.

On the next trip through the loop, **I** is 1, and this exchange is made:

```
I is 1
PassWordLength is 7
PassWordLength - I - 1 is 5
```

```
   n  u  f  e  v  a  h\0
  |_|_|_|_|_|_|_|_|_|_|...          UserPassWord
   0  1  2  3  4  5  6  7  8  9
      v        v
      |        |
      -        -
      |-    -|
      -        -
      |        |
      v        v
   h  a  f  e  v  u  n\0
  |_|_|_|_|_|_|_|_|_|_|...          UserPassWord
   0  1  2  3  4  5  6  7  8  9
```

Now the calculation to determine the two letters to exchange becomes clear. **UserPassWord[1]** and **UserPassWord[5]** must be exchanged. **I** is one, and **PassWordLength - [I] - 1** is five. Exchange these letters.

The loop executes once more and **I** is 2. Exchange **UserPassWord[2]** and **UserPassWord[4]**. Now **I** is incremented, giving 3. The **for** loop continuation condition now fails because **I** is equal to **PassWordLength / 2**. The string is inverted. This technique works with strings of any length.

ANATOMY: comparing strings with strcmp

The system function **strcmp** (pronounced "stir-comp," meaning "string comparison") compares two strings for equality or inequality. **strcmp** takes two parameters, the two strings to be checked:

```
result = strcmp(UserPassWord,PASSWORD) ;
```

strcmp examines each character in each string and returns one of three values·

zero: if the two strings are EQUAL
a number greater than zero: if the first string is GREATER than the second
a number less than zero: if the first string is LESS than the second

Strings are *equal* if every character in each string matches the corresponding character in the other:

```
A B  C  D E  F  G  H  I  \0
i_i_i_i_i_i_i_i_i_i_i            first string
 ^ ^ ^ ^ ^ ^ ^ ^ ^ ^

i  i  i  i  i  i  i  i  i  i
 ^ ^ ^ ^ ^ ^ ^ ^ ^ ^

A  B  C  D E  F  G  H  I  \0
i_i_i_i_i_i_i_i_i_i_i            second string
```

The first string is less than the second string if it is shorter than the first string and all characters match otherwise:

```
A  B  C  D E  \0
i_i_i_i_i_i_i                   first string
 ^ ^ ^ ^ ^ ^

i  i  i  i  i  i
 ^ ^ ^ ^ ^ ^

A  B  C  D E  F  G  H  I  \0
i_i_i_i_i_i_i_i_i_i_i            second string
```

or if a character in the first string is smaller than the corresponding character in the second string:

```
A  B  C  D O  F  G  H  I  \0
i_i_i_i_i_i_i_i_i_i_i            first string
 ^ ^ ^ ^ ^

i  i  i  i  i
 ^ ^ ^ ^ ^

A  B  C  D E  F  G  H  I  \0
i_i_i_i_i_i_i_i_i_i_i            second string
```

The ASCII collating sequence is used in **C** compilers to define which characters are greater than or less than a character.

As might be expected, the first string is greater than the second string if either the first string is longer than the second, or if a character in the first string is greater than the corresponding character in the second string—using the ASCII collating sequence.

The program uses **strcmp** to see if the unscrambled **UserPassWord** is equal to the **PASSWORD** that is known to the system:

```
if (strcmp(UserPassWord,PASSWORD) != EQUALS) {
    print a message
    exit the program
}
```

Writing strcmp

As with all the string functions discussed up to this point, **strcmp** is easy to write. The strategy is to compare each character in the string for equality. If the characters compared are the null character, the entire string has been traversed, and the two strings are equal. Zero is then returned. If a mismatch is found, a non-zero number is returned to show the result of the comparison as described above. Here's the code:

```
int strcmp(String1,String2)
char      String1[] ;
char      String2[] ;
{       /* strcmp */
    int    Location ;

    Location = 0 ;
    /* Search through while the corresponding
     * characters are equal.
     */
    while (String1[Location] == String2[Location]) {
         if (String1[Location++] == '\0')
             return(0) ;
    }
    return(String1[Location] - String2[Location]) ;
}       /* strcmp */
```

Begin examining the zero-th characters in each string for equality. The **while** loop continues when the corresponding characters in each string are equal. If the characters being examined are equal and they are *null characters*, this task is finished. Zero is returned, indicating the strings are equal.

If any corresponding character in the strings is unequal, a number calculated by subtracting the two characters is returned. What does this mean?

Compare two characters **A** and **B** from **String1** and **String2**, respectively. They are unequal. The ASCII collating values for the characters are:

```
A is 65     B is 66
```

Arithmetic is performed on the characters by first converting them to their ASCII collating values, then manipulating these numbers. Indeed, the characters are always stored internally as the ASCII collating values, and are converted only on output to us as a convenience.

The statement:

```
return(String1[Location] - String2[Location]) ;
```

does this subtraction:

```
return('A' - 'B')
```
or
```
return(65 - 66)  -----> return -1, a number
                        less than zero.
```

If **String1** has the character with the greater collating value, a number greater than zero is returned through the same calculation.

ANATOMY: multiple returns from a function

strcmp has two **return** statements: one inside the **while** loop and the other at the end of the function.C lets us have as many **return** statements as are needed inside a function; whenever the **return** is executed we leave the function just as if we had left through the bottom of the function. This mechanism lets us escape easily from the middle of a loop and return immediately with a special value.

Finding a String in a File

In large text files it is often helpful to display all lines that contain a specified string. The objective is:

Get the name of a file to be processed from the
user, and a search string to be located.
Open the file and read it line by line.
If a line contains the search string,
display it to **stdout**. Make the search
find the string whether letters are in upper
or lower case in the file being processed.

The code is surprisingly simple.

HAZARD: microcomputer C users please note!

Some microcomputer **C** compilers do not use the common definition for **index**. The complete source code is included as part of the program below. Note some **C** compilers do not allow a function that you define to have the same name as a system-defined function name. (See Appendix A and your compiler documentation for details.)

```
#include <stdio.h>
#include <ctype.h>
#define MAXSTRLEN    255
#define VOID         int

main()
{     /* main */
    char       CurrentLine[MAXSTRLEN] ;
    char       FileName[MAXSTRLEN] ;
    FILE       *InFile ;
    char       SearchString[MAXSTRLEN] ;

    /* Open the input file.
     */
    printf("Enter the name of the file to search: ") ;
    fgets(FileName,MAXSTRLEN,stdin) ;
    StripNewLines(FileName) ;
    if (!(InFile = fopen(FileName,"r"))) {
        printf("I can't find the file %s.\n",FileName) ;
        exit(0) ;
    }
    /* Get the search string.
     */
    printf("Enter your search string: ") ;
```

```
        fgets(SearchString,MAXSTRLEN,stdin) ;

        /* Remove all newlines and shift
         * all letters to lower case.
         */
        StripNewLines(SearchString) ;
        LowerString(SearchString) ;

        /* Now, search the file.  Read each line in turn.
         * If fgets returns a zero, there are no more
         * lines to read.  Continue until that time.
         */
        while (fgets(CurrentLine,MAXSTRLEN,InFile) != 0) {
            /* First, convert our line to have only
             * lower case letters
             */
            LowerString(CurrentLine) ;

            /* If the string is found, write it out.
             */
            if (index(CurrentLine,SearchString) != -1)
                fputs(CurrentLine,stdout) ;
        }
}       /* main */

int index(LineToCheck,Pattern)
/* index returns the number of the character in the string
 * LineToCheck where Pattern is first found.  It returns -1 if
 * Pattern is not found.
 */
char    LineToCheck[] ;
char    Pattern[] ;
{       /* index */
    int CurrentBase ;
    int LineIndex ;
    int PatternIndex ;

    /* This outer loop looks at each character in
     * LineToCheck, one after another.
     */
    for (CurrentBase = 0 ; LineToCheck[CurrentBase] != '\0' ;
                CurrentBase++) {
        /* LineIndex is the starting place to look in
         * LineToCheck.  Look through the line while there
         * are characters in Pattern, and while the characters
         * compared are identical.
         */
        for (LineIndex = CurrentBase,PatternIndex = 0 ;
                Pattern[PatternIndex] != '\0' &&
                Pattern[PatternIndex] == LineToCheck[LineIndex] ;
                LineIndex++,PatternIndex++)
            ;       /* no body */

            /* If all characters are completely matched in
             * Pattern, return CurrentBase, the position in
             * LineToCheck where we are successful.
             */
            if (Pattern[PatternIndex] == '\0')
                return (CurrentBase) ;
        }
        return (-1) ;           /* We failed */
}       /* index */
```

```
VOID LowerString(StringToProcess)
char      StringToProcess[] ;
{       /* LowerString */
      int        I ;

      /* Advance a character at a time, shifting each to
       * lower case, until the terminator is found.
       */
      for (I = 0 ; StringToProcess[I] ; I++)
            StringToProcess[I] = tolower(StringToProcess[I]) ;
}       /* LowerString */

VOID StripNewLines(StringToProcess)
char      StringToProcess[] ;
{       /* StripNewLines */
      int        I ;

      /* Advance a character at a time until
       * the zero terminator is found.
       */
      for (I = 0 ; StringToProcess[I] ; I++)

            if (StringToProcess[I] == '\n') {
                  StringToProcess[I] = '\0' ;
                  break ;
            }
}       /* StripNewLines */
```

The program falls into these sections: first open the file for input; then get the search string and clean it free of newlines and upper case letters; then search the input file for the desired string.

ANATOMY: the not operator

We've used the **C** logical operators **&&** (and) and ‖ (or). **C** also provides the *not* operator. The *not* operator makes a condition true when the value to which it applies is false. The *not* operator is written as a single exclamation point (!) before its operand:

```
!A
```

means "not-A."

```
!A
```
is <u>true</u> when **A** is <u>false</u>:

```
      if A is:        !A is:
      --------        ------
      TRUE            FALSE
      FALSE           TRUE
```

This operator allows simple tests for successful file opening in the program above. Write:

```
if (!(InFile = fopen(FileName,"r"))) {
      printf("I can't find the file %s.  Check the directory.\n",
      FileName) ;
      exit(0) ;
}
```

First, call **fopen** to open the file. Assign the result to **InFile**. If **fopen** successfully completes the opening, **InFile** is a non-zero number (see our discussion of **fopen** above). Remembering that a non-zero number means TRUE in **C**, evaluate the **if** expression as:

```
if (!(TRUE)) {
    printf("I can't find the file %s.   Check the directory.\n",
    FileName) ;
    exit(0) ;
}
```

!(TRUE) is false, so the **if** action is not performed.

If, on the other hand, the file opening fails, **fopen** returns a zero. Remembering that a zero number means FALSE in **C**, the **if** expression is evaluated as:

```
if (!(FALSE)) {
    printf("I can't find the file %s.   Check the directory.\n",
    FileName) ;
    exit(0) ;
}
```

!(FALSE) is true. So, execute the **if** action.

This code is incorrect:

```
if (InFile != fopen(FileName,"r")) {
    printf("I can't find the file %s.   Check the directory.\n",
    FileName) ;
    exit(0) ;
}
```

fopen is called and returns a pointer to a file. If this value is not equal to the current value of **InFile**, the **if** action is executed. This statement never initializes **InFile**—the assignment must be enclosed in parentheses.

This initially confusing shorthand is commonly used in **C** programs. Spend some time developing an understanding of the not operator. It will be time well invested.

ANATOMY: reading from text files with fgets and handling end-of-file

When text is read from the user, it is known when the end of the input has been reached because the program usually asks for a specific number of items to be entered, and the program waits until entry is complete.

Many applications which read from text files on disk don't know how much text to read. The program must continue to read until the end of the input file is reached. Our program uses **fgets** to read a line at a time from the input file. Each time a line is read, the program advances in the file to the next line to be read.

Let's say the input file has the text in the box below. When this file is read from for the first time, it is:

```
------------------------------------
| This is the first line.          |
| This is the second line.         |
| This is the third line.          |
|      . . .                       |
| <End-of-file>                    |
------------------------------------
```

< End-of-file > has been explicitly marked at the bottom of the box.

When reading from this file for the first time using **fgets**, the following is read into **CurrentLine**:

```
This is the first line.
```

which is followed by a newline and a zero terminator. On the next reading from the file, we see:

```
----------------------------
| This is the second line.  |
| This is the third line.   |
|      . . .                |
| <End-of-file>             |
----------------------------
```

The file appears without the line just read. The line is still really there. It wasn't erased from the disk. But it is no longer visible. When **fgets** is called again, we read:

```
This is the second line.
```

What happens when there are no more lines? **fgets** returns the number zero; there is no more input data. If **fgets** successfully reads a line, it returns a non-zero value.

The program uses this **while** loop to test for end-of-file after every read:

```
while (fgets(CurrentLine,MAXSTRLEN,InFile) != 0) {
    /* First convert our line to have
     * only lower case letters.
     */
    LowerString(CurrentLine) ;

    /* If the string is found, write it out.
     */
    if (index(CurrentLine,SearchString) != -1)
        puts(CurrentLine,stdout) ;
}
```

Test the number returned by **fgets**. **while** it is not zero, continue processing the text.

We will meet end-of-file again when reading from a file character-by-character with **getc** and block-by-block with **fread**.

ANATOMY: finding a pattern in a string using index

C has the function **index** to find a pattern string inside a master string. This is the way **index** is used:

```
Place = index(CurrentLine,PatternString) ;
                    ^               ^
                    |               |
        string to ---        --- string to
        look through            search for
```

index then returns the array index where the pattern string is found inside the master string. If the pattern string is not found, **index** returns minus one.

Let's consider this string:

```
T h i s   i s   1 . \0
|_|_|_|_|_|_|_|_|_|_|_|   master string
 0 1 2 3 4 5 6 7 8 9 10
```

And the search is for this pattern:

```
i s \0
|_|_|_|   search string
0 1 2
```

index first positions the pattern string at the zero-th character in the master string
and sees if the two match:

```
T h i s   i s   1 . \0
|_|_|_|_|_|_|_|_|_|_|_|_|   master string
0 1 2 3 4 5 6 7 8 9 10
^
|
^

i s \0
|_|_|_|   pattern string
0 1 2
            Trying for match in master string position 0.
```

It fails. **index** continues to move the pattern string along each succeeding position
in the master string until it either finds the match, or it runs out of characters to search
in the master string.

   index's second try looks like this:

```
T h i s   i s   1 . \0
|_|_|_|_|_|_|_|_|_|_|_|_|   master string
0 1 2 3 4 5 6 7 8 9 10
  ^
  |
  ^

  i s \0
  |_|_|_|   pattern string
  0 1 2
            Trying for match in master string position 1.
```

This fails, too.

The third try succeeds:

```
T h i s   i s   1 . \0
|_|_|_|_|_|_|_|_|_|_|_|_|   master string
0 1 2 3 4 5 6 7 8 9 10
    ^
    |
    ^

    i s \0
    |_|_|_|   pattern string
    0 1 2
            Trying for match in master string position 2.
```

   The pattern string is found in the master string starting in array position two. **index**
returns the number two to its caller, indicating a successful match and the correct
position.

   Note: **index** only returns the *first* occurrence of the pattern string in the master
string. In the example, the master string contains the pattern string in two places:

```
        "is"
        -----
        |   |
        v   v
       ---  ---
 T h i s   i s   1 . \0
|_|_|_|_|_|_|_|_|_|_|_|_|            master string
 0 1 2 3 4 5 6 7 8 9 10
```

index returns only 2, never 5.

Writing index

index is the most involved string function we will study. It must do a string comparison repeatedly as it goes through the string.

The above source code uses **LineToCheck** to mean the master string. It uses **Pattern** to mean the pattern string for which we are searching. **CurrentBase** is the position within **LineToCheck** that is being searched.

This is the strategy:

> Set **CurrentBase** to zero, starting the search with the zero-th character in **LineToCheck**. If the comparison starting at this position fails, increment **CurrentBase** to check each succeeding position until the file has no more characters.

```
for (CurrentBase = 0 ; LineToCheck[CurrentBase] != '\0' ;
        CurrentBase++) {
```

LineIndex is the array index where, in **LineToCheck**, the character-by-character comparison with **Pattern** starts. Each time a comparison is made, **PatternIndex** is set to zero to begin the comparison with the zero-th character in **Pattern**.

The comparison is done in this **for** loop:

```
for (LineIndex = CurrentBase,PatternIndex = 0 ;
    Pattern[PatternIndex] != '\0' &&
    Pattern[PatternIndex] == LineToCheck[LineIndex] ;
    LineIndex++,PatternIndex++)
        ;    /* no body */
```

The only action performed is to compare characters in the continuation condition. No other action is performed.

The loop terminates under two conditions:

1. The compared characters are unequal.
2. All characters in **Pattern** have been compared.

If all characters have been successfully compared, **Pattern[PatternIndex]** is the null character. **CurrentBase** is returned, the starting position in **LineToCheck** where the successful comparison began.

An unsuccessful match occurs if we run out of characters in **LineToCheck** in the outer loop before a successful match is found.

This condition happens if the outer loop finishes with the continuation condition failing:

```
. . . ; LineToCheck[CurrentBase] != '\0' ; . . .
```

The last statement in **index** is **return(-1)**. This means failure and is only reached if all possible matches have failed.

7

Paths And Pointers

Introduction To Pointers

A major strength of **C** is its handling of pointers. Most **C** programs heavily use pointers, so understanding the ground rules behind using pointers is especially important. Don't rush this chapter. Reread it as you go until you are confident of a high level of comprehension. Work through the examples patiently and in detail.

A Tale of Many Houses

Rather than jump right into pointers, we'll take an indirect, anecdotal approach. Let us discuss delivering mail to many houses on a block. Assume we are describing delivering mail to someone who has never done it before.

Explanation One

It is essential that mail be delivered to everyone in a particular block. Visualize the "block" in this way:

```
        !__!__!__!__!__!__!__!__!__!
house    0  1  2  3  4  5  6  7  8
```

On this block there are nine houses, numbered zero through eight. (Of course houses aren't normally numbered starting from zero, but allow the license.) Start the mail delivery with house number zero. All the mail with the address zero is delivered there. Now, add one (1) to the address of the house to which a delivery has just been made (0 + 1 gives 1). Now, go to the house with the next address in the block. The starting picture looks like:

```
        !__!__!__!__!__!__!__!__!__!
house    0  1  2  3  4  5  6  7  8
         ^
         !
           -- Go to the zero-th house and deliver
              the  mail.  Take its address (0), add
              one and get the next address (1).
```

109

Now, at house one, deliver all the appropriate mail there.

```
         !__!__!__!__!__!__!__!__!
house     0  1  2  3  4  5  6  7  8
             ^
             !
             -- Go to the first house and deliver
                the mail.  Take its address (1), add
                one and get the next address (2).
```

Again, add one to the address of the house (1 + 1 gives 2), and go to house two.

Continue to deliver mail to each house on the block, then add one to its address and go to the house with that next address. Stop on arrival at the last address in the block.

HOW THIS EXAMPLE RELATES TO C

This model of mail delivery is much like **arrays**. Start with the zero-th element in the array and process it by its array number. Then, increment the array number and process that element. Continue incrementing the array number and processing that element until done with all elements. Each house is referred to by an address number, just as all array elements are referred to by an element number.

Explanation Two

As an alternate approach, think of a path leading to the zero-th house on the block. This is the picture at the start:

```
 !__!__!__!__!__!__!__!__!
 ^
 !
 !
path to the zero-th house
```

Follow the path and deliver all the mail to its destination.

Move the path to the next house. (Yes, in the **C** world there are movable paths.) The address of the house is not known by number, but it's the one following the last one referred to. The picture is now:

```
 !__!__!__!__!__!__!__!__!
     ^
     !
     !
    path to the next house
```

Follow this path to its destination and deliver all the appropriate mail.

Continue, moving the path to the next house, delivering mail until the entire block is finished.

HOW THIS EXAMPLE RELATES TO C

This model is like pointers. Get a pointer to the beginning of some data. The pointer is not itself the data to process, but it is followed to the data. Once arrived at the data, process it, as is always done.

Pointers in **C** are movable. Move a pointer to the next item or to the previous item in the block. After moving the pointer, the new pointer can be followed to this piece of data.

When a path to a house is followed, its house address is not used. Similarly, when pointers in **C** are used, refer to the information using the pointer, not through an array index.

Our First Program with Pointers

This brief program is an example of the use of pointers. It writes a character string, character by character:

```
#include <stdio.h>
#define MAXSTRLEN        255

main()
{       /* main */
    char            *CurCharPtr ;
    char            String [MAXSTRLEN] ;

    printf("Enter a line of text: ") ;    /* write a prompt */
    fgets(String,MAXSTRLEN,stdin) ;       /* read the line */

    /* Print each character until
     * a zero terminator is found.
     */
    for (CurCharPtr = &String[0] ; *CurCharPtr != '\0' ;
                    CurCharPtr++)
        printf("The next character is: %c\n",*CurCharPtr) ;
}       /* main */
```

ANATOMY: declaring pointers

Pointer variables are declared before they are used; as with any other variable. To declare a pointer to a character, write:

```
char    *CurCharPtr ;
```

The star (*) in the declaration means ''create a pointer,'' a path that, when followed to its destination, arrives at a character.

In **C**, all pointers have a *base type*: the type of data the pointer points to. For example:

```
int         *IntPointer ;      /* base type int */
double      *DoubPointer ;     /* base type double */
```

IntPointer is a *pointer* that points to an integer; if **IntPointer** is followed, we find an integer. Similarly, **DoubPointer** is a *pointer* that points to a double. In each case, when a pointer is followed to its destination, a value is found there which has the base type that was declared.

ANATOMY: giving pointers a value, and the mysterious ampersand

When a pointer is declared, it is a path to nowhere in particular. It doesn't point to anything. Before using it, you have to give it a value, just as you would any other variable.

In this example, the pointer **CurCharPtr** points to the zero-th element of **String** in the **for** statement:

```
for (CurCharPtr = &String[0] ; *CurCharPtr != '\0' ;
               CurCharPtr++)
```

The clause:

```
CurCharPtr = &String[0] ...
```

means "make **CurCharPtr** point to the zero-th element of **String**." **CurCharPtr** now looks like this:

```
!__!__!__!__!__!__!__!__!__!__!__ ...
 0   1   2   3   4   5   6   7   8   9   10          String
 ^
 !
  --- CurCharPtr = &String[0]
```

When **CurCharPtr** is followed to its destination, the zero-th element of **String** is reached. The ampersand operator **&** returns a pointer to anything. A pointer to any variable can be created simply by prefixing it with an ampersand.

Assume **Q** is an integer and **NewPtr** is a pointer to an integer. This set of statements:

```
int     Q ;
int     *NewPtr ;
NewPtr = &Q ;
```

makes **NewPtr** point to **Q**. This means that when **NewPtr** is followed to its destination, **Q** is reached.

ANATOMY: following pointers to their destination with the star operator

Follow a pointer to its destination by using the star operator *****. In:

```
*CurCharPtr
```

the pointer **CurCharPtr** is followed to its destination and access the value living there. In the above example, if **CurCharPtr** points at **String[0]**, as shown here:

```
H   i       t   h   e   r   e   !
!__!__!__!__!__!__!__!__!__!__!__ ...
 0   1   2   3   4   5   6   7   8   9   10          String
 ^
 !
  --- CurCharPtr = &String[0]
```

then ***CurCharPtr** has the value *H*. Follow **CurCharPtr** to its destination and look at the value there.

Remember these points; they are crucial:

- **CurCharPtr** is a pointer. It is *not* the data directly used.
- ***CurCharPtr** is the *value* derived when the pointer is followed to its destination.

ANATOMY: moving pointers

To move a pointer to the next data item, use the autoincrement operator. If **CurCharPtr** points to **String[0]**:

```
H   i     t  h  e  r  e  !  \0
|__|__|__|__|__|__|__|__|__|__|__ ...
0   1  2  3  4  5  6  7  8  9  10       String
^
|
CurCharPtr
```

it can be moved to the next character in **String** by writing:

```
CurCharPtr++
```

The result is:

```
H   i     t  h  e  r  e  !  \0
|__|__|__|__|__|__|__|__|__|__|__ ...
0   1  2  3  4  5  6  7  8  9  10       String
   ^
   |
CurCharPtr
```

Now, when **CurCharPtr** is followed to its destination, ***CurCharPtr** is *i*. Either the autopreincrement or autopostincrement operators work. To move a pointer to the previous data item, use the autodecrement operator.

If we have:

```
H   i     t  h  e  r  e  !  \0
|__|__|__|__|__|__|__|__|__|__|__ ...
0   1  2  3  4  5  6  7  8  9  10       String
            ^
            |
        CurCharPtr
```

it can be moved to the previous character in **String** by writing:

```
CurCharPtr--
```

Then we have:

```
H   i     t  h  e  r  e  !  \0
|__|__|__|__|__|__|__|__|__|__|__ ...
0   1  2  3  4  5  6  7  8  9  10       String
         ^
         |
       CurCharPtr
```

*CurCharPtr is *h*. Either the autopreincrement or autopostdecrement operators work.

Sometimes it may be desirable to move a pointer several data items from its current spot.

If this is the start:

```
H   i       t   h   e   r   e   !   \0
|__|__|__|__|__|__|__|__|__|__|__|__  ...
 0   1   2   3   4   5   6   7   8   9  10          String
 ^
 ¦
CurCharPtr
```

CurCharPtr can be moved down three characters by writing:

```
CurCharPtr += 3 ;
```

Then, the result is:

```
H   i       t   h   e   r   e   !   \0
|__|__|__|__|__|__|__|__|__|__|__|__  ...
 0   1   2   3   4   5   6   7   8   9  10          String
             ^
             ¦
            CurCharPtr
```

CurCharPtr can be moved back to its original position by writing:

```
CurCharPtr -= 3 ;
```

Then, the result is:

```
H   i       t   h   e   r   e   !   \0
|__|__|__|__|__|__|__|__|__|__|__|__  ...
 0   1   2   3   4   5   6   7   8   9  10          String
 ^
 ¦
CurCharPtr
```

Simply add (to move forward) or subtract (to move backward) an integer value to reposition the pointer.

Integer values may only be added or subtracted to pointers. Pointers may not be multiplied or divided by integer values.

How Pointers Work in Programs

This set of statements was used above:

```
char            *CurCharPTr ;
char            String [MAXSTRLEN] ;

fgets(String,MAXSTRLEN,stdin) ;         /* read the line */
for (CurCharPtr = &String[0]; *CurCharPtr != '\0' ;
        CurCharPtr++)
    printf("The next character is: %c\n",*CurCharPtr) ;
```

The call to **fgets** reads a line of text from **stdin** and puts it in **String**. If the line **Hi there!** is entered, **fgets** gives **String** the value:

```
H  i      t  h  e  r  e  !\n\0
|_|_|_|_|_|_|_|_|_|_|_|_|
 0 1 2 3 4 5 6 7 8 9 10              String
```

Remember, **fgets** includes the newline the user typed to end the line.

The **for** loop works as follows. First set **CurCharPtr** to point at **String[0]**:

```
for (CurCharPtr = &String[0] ; ...
```

```
H i   t h e r e ! \n 0
|_|_|_|_|_|_|_|_|_|_|_|          String
0 1 2 3 4 5 6 7 8 9 10
^
|
  --- CurCharPtr = &String[0]
```

Now, execute the body of the loop:

```
printf("The next character is: %c\n",*CurCharPtr) ;
```

The value displayed here is ***CurCharPtr**. Follow **CurCharPtr** and find the letter *H*. This is the letter that is displayed. Now, do the increment operation:

```
. . . ; CurCharPtr++)
```

This moves **CurCharPtr** to the next character:

```
H i   t h e r e ! \n 0
|_|_|_|_|_|_|_|_|_|_|_|          String
0 1 2 3 4 5 6 7 8 9 10
  ^
  |
CurcharPtr
```

Next, do the loop continuation test:

```
. . . ; *CurCharPtr != '\0' ; . . .
```

Follow the new value of **CurCharPtr** to its destination and test if that character is not equal to the null character. It isn't, so continue looping and displaying characters. Display each character **CurCharPtr** points to, then move **CurCharPtr** to the next character in turn. At this point, the effect is:

```
H i   t h e r e ! \n \0
|_|_|_|_|_|_|_|_|_|_|_|          String
0 1 2 3 4 5 6 7 8 9 10
                  ^
                  |
              CurCharPtr
```

Output the newline, then increment **CurCharPtr**. **CurCharPtr** points to the null character, ending the string.

```
H i   t h e r e ! \n \0
|_|_|_|_|_|_|_|_|_|_|_|          String
0 1 2 3 4 5 6 7 8 9 10
                    ^
                    |
                CurCharPtr
```

Now, when the loop continuation is tested, it fails and the loop stops.

A Simple Rewrite

C has a simpler construction to get a pointer to the first data item in an array. The program is simplified by using this feature:

```
#include <stdio.h>
#define MAXSTRLEN        255

main()
{       /* main */
    char        *CurCharPtr ;
    char        String[MAXSTRLEN] ;

    printf("Enter a line of text: ") ;   /* write a prompt */
    fgets(String,MAXSTRLEN,stdin) ;      /* read the line */

    /* Print each character until
     * a zero terminator is found.
     */
    for (CurCharPtr = String ; *CurCharPtr != '\0' ;
                CurCharPtr++)
        printf("The next character is: %c\n",*CurCharPtr) ;
}       /* main */
```

ANATOMY: pointer-initialization and arrays

The first program used the ampersand operator to initialize **CurCharPtr** in our **for** loop:

```
for (CurCharPtr = &String[0] ; *CurCharPtr != '\0' ;
            CurCharPtr++)
```

Using the **&** operator, explicitly request a pointer to **String[0]**.

Now—a shorthand—if an array name without a subscript is used, we automatically get a pointer to the zero-th element of the array:

```
for (CurCharPtr = String ; *CurCharPtr != '\0' ;
            CurCharPtr++)
```

This statement uses **String** (the name of our character array) without an array subscript, meaning a pointer to the zero-th element of **String**. **CurCharPtr** is automatically set to point to the first character in the array.

When Are Pointers Useful?

Pointers are particularly useful when dealing with groups of information (such as arrays), to move easily to the next item in the group. Using pointers, a particular element is not referred to by number. Many mathematical and engineering problems are best solved using arrays. Most character string and file manipulation functions are best written through the use of pointers.

Now, to consolidate our advanced knowledge, we will rewrite many of the string handling functions from the last chapter, this time using pointers.

Rewriting strlen

Remember **strlen** counts character-by-character until it finds the null character that terminates the string. It then returns the count. This is the function when it used arrays:

```
int strlen(String)
char    String[] ;
{       /* strlen */
     int         Counter ;

     for (Counter = 0 ; String[Counter] ; Counter++)
     ;
     return(Counter) ;
}       /* strlen */
```

Now, rewrite it to use pointers instead of arrays:

```
int strlen(String)
char    *String ;
{       /* strlen */
     int         Counter ;

     Counter = 0 ;
     while (*String++)
          Counter++ ;
     return(Counter) ;
}       /* strlen */
```

Instead of looking at the parameter **String** as an indefinitely long array of characters, look at it as a character pointer which points to a zero-terminated character string.

This brings up another important point: array-parameters of indefinite length are the same as pointer-parameters pointing to the same base type as the array. Whichever is needed to solve the problem can be used. We will return to this later.

When the loop is entered, the pointer **String** is already pointing at the beginning of the string. **Counter** is set to zero before the **while** loop begins. This is the first pass through the loop:

```
H  e  r  e     w  e     g  o  !  \0
|_|_|_|_|_|_|_|_|_|_|_|_|_|
^
|
String
          Counter is 0
```

The **while** continuation condition is:

```
while (*String++)
```

This means "first apply the * operator to **String** and get the character to which it points." In this example, it is *H*. While the character pointed to is *not* the null character zero, a true continuation condition exists.

After the test is made, **String** is incremented. This moves **String** to point to the next character in the string. **Counter** is incremented in the loop body and continues. Note the order of operations; it is crucial to the correct execution of the code.

After some time, we have:

```
H  e  r  e     w  e     g  o  !  \0
|_|_|_|_|_|_|_|_|_|_|_|_|_|
                         ^
                         |
                      String
          Counter is 10
```

Evaluate the **while** continuation condition by seeing if ***String** is the null character. It still is, so **String** and **Counter** are incremented. Now:

```
H e r e    w e    g o ! \0
|_|_|_|_|_|_|_|_|_|_|_|_|
                        ^
                        |
                     String

             Counter is 11
```

Again, the continuation condition is evaluated. ***String** is now *zero,* and the loop stops before **Counter** is incremented. Then **String** is incremented. It now points off the end of the string, but it not used anymore. Return **Counter**.

The pointer implementation is much more elegant in this application!

ANATOMY: order of evaluation

In expressions such as:

```
*A + 5
```

the pointer **A** is followed to its value and five is added to that value. In expressions such as:

```
*String++
```

String is followed to its value and the pointer **String** is incremented afterwards. An important note: the increment operation applies in this example to the pointer, not to the value found there.

ANATOMY: changing parameter values inside a function

strlen uses the parameter **String** in its work. **String** is a pointer, not the characters themselves. **strlen** changes the value of **String** during the function's life. Does this alter the value of the string's pointer in the calling function? This diagram illustrates the problem:

```
-----------------------------------------------
| main                                        |
|    char Buffer [255] ;                       |
|    int  Len ;                                |
|                                             |
|    fgets(Buffer,255,stdin) ;                 |
|    Len = strlen(Buffer) ;                    |
-----------------------|                       |
| |          . . .                            |
| ---------------------------------------------
-----------
        |
   --------v------------------------------
   | strlen(String)                       |
   |                                      |
   |                                      |
   |                                      |
   ----------------------------------------
```

When the value of **String** is changed inside **strlen**, is **Buffer** affected?

No! **C** functions *never* change the value of their parameters. **C** makes a copy of the pointer to **Buffer** when **strlen** is called. This copy is changed, but never the original.

The diagram is better drawn:

```
 -------------------------------------------
| main                                      |
|    char Buffer[255] ;                     |
|    int  Len ;                             |
|                                           |
|    fgets(Buffer,255,stdin) ;              |
|    Len = strlen(Buffer) ;                 |
 -----------------------------|             |
|  |          . . .                         |
|  |   --------------------------------------
 ------------
       |
    ----------
   | new copy |
    ----------
       |
 ---------v-------------------------------
| strlen(String)                          |
|                                         |
|                                         |
 -----------------------------------------
```

The calling routine never sees the new copy of the parameter. The copy is created and destroyed automatically.

Rewriting StripNewLines

The function for converting uppercase letters in a string to lower case is easily written using pointers:

```
VOID StripNewLines(StringToProcess)
char    *StringToProcess ;
{       /* StripNewLines */
    while (*StringToProcess && *StringToProcess != '\n')
        StringToProcess++ ;
    *StringToProcess = '\0' ;
}       /* StripNewLines */
```

Begin by checking the loop continuation condition:

```
while (*StringToProcess && *StringToProcess != '\n')
```

First, ask if ***StringToProcess** (the character pointed to by **StringToProcess**) is a non-null character?'' If it is, then ask if ***StringToProcess** is not a newline? If both conditions are true, continue moving **StringToProcess** along until the condition fails, becomes false.

When the loop terminates, **StringToProcess** points to either a null character or a newline. In either case, set the character pointed to by **StringToProcess** to a null character.

ANATOMY: using pointer expressions on the left side of an assignment

In **StripNewLines**, a string and pointer combination like this may occur:

```
N e w   o n e\n\0
|_|_|_|_|_|_|_|_|_|
          ^
          |
       StringToProcess
```

The intent is to change the character pointed to by **StringToProcess**. Simply use the star operator and the pointer name on the left hand side of the assignment statement:

```
*StringToProcess = '\0' ;
```

This statement determines the value of the right hand side of the statement and assigns it to the character pointed to by **StringToProcess**.

Rewriting strcat

strcpy and **strcat** are similar functions. Rewrite **strcat** here. It would be a valuable exercise for you to rewrite **strcpy**.

```
VOID strcat(ToString,FromString)
char    *FromString ;
char    *ToString ;
{       /* strcat */
   /* Advance to the end of ToString.
    */
   while (*ToString)
       ToString++ ;

   /* Now copy.
    */
   do {
       *ToString++ = *FromString ;
   } while (*FromString++) ;
}       /* strcat */
```

Analyze these two simple loops. In the example in Chapter Six, these two strings were concatenated:

```
T e s t i n g\0
|_|_|_|_|_|_|_|_|_|_|_|_|_|_|_|_|_|
0 1 2 3 4 5 6 7 8 9 10 12  14  16
^
|
ToString

A g a i n\0
|_|_|_|_|_|_|
0 1 2 3 4 5
^
|
FromString
```

The first **while** loop moves the pointer **ToString** over to its null character. Run the loop:

```
while (*ToString)
    ToString++ ;
```

It checks ***ToString** to see if it is not a null character. If the test succeeds, it increments **ToString**. When the loop stops, the strings look like this:

```
T  e  s  t  i  n  g\0
|_|_|_|_|_|_|_|_|_|_|_|_|_|_|_|_|_|_|
0  1  2  3  4  5  6  7  8  9  10  12    14    16
                      ^
                      |
              ToString

              A  g  a  i  n\0
              |_|_|_|_|_|_|_|
              0  1  2  3  4  5
              ^
              |
          FromString
```

Now, copy each new character. The **do/while** loop continues as long as ***FromString** is not a null character. On the first trip, copy ***FromString** into ***ToString**:

```
T  e  s  t  i  n  g  A
|_|_|_|_|_|_|_|_|_|_|_|_|_|_|_|_|_|_|
0  1  2  3  4  5  6  7  8  9  10  12    14    16
                      ^
                      |
              ToString

              A  g  a  i  n\0
              |_|_|_|_|_|_|_|
              0  1  2  3  4  5
              ^
              |
          FromString
```

After doing the copy, autoincrement **ToString**:

```
T  e  s  t  i  n  g  A
|_|_|_|_|_|_|_|_|_|_|_|_|_|_|_|_|_|_|
0  1  2  3  4  5  6  7  8  9  10  12    14    16
                         ^
                         |
              ToString

              A  g  a  i  n\0
              |_|_|_|_|_|_|_|
              0  1  2  3  4  5
              ^
              |
          FromString
```

Now, test to see if ***FromString** is a null character. It is not. Increment **FromString** and continue the loop. When the next assignment is done, the strings look like this:

```
T e s t i n g A g
|_|_|_|_|_|_|_|_|_|_|_|_|_|_|_|_|_|_|
 0 1 2 3 4 5 6 7 8 9 10 12   14   16
               ^
               ¦
            ToString
```

```
            A  g  a  i  n\0
            |_|_|_|_|_|_|_|
             0  1  2  3  4  5
             ^
             ¦
          FromString
```

Continue assigning and moving pointers until the null character pointed to by **FromString** is reached. The strings look like this:

```
T e s t i n g A g a i  n\0
|_|_|_|_|_|_|_|_|_|_|_|_|_|_|_|_|_|_|
 0 1 2 3 4 5 6 7 8 9 10 12   14   16
                       ^
                       ¦
                    ToString
```

```
            A  g  a  i  n\0
            |_|_|_|_|_|_|_|
             0  1  2  3  4  5
                         ^
                         ¦
                    FromString
```

Test ***FromString**, and it is the null character. Stop looping, and return.

Rewriting strcmp

The string comparison function looks like this using pointers:

```
int strcmp(String1,String2)
char       *String1 ;
char       *String2 ;
{          /* strcmp */
    /* Search through while the corresponding
     * characters are equal.
     */
    for ( /* No initialization */ ; *String1 == *String2 ;
              String1++,String2++)
        if (*String1 == '\0')
            return(0) ;
    return(*String1 - *String2) ;
}          /* strcmp */
```

The **for** loop checks each character pointed to by **String1** and **String2** for equality. Next, **String1** is checked for a null character. If it points to a null character, the end of the loop has been reached, and can be exited. If this second test fails, increment **String1** and **String2** to point to the next character in the string.

If ***String1** and ***String2** are unequal, leave the **for** loop. As before, the values of these two unequal characters are returned subtracted from each other.

More Pointed Topics

To start using pointers effectively in longer programs, some special topics in using pointers must be covered. This chapter provides a group of important odds-and-ends.

How Do Pointers and Arrays Work Together?

In Chapter 7, we saw that an array parameter of indefinite length passed to a function is the same as a pointer parameter having the same base type as the array. What is the difference between pointers and arrays?

Let's assume **IntArray**, an array of integers, and **IntPointer**, an integer pointer, are set up this way:

```
int        IntArray[11] ;
int        *IntPointer ;
```

```
 --- --- --- --- --- --- --- --- --- --- ---
|15 |27 |81 | 0 | 5 |17 |22 | 0 | 8 | 5 |15 |
 --- --- --- --- --- --- --- --- --- --- ---
  0   1   2   3   4   5   6   7   8   9   10
  ^
  |
IntPointer
```

IntArray has been initialized to the values shown. Also, **IntPointer** has been set to point to **IntArray[0]** with the statement:

```
IntPointer = IntArray ;
```

Using an array name without a subscript is the same as having a pointer to the zero-th element of the array.

How can we refer to the zero-th element of **IntArray**? Two notations which mean the same thing can be used:

```
IntArray[0]          array notation
*IntPointer          pointer notation
```

That's straightforward. But how can reference be made to the next element of **IntArray**? Again, here are two equivalent notations:

```
IntArray[1]          array notation
*(IntPointer + 1)    pointer notation
```

The pointer notation means "move the path currently pointed to by **IntPointer** forward by one data-item and then get the integer pointed to by that new pointer." Remember:

```
*(IntPointer + 1)
```

is not the same as:

```
*IntPointer + 1
```

The first form moves the pointer **IntPointer** one data-value forward and follows this new pointer to the data at its destination. The second form takes the integer value pointed to by **IntPointer**, and adds one.

Similarly, the fifth element of the array can be referenced in two ways:

```
IntArray[5]        array notation
*(IntPointer + 5)  pointer notation
```

Note the pattern! If **IntPointer** points to the zero-th element of **IntArray**, the **I**-th array element in **IntArray** can be referenced as:

```
IntArray[I]        array notation
*(IntPointer + I)  pointer notation
```

The first form uses the **I**-th element in **IntArray**; the second moves **IntPointer** forward by **I** data-items, then gets the integer pointed to by this new pointer.

Go still further. Remember using an array name without a subscript is the same as a pointer to the zero-th element of the array. This means these notations can be used interchangeably:

```
IntArray[I]        array notation
*(IntArray + I)    pointer notation
```

Here, instead of creating a temporary pointer variable, the array name **IntArray** is used directly.

Internally, **C** always uses the pointer notation. Array references are converted to pointers before anything else happens. Arrays in **C** are for those cases where it is more natural to refer to elements directly by number, or where using the star operator is clumsy. Many mathematical and engineering problems are best solved using arrays. Most of the examples in this book are best solved with pointers.

Are Arrays Ever Required?

Take the last example again, but this time omit the array declaration.

```
int       *IntPointer ;
```

Now what does ***(IntPointer + 5)** mean? *It has no meaning!* **IntPointer** doesn't yet point to anything. If a random value in memory is referenced, the results are usually disastrous. Using the value of an *uninitialized* pointer is a common mistake in **C** programs.

But here's a problem. If the pointer itself doesn't define a place to store the data, how is it done?

Arrays must be used to declare the data areas. (As with most things, there is an exception to this rule discussed in Chapter Twelve.) C doesn't care whether array or pointer notations are used to access the information, but the data area must be declared with an array. In this way, space is reserved in the programs for the data.

This means that, even if character pointers are used to do the string manipulations within the program, the character strings must be declared using character arrays.

ANATOMY: multi-dimensional arrays

Mathematics, science, and engineering problems often need arrays of more than one dimension. C allows arrays to have as many dimensions as needed.

To declare an array with more than one dimension, declare the array, as always, the size of each dimension of the array in square brackets following the array name. Do not use a special character to separate the square brackets, and do not put more than one number inside any single set of square brackets.

For example:

```
double    MultiDim[5][5] ;
```

MultiDim is a two-dimensional array:

```
        0   1   2   3   4
       --  --  --  --  --
   0 |   |   |   |   |   |
       --  --  --  --  --
   1 |   |   |   |   |   |
       --  --  --  --  --
   2 |   |   |   |   |   |
       --  --  --  --  --
   3 |   |   |   |   |   |
       --  --  --  --  --
   4 |   |   |   |   |   |
       --  --  --  --  --
```

Each square accommodates one **double**. Each element is referred to with two array indices. For example:

```
MultiDim[1][4] = 17.0 * MultiDim[2][2] ;
```

Note the use of multiple sets of square brackets, each containing an array subscript. (Also note the star operator here is multiplication, not a pointer operation!)

Arrays of multiple dimensions are natural for matrix arithmetic commonly used in mathematics and science.

The next section shows how multiple-dimensioned arrays are helpful in non-mathematical work.

Dressing Up the Histogram Program

The end of Chapter 5 presented a histogram program which produced good-looking, useful output. We now know enough to label each of the items with a name the user enters. The new **main**, **PrintRuler**, and **WriteHistogram** functions are reproduced here; the remainder of the program is unchanged and may be entered as written in Chapter 5. This version's code is named "histo-7":

```
#define MAXNAMELENGTH    11

main()
{       /* main */
    char    Dummy[MAXNAMELENGTH] ;
    int     EntryCount ;    /* looping variable--
                             * the current entry number
                             */
    char    FileName [MAXNAMELENGTH] ;
    char    Labels[MAXNUMENTRIES][MAXNAMELENGTH] ;
                            /* labels for our entries */
    FILE    *OutFile ;      /* where we're writing information */
    int     NumEntries ;    /* total number of entries */
    double  ScalingMultiplier ; /* our scaling value */
    double  Value[MAXNUMENTRIES] ; /* all values the user enters */

    printf("Enter the output filename: ") ;
    fgets(FileName,MAXNAMELENGTH,stdin) ;
    StripNewLines(FileName) ;

    if ((OutFile = fopen(FileName,"w")) == 0) {
        fprintf(stderr,"Can't open %s for output.\n",FileName) ;
        exit(0) ;
    }
    ClearScreen() ;
    printf("How Many Entries Will You Make? ") ;
    scanf("%d",&NumEntries) ;
    while (NumEntries > MAXNUMENTRIES || NumEntries < 1) {
        printf("\n\tI Can Only Accept a Number Between 1 and %d!\n",
                    MAXNUMENTRIES) ;
        printf("\nHow Many Entries Will You Make? ") ;
        scanf("%d",&NumEntries) ;
    }

    /* Dispose of the characters scanf leaves behind.
     */
    fgets(Dummy,MAXNAMELENGTH,stdin) ;

    /* Get the names.
     */
    for (EntryCount = 0 ; EntryCount < NumEntries ; EntryCount++) {
        printf(
        "For Entry %d, Type a Label (less than 10 characters): ",
                EntryCount + 1) ;
        fgets(Labels[EntryCount],MAXNAMELENGTH,stdin) ;
        StripNewLines(Labels[EntryCount]) ;
    }
    printf("\n") ;
    /* Get the entries.
     */
    for (EntryCount = 0 ; EntryCount < NumEntries ;
                    EntryCount++) {
        printf("For Entry %d, Type a Value: ", EntryCount + 1) ;
        scanf("%lf",&Value[EntryCount]) ;
    }

    ScalingMultiplier = FindScalingFraction(Value,
                        NumEntries,MAXNUMSTARS) ;
    WriteHistogram(stdout,Value,NumEntries,ScalingMultiplier,
                    Labels) ;
```

```
        WriteHistogram(OutFile,Value,NumEntries,ScalingMultiplier,
                       Labels) ;
        fclose(OutFile) ;
}       /* main */

VOID PrintRuler(TargetFile)
FILE    *TargetFile ;
/* PrintRuler writes a ruler line to TargetFile.
 */
{       /* PrintRuler */
    int    Ruler ;

    fprintf(TargetFile,"\nSCALE            | ") ;
    for (Ruler = 0 ; Ruler < 10 ; Ruler++)
        fprintf(TargetFile,"----+") ;
}       /* PrintRuler */

VOID WriteHistogram(TargetFile,InputArray,NumElements,ScalingFactor,
                    Names)
double  InputArray[] ;
char    Names[MAXNUMENTRIES][MAXNAMELENGTH] ;
int     NumElements ;
double  ScalingFactor ;
FILE    *TargetFile ;
{       /* WriteHistogram */
    int  ElementCount ;
    int  NumStarsToWrite ;
    int  StarCount ;

    /* Cycle through each element, printing each on a separate line.
     */
    for (ElementCount = 0 ; ElementCount < NumElements ;
                    ElementCount++) {

      /* First, print the label and number to write on the line,
       * then a bar to signal the start of the graph.
       */
      fprintf(TargetFile,"%10s %5.1f | ",
              Names[ElementCount],InputArray[ElementCount]) ;

      /* Calculate the number of stars to write by multiplying the
       * value by the ScalingFactor.  Note that the multiplication
       * is done with floating point arithmetic, but the final answer
       * is converted to an integer with a cast.
       */
      NumStarsToWrite =
         (int)(InputArray[ElementCount] * ScalingFactor) ;

      /* Now write the stars and a newline.
       */
      for (StarCount = 0 ; StarCount < NumStarsToWrite ;
                    StarCount++)
          putc('*',TargetFile) ;
      fprintf(TargetFile,"\n") ;
    }
    /* Print the ruler line at the end of every histogram.
     */
    PrintRuler(TargetFile) ;
}       /* WriteHistogram */
```

ANATOMY: two dimensional arrays of characters

Think of two dimensional arrays of characters as *arrays of strings*. For example:

```
char      Labels [4][20] ;
```

```
0         5        10        15        19
```

```
0 |_|_|_|_|_|_|_|_|_|_|_|_|_|_|_|_|_|_|_|_|
1 |_|_|_|_|_|_|_|_|_|_|_|_|_|_|_|_|_|_|_|_|
2 |_|_|_|_|_|_|_|_|_|_|_|_|_|_|_|_|_|_|_|_|
3 |_|_|_|_|_|_|_|_|_|_|_|_|_|_|_|_|_|_|_|_|
```

Labels can store 80 individual characters. Instead of thinking of storing individual characters, think of storing arrays of strings (arrays of arrays of characters):

```
0         5        10 .      15        19
```

```
0 |_|_|_|_|_|_|_|_|_|_|_|_|_|_|_|_|_|_|_|_|   Labels[0]

1 |_|_|_|_|_|_|_|_|_|_|_|_|_|_|_|_|_|_|_|_|   Labels[1]

2 |_|_|_|_|_|_|_|_|_|_|_|_|_|_|_|_|_|_|_|_|   Labels[2]

3 |_|_|_|_|_|_|_|_|_|_|_|_|_|_|_|_|_|_|_|_|   Labels[3]
```

Four independent strings can be read into **Labels** using **fgets**. For example:

```
fgets(Labels[0],20,stdin) ;
fgets(Labels[3],20,stdin) ;
```

reads two strings into **Labels[0]** and **Labels[3]**. **fgets** returns, as always, with the strings inserted in the desired character arrays. For example, depending on input, we may see:

```
0         5        10        15        19
```

```
0 |T|h|i|s|_|i|s|_|s|t|r|i|n|g|_|1|\n|\0|_|_|   Labels[0]
1 |_|_|_|_|_|_|_|_|_|_|_|_|_|_|_|_|_|_|_|_|   Labels[1]
2 |_|_|_|_|_|_|_|_|_|_|_|_|_|_|_|_|_|_|_|_|   Labels[2]
3 |T|h|i|s|_|i|s|_|#|2|\n|\0|_|_|_|_|_|_|_|_|   Labels[3]
```

Notice the notation used to **fgets**. To read information into any of these four strings, write:

```
fgets(Labels[0],20,stdin) ;
```

```
0         5        10        15        19
```

```
0 |T|h|i|s|_|i|s|_|s|t|r|i|n|g|_|1|\n|\0|_|_|   Labels[0]
1 |_|_|_|_|_|_|_|_|_|_|_|_|_|_|_|_|_|_|_|_|   Labels[1]
2 |_|_|_|_|_|_|_|_|_|_|_|_|_|_|_|_|_|_|_|_|   Labels[2]
3 |T|h|i|s|_|i|s|_|#|2|\n|\0|_|_|_|_|_|_|_|_|   Labels[3]
```

Use only the first subscript to see an element of **Labels** as a string.

Remember, individual characters in the array can also be examined. To refer to the zero-th character in the second string in **Labels**, write:

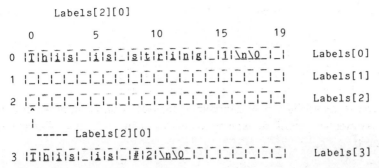

The second subscript means we want to see a single character inside any of these strings.

The above program asks the user to enter as many labels for the histogram as there are entries. **fgets** reads these strings into the array **Labels**. These strings are passed to **WriteHistogram** and then are written as identifiers in the histogram.

ANATOMY: passing multi-dimensional arrays as parameters

Labels is passed to **WriteHistogram**. It is a two-dimensional array. Note how the parameter is declared:

```
VOID WriteHistogram(TargetFile,InputArray,NumElements,
           ScalingFactor,Names)
char     Names[MAXNUMENTRIES][MAXNAMELENGTH] ;
```

If an array with multiple dimensions is passed to a function, the size of the first dimension can vary but the second dimension must be fixed. For example, **C** will not accept this construction:

```
char     Names[][] ;
```

This parameter declaration is permissible:

```
char     Names[][MAXNAMELENGTH] ;
```

The second declaration causes an array of character strings to be passed. The number of strings is unspecified, but the length of each string is **MAXNAMELENGTH** characters.

A Revision Using pointers

Rewrite the two routines to eliminate passing multi-dimensional arrays in HISTOGRAM-8 under the filename "histo-8":

```
#define MAXNAMELENGTH    11

main()
{        /* main */
    char    Dummy[MAXNAMELENGTH] ;
    int     EntryCount ;    /* looping variable--
                             * the current entry number
                             */
    char    FileName[MAXNAMELENGTH] ;
    char    Labels[MAXNUMENTRIES][MAXNAMELENGTH] ;
```

```
                              /* labels for our entries */
   char    *LabelPtr[MAXNUMENTRIES] ;
                              /* pointers to our labels */
   FILE    *OutFile ;        /* where we're writing information */
   int     NumEntries ;      /* total number of entries */
   double  ScalingMultiplier ; /* our scaling value */
   double  Value[MAXNUMENTRIES] ; /* all values the user enters */

   printf("Enter the output filename: ") ;
   fgets(FileName,MAXNAMELENGTH,stdin) ;
   StripNewLines(FileName) ;

   if ((OutFile = fopen(FileName,"w")) == 0) {
       fprintf(stderr,"Can't open %s for output.\n",FileName) ;
       exit(0) ;
   }

   ClearScreen() ;
   printf("How Many Entries Will You Make? ") ;
   scanf("%d",&NumEntries) ;
   while (NumEntries > MAXNUMENTRIES || NumEntries < 1) {
       printf("\n\tI Can Only Accept a Number Between 1 and %d!\n",
                   MAXNUMENTRIES) ;
       printf("\nHow Many Entries Will You Make? ") ;
       scanf("%d",&NumEntries) ;
   }

   /* Set up the pointers to the names.
    */
   for (EntryCount = 0 ; EntryCount < MAXNUMENTRIES ; EntryCount++)
       LabelPtr[EntryCount] = Labels[EntryCount] ;

   /* Dispose of the characters scanf left behind.
    */
   fgets(Dummy,MAXNAMELENGTH,stdin) ;

   /* Get the names.
    */
   for (EntryCount = 0 ; EntryCount < NumEntries ; EntryCount++) {
       printf(
         "For Entry %d, Type a Label (10 Characters Maximum): ",
                   EntryCount + 1) ;
       fgets(LabelPtr[EntryCount],MAXNAMELENGTH,stdin) ;
       StripNewLines(LabelPtr[EntryCount]) ;
   }

   printf("\n") ;
   /* Get the entries.
    */
   for (EntryCount = 0 ; EntryCount < NumEntries ; EntryCount++) {
       printf("For Entry %d, Type a Value: ",EntryCount + 1) ;
       scanf("%lf",&Value[EntryCount]) ;
   }

   ScalingMultiplier = FindScalingFraction(Value,
                           NumEntries,MAXNUMSTARS) ;
   WriteHistogram(stdout,Value,NumEntries,ScalingMultiplier,
                           LabelPtr) ;
   WriteHistogram(OutFile,Value,NumEntries,ScalingMultiplier,
                           LabelPtr) ;
   fclose(OutFile) ;
}      /* main */
```

```
VOID PrintRuler(TargetFile)
FILE    *TargetFile ;
/* PrintRuler writes a ruler line to TargetFile.
 */
{       /* PrintRuler */
    int    Ruler ;

    fprintf(TargetFile,"\nSCALE              | ") ;
    for (Ruler = 0 ; Ruler < 10 ; Ruler++)
        fprintf(TargetFile,"----+") ;
}       /* PrintRuler */

VOID WriteHistogram(TargetFile,InputArray,NumElements,ScalingFactor,
                    Names)
double. InputArray[] ;
char    *Names[] ;
int     NumElements ;
double  ScalingFactor ;
FILE    *TargetFile ;
{       /* WriteHistogram */
    int   ElementCount ;
    int   NumStarsToWrite ;
    int   StarCount ;

    /* Cycle through each element, printing each on a
     * separate line.
     */
    for (ElementCount = 0 ; ElementCount < NumElements ;
                    ElementCount++) {

        /* First, print the label and number to write on the line,
         * then a bar to signal the start of the graph.
         */
        fprintf(TargetFile,"%10s %5.1f | ",
            Names[ElementCount],InputArray[ElementCount]) ;

        /* Calculate the number of stars to write by multiplying the
         * value by the ScalingFactor.  Note that the multiplication
         * is done with floating point arithmetic, but the final
         * answer is converted to an integer with a cast.
         */

        NumStarsToWrite =
            (int)(InputArray[ElementCount] * ScalingFactor) ;

        /* Now write the stars and a newline.
         */
        for (StarCount = 0 ; StarCount < NumStarsToWrite ;
                    StarCount++)
            putc('*',TargetFile) ;
        fprintf(TargetFile,"\n") ;
    }

    /* Print the ruler line at the end of every histogram.
     */
    PrintRuler(TargetFile) ;
    /* WriteHistogram */
```

ANATOMY: arrays of pointers

In the above example, **Labels** is an array of character strings:

```
char        Labels[4][20] ;
```

```
    0         5        10        15        19
```

It's easy to make a pointer to the beginning of any of these strings. Assume a variable **LabelPtr** points to the beginning of **Labels[2]**. The code is:

```
char        Labels[4][20] ;
char        *LabelPtr ;

LabelPtr = Labels[2] ;
```

This sets **LabelPtr** to point to the zero-th character of **Labels[2]**:

Suppose a pointer is wanted at the beginning of every string in the array. These could be named **Label0Ptr**, **Label1Ptr**, and so forth:

This gets cumbersome when there are many strings. **C** allows us to declare arrays of character pointers. Let's declare an array of pointers:

```
char        *LabelPtr[4] ;
```

Note the syntax: the base type of the array is "pointer to character." Code **char**
***LabelPtr**. To say four of these pointers are needed, follow the array name with
an array length in square brackets as before. Each element of **LabelPtr** can be set
to point to the corresponding string in **Labels**:

```
for (Counter = 0 ; Counter < 5 ; Counter++)
    LabelPtr[Counter] = Labels[Counter] ;
```

Diagram this:

The **LabelPtr** elements point to the corresponding string in **Labels**. Since pointers
to strings can be used interchangeably with the string names, **LabelPtr** names can
be used instead of **Label** names to do the work:

```
/* Get the names.
 */
for (EntryCount = 0 ; EntryCount < NumEntries ; EntryCount++) {
    printf(
        "For Entry %d, Type a Label (10 Characters Maximum): ",
            EntryCount + 1) ;
    fgets(LabelPtr[EntryCount],MAXNAMELENGTH,stdin) ;
}
```

LabelPtr[EntryCount] is used in the call to **fgets**. Just as before, the character
pointer works as well as an array name without a subscript. Remember that because
Labels is two-dimensional, using **Labels** with one subscript as we did at first is like
using a regular string name (i.e., character array) without a subscript.

Using a one-dimensional array of pointers to simplify parameter passing, we can
make the format parameter in **WriteHistogram**:

```
VOID WriteHistogram(TargetFile,InputArray,NumElements,
        ScalingFactor,Names)
char    *Names[] ;
```

Reading From the Command Line—Histogram-9

Almost every program written to this point asks the user to enter information in
response to some prompt as the program runs. Many times, a user likes to enter

values from the command line. This is easily done with **C**. Revise the program to ask the user which file should be used for output. Name it "histo-9":

```
#define MAXNAMELENGTH    11

main(argc,argv)
int        argc ;
char       *argv[] ;
{       /* main */
    char    Dummy[MAXNAMELENGTH] ;
    int     EntryCount ;    /* looping variable--
                             * the current entry number
                             */
    char    Labels[MAXNUMENTRIES][MAXNAMELENGTH] ;
                                        /* labels for our entries */
    char    *LabelPtr[MAXNUMENTRIES] ;       /* pointers to labels */
    FILE    *OutFile ;          /* where we're writing information */
    int     NumEntries ;                /* total number of entries */
    double  ScalingMultiplier ;                 /* our scaling value */
    double  Value[MAXNUMENTRIES] ; /* all values the user enters */

    if (argc < 2) {
        fprintf(stderr,"Usage: histo-9 outputname") ;
        exit(0) ;
    }

    if ((OutFile = fopen(argv[1],"w")) == 0) {
        fprintf(stderr,"Can't open %s for output.\n",argv[1]) ;
        exit(0) ;
    }

    ClearScreen() ;

    printf("How Many Entries Will You Make? ") ;
    scanf("%d",&NumEntries) ;
    while (NumEntries > MAXNUMENTRIES || NumEntries < 1) {
        printf("\n\tI Can Only Accept a Number Between 1 and %d!\n",
                MAXNUMENTRIES) ;
        printf("\nHow Many Entries Will You Make? ") ;
        scanf("%d",&NumEntries) ;
    }

    /* Set up the pointers to the names.
     */
    for (EntryCount = 0 ; EntryCount < MAXNUMENTRIES ; EntryCount++)
        LabelPtr[EntryCount] = Labels[EntryCount] ;

    /* Dispose of the characters scanf left behind.
     */
    fgets(Dummy,MAXNAMELENGTH,stdin) ;

    /* Get the names.
     */
    for (EntryCount = 0 ; EntryCount < NumEntries ;
                        EntryCount++) {
        printf(
          "For Entry %d, Type a Label (less than 10 characters): ",
                EntryCount + 1) ;
        fgets(LabelPtr[EntryCount],MAXNAMELENGTH,stdin) ;
        StripNewLines(LabelPtr[EntryCount]) ;
    }

    printf("\n") ;
    /* Get the entries.
     */
    for (EntryCount = 0 ; EntryCount < NumEntries ; EntryCount++) {
```

```
            printf("For Entry %d, Type a Value: ",
                    EntryCount + 1) ;
            scanf("%lf",&Value[EntryCount]) ;
        }

    ScalingMultiplier = FindScalingFraction(Value,
                            NumEntries,MAXNUMSTARS) ;

    WriteHistogram(stdout,Value,NumEntries,ScalingMultiplier,
                        LabelPtr) ;
    WriteHistogram(OutFile,Value,NumEntries,ScalingMultiplier,
                        LabelPtr) ;
    fclose(OutFile) ;
}       /* main */

VOID PrintRuler(TargetFile)
FILE    *TargetFile ;
/* PrintRuler writes a ruler line to TargetFile.
 */
{       /* PrintRuler */
    int     Ruler ;

    fprintf(TargetFile,"\nSCALE            | ") ;
    for (Ruler = 0 ; Ruler < 10 ; Ruler++)
        fprintf(TargetFile,"----+") ;
}       /* PrintRuler */

VOID ClearScreen()
/* ClearScreen writes NUMTOCLEAR newlines to the screen.
 */
{       /* ClearScreen */
    int  Counter ;

    for (Counter = 0 ; Counter < NUMTOCLEAR ; Counter++)
        putchar('\n') ;
}       /* ClearScreen */

double FindScalingFraction(InputArray,NumElements,MaxSize)
double  InputArray[] ;
int     MaxSize ;
int     NumElements ;
/* FindScalingFraction returns the multiplier which scales
 * every element of InputArray to be no larger than MaxSize.
 */
{       /* FindScalingFraction */
    int         CurElement ;
    double      MaxElement ;

    /* Find the largest element in InputArray by looking at each
     * element in turn and, if the element under examination is larger
     * than the old value of MaxElement (initially set to zero), make
     * MaxElement equal to that value.
     */
    for (CurElement = 0,MaxElement = 0.0 ; CurElement < NumElements ;
                        CurElement++)
        MaxElement = (InputArray[CurElement] > MaxElement) ?
                    InputArray[CurElement] : MaxElement ;

    /* The scaling multiplier is the maximum number divided
     * by the MaxElement, the largest element in the array.
     */
    return((double)MaxSize / MaxElement) ;
}       /* FindScalingFraction */
```

```
VOID StripNewLines(StringToProcess)
char    StringToProcess[] ;
{       /* StripNewLines */
    int         I ;

    /* Advance a character at a time until
     * the zero terminator is found.
     */
    for (I = 0 ; StringToProcess[I] ; I++) {

        /* If the character being examined is a
         * newline, replace it with a null and
         * stop looping. */
        if (StringToProcess[I] == '\n') {
            StringToProcess[I] = '\0' ;
            break ;
        }
    }
}       /* StripNewLines */

VOID WriteHistogram(TargetFile,InputArray,NumElements,ScalingFactor,
                    Names)
double  InputArray[] ;
char    *Names[] ;
int     NumElements ;
double  ScalingFactor ;
FILE    *TargetFile ;
{       /* WriteHistogram */
    int ElementCount ;
    int NumStarsToWrite ;
    int StarCount ;

    /* Cycle through each element, printing each on a
     * separate line.
     */
    for (ElementCount = 0 ; ElementCount < NumElements ;
                    ElementCount++) {

        /* First, print the label and number to write on the line,
         * then a bar to signal the start of the graph.
         */
        fprintf(TargetFile,"%10s %5.1f | ",
            Names[ElementCount],InputArray[ElementCount]) ;

        /* Calculate the number of stars to write by multiplying the va
         * by the ScalingFactor.  Note that the multiplication is done
         * with floating point arithmetic, but the final answer is
         * converted to an integer with a cast.
         */
        NumStarsToWrite =
                (int)(InputArray[ElementCount] * ScalingFactor) ;

        /* Now write the stars and a newline.
         */
        for (StarCount = 0 ; StarCount < NumStarsToWrite ;
                        StarCount++)
            putc('*',TargetFile) ;
        fprintf(TargetFile,"\n") ;
    }

    /* Print the ruler line at the end of every histogram.
     */
    PrintRuler(TargetFile) ;
}       /* WriteHistogram */
```

NOTE: Only **main** changes. The remaining functions for HISTOGRAM-9 are the same as written for HISTOGRAM-8.

ANATOMY: main has parameters, too

So far, many functions with parameters have been written. **main**, too, has parameters which can be used. When it is necessary to read values from the command line, declare:

```
main(argc,argv)
int      argc ;
char     *argv[] ;
```

The names **argc** (pronounced "arg-see") and **argv** (pronounced "arg-vee") are standard in almost all **C** programs.

argc is a count of the number of items the user typed on the command line. The command line values are numbered this way:

```
pgmname   value1    value2    value3    value4
   0         1         2         3         4
```

As usual, values are numbered from zero to one less than **argc**. The command line values are numbered from left to right. A command line value is separated by white space (a blank or tab) from other values.

Thus, if the user types this command line:

```
ourpgm   entry1 entry2 entry3 entry4
```
argc is 5.

HAZARD: microcomputers and argv[0]

Some microcomputer operating systems do not let applications programs know what the first name on the command line is—which is the program's name itself. Most **C** systems running on these machines return a dummy value as **argv[0]**.

argv is an array of character pointers:

```
char      *argv[] ;
```
The run-time system automatically sets **argv**'s elements to point to the first character in each of the command line values:

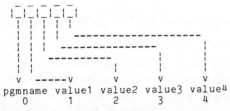

```
v  -----v        v         v         v
pgmname value1 value2 value3 value4
   0       1       2       3       4
```

With these pointers, items from the command line can be used directly. To use the first value (not the zero-th), write:

```
argv[1]
```
This refers to **value1** in the example.

Using argc and argv

The program first checks the value of **argc**:

```
if (argc < 2) {
    fprintf(stderr,"Usage: histogrm outputname") ;
    exit(0) ;
}
```

If the user enters the command line correctly:

```
histogrm myfile
```

there are two values on the command line. Therefore, **argc** is **2**. If the user forgets to enter the second argument, **argc** is **1**, in which case an error is signaled and the program is stopped. In the example, the command line must have the output filename before the program can continue.

When the number of values is entered on the command line, the filename the user entered is referenced. Again, the values are numbered from zero. The filename is pointed to by **argv[1]**, as in the following example:

```
if ((OutFile = fopen(argv[1],"w")) == 0) {
    fprintf(stderr,"Can't open %s for output.\n",argv[1]) ;
    exit(0) ;
}
```

As usual, the character pointer is used as the first argument to **fopen**. Whatever file the user names on the command line is created, and the program continues.

If the program needs additional arguments from the command line, refer to them as **argv[2]**, **argv[3]**, and so on.

What About Redirection?

What if the user entered a redirection command in addition to the filename? Consider this example:

```
histogrm <inputfile myfile
```

Which is the value on the command line the program will open?

```
<inputfile     or     myfile
```

The example command-line means read all input that would normally come from the user's console from **inputfile** instead. Remember this process is called "redirection;" **stdin** is redirected to come from **inputfile**. When a C program is run, all redirection is set up before **argc** and **argv** are constructed. In this example, first redirect **stdin** from **inputfile**. After redirecting **stdin**, the name **inputfile** effectively disappears from the command line. As before, this leaves **histogrm myfile**.

The program always sees a command line set up without the redirection arguments.

Complete Code for Histogram-10

Here is the final version of programs in the histogram series. The complete code is given here. In the code, the program is called "histo-10" to meet the eight-character maximum requirements for naming files on microcomputers:

```c
#include <stdio.h>

#define MAXNAMELENGTH    11
#define MAXNUMSTARS      50
#define MAXNUMENTRIES    50
#define NUMTOCLEAR       25
#define VOID int

extern  double FindScalingFraction() ;  /* function declaration */

main(argc,argv)
int      argc ;
char     *argv[] ;
{      /* main */
    char         Dummy[MAXNAMELENGTH] ;
    int     EntryCount ;    /* looping variable -- the
                             current entry number */
    char    Labels[MAXNUMENTRIES][MAXNAMELENGTH] ;  /* labels for
                                             our entries */
    char    *LabelPtr[MAXNUMENTRIES] ;   /* pointers to labels */
    FILE    *OutFile ;      /* where we're writing information */
    int     NumEntries ;    /* total number of entries */
    double  ScalingMultiplier ; /* our scaling value */
    double  Value[MAXNUMENTRIES] ; /* all values the user enters */

    if (argc < 2) {
        fprintf(stderr,"\n\tUsage: histo-10 outputname\n") ;
        exit(0) ;
    }

    if ((OutFile = fopen(argv[1],"w")) == 0) {
        fprintf(stderr,"\n\tCan't open %s for output.\n",argv[1]) ;
        exit(0) ;
    }

    ClearScreen() ;
    printf("How Many Entries Will You Make? ") ;
    scanf("%d",&NumEntries) ;
    while (NumEntries > MAXNUMENTRIES || NumEntries < 1) {
        printf("\n\tI Can Only Accept a Number Between 1 and %d!\n",
               MAXNUMENTRIES) ;
        printf("\nHow Many Entries Will You Make? ") ;
        scanf("%d",&NumEntries) ;
    }

    /* Set up the pointers to the names.
     */
    for (EntryCount = 0 ; EntryCount < MAXNUMENTRIES ;
         EntryCount++)
        LabelPtr[EntryCount] = Labels[EntryCount] ;

    /* Get the labels and values.
     */
```

```
        for (EntryCount = 0 ; EntryCount < NumEntries ; EntryCount++) {
            /* Dispose of the characters scanf leaves behind.
             */
            fgets(Dummy,MAXNAMELENGTH,stdin) ;
            printf(
                "\nFor Entry %d, Type a Label (10 Characters Maximum): ",
                             EntryCount + 1) ;
            fgets(LabelPtr[EntryCount],MAXNAMELENGTH,stdin) ;
            StripNewLines(LabelPtr[EntryCount]) ;

            printf("\nFor Entry %d, Type a Value: ", EntryCount +1) ;
            scanf("%lf",&Value[EntryCount]) ;
        }

        ScalingMultiplier = FindScalingFraction(Value,NumEntries,
                                MAXNUMSTARS) ;
        WriteHistogram(stdout,Value,NumEntries,ScalingMultiplier,
                                LabelPtr) ;
        WriteHistogram(OutFile,Value,NumEntries,ScalingMultiplier,
                                LabelPtr) ;
        fclose(OutFile) ;
}       /* main */

VOID ClearScreen()
/* ClearScreen writes NUMTOCLEAR newlines to the screen.
 */
{       /* ClearScreen */
    int  Counter ;
    for (Counter = 0 ; Counter < NUMTOCLEAR ; Counter++)
        putchar('\n') ;
}       /* ClearScreen */

double  FindScalingFraction(InputArray,NumElements,MaxSize)
double  InputArray[] ;
int     MaxSize ;
int     NumElements ;
/* FindScalingFraction returns the multiplier which scales
 * every element of InputArray to be no larger than MaxSize.
 */
{       /* FindScalingFraction */
    int         CurElement ;
    double      MaxElement ;

    /* Find the largest element in InputArray by looking at
     * each element in turn and if the element under examination
     * is larger than the old value of MaxElement (initially set
     * to zero), make MaxElement equal to that value.
     */
    for (CurElement = 0,MaxElement = 0.0 ; CurElement < NumElements ;
                    CurElement++)
        MaxElement = (InputArray[CurElement] > MaxElement) ?
                        InputArray[CurElement] : MaxElement ;
    /* The scaling multiplier is the maximum number divided
     * by the MaxElement, the largest element in the array.
     */

    return((double)MaxSize / MaxElement) ;
}       /* FindScalingFraction */

VOID PrintRuler(TargetFile)
FILE    *TargetFile ;
/* PrintRuler writes a ruler line to TargetFile.
 */
{       /* PrintRuler */
```

```
      int    Ruler ;

      /* This replaces the literal, longhand writing of the ruler
       * by first printing a heading followed by ten repetitions of
       * the value ----+.     */
      fprintf(TargetFile,"\n\t   SCALE | ") ;
      for (Ruler = 0 ; Ruler < 10 ; Ruler++)
          fprintf(TargetFile,"----+") ;
}         /* PrintRuler */

VOID StripNewLines(StringToProcess)
char    *StringToProcess ;
{         /* StripNewLines */
    while (*StringToProcess && *StringToProcess != '\n')
        StringToProcess++ ;
    *StringToProcess = '\0' ;
}         /* StripNewLines */

VOID WriteHistogram(TargetFile,InputArray,NumElements,ScalingFactor,
                    Names)
double  InputArray[] ;
char    *Names[] ;
int     NumElements ;
double  ScalingFactor ;
FILE    *TargetFile ;
{         /* WriteHistogram */
    int   ElementCount ;
    int   NumStarsToWrite ;
    int   StarCount ;

    /* Cycle through each element, printing each on a
     * separate line.
     */
    for (ElementCount = 0 ; ElementCount < NumElements ;
                    ElementCount++) {

        /* First, print the label and number to write on the line,
         * then a bar to signal the start of the graph.
         */
        fprintf(TargetFile,"%10s %5.1f | ",
            Names[ElementCount],InputArray[ElementCount]) ;

        /* Calculate the number of stars to write by multiplying
         * the value by the ScalingFactor. Note that the multi-
         * plication is done with floating point arithmetic, but
         * the final answer is converted to an integer with a cast.
         */
        NumStarsToWrite =
                (int)(InputArray[ElementCount] * ScalingFactor) ;
        /* Now write the stars and a newline.
         */
        for (StarCount = 0 ; StarCount < NumStarsToWrite ; StarCount++)
            putc('*',TargetFile) ;
        fprintf(TargetFile,"\n") ;
    }

    /* Print the ruler line at the end of every histogram.
     */
    PrintRuler(TargetFile) ;
}         /* WriteHistogram */
```

Part Two

Useful Programs

Rather than continue to teach **C** programming through the use of graded examples, the second half of this book directly presents a group of programs that are especially useful as well as instructive.

Chapter 9 presents **EPSET**, a source code configurator program for those who have software-configurable dot-matrix printers. While it appears to be and is a relatively simple program, **EPSET** uses code macros that introduce a valuable way to apply **# define** compiler directives.

Chapter 10 presents **TXTRDR1** which does statistical analyses of text files by counting words, lines, and sentences.

Chapter 11 builds on **TXTRDR1**, describing two more programs for text analysis, **TXTRDR2** and **TXTRDR3**. In addition to doing relatively simple word and sentence counting, **TXTRDR2** and **TXTRDR3** produce a qualitative index of how "easy" the text is to read. Several important features of **C** are introduced and discussed.

Chapter 12 presents **WFREQ**, a word frequency analyzer for text. Again building on programs described previously, **WFREQ** uses **C**'s dynamic memory allocation mechanism to store room for words as they are read. **WFREQ** also introduces sorting methods.

Chapters 13 and 14 present two valuable tools for **C** programmers: **XREF** and **CALLS**. **XREF** prints a listing of the location of every identifier used in a **C** program. **CALLS** prints a graph of how functions in a program call each other. These programs use list processing and dynamic memory allocation to create compound data structures.

A Note on Reconstructing the Programs

The larger programs are broken into sections. To reconstruct them, copy the source code for each section into a file. The functions should be ordered with the definitions and declarations first, **main** as the first function in the file, and all supporting functions following in alphabetical order.

Except for **EPSET** which, as presented, refers to a specific printer, these programs are written in portable **C** code that is not hardware-dependent and makes no reference to the peculiarities of a particular machine. These programs require a **C** compiler that supports the full **C** language and a standard system library compatible with UNIX. The programs in Chapters 9 through 14 have all been compiled and tested under MSDOS and CP/M-86. Some of them have also been ported without change to these operating systems: UNIX, Data General's AOS/VS, and CP/M-80.

9

EPSET: A Printer Configurator

A printer attached to a computer frequently has to be configured; commanded to change pitch, line spacing, print emphasized or bold characters, and so on. Many printers recognize unique sets of codes that, when transmitted to the printers, configure the printers, causing them operate in a desired mode.

EPSET is introduced in this chapter as a model for a program dedicated to controlling a printer's modes from the computer terminal's keyboard. The printer whose codes are used in our example is the Epson MX80., a popular dot-matrix printer. If you are using a different printer and the printer's documentation provides the codes (often called "escape sequences"), the **EPSET** program can easily be changed to incorporate the escape sequences that are appropriate to your printer.

The program's objective is:

Display the possible printer options and
permit the user to select one at a time
through appropriate inputs from the keyboard.
Send the correct control codes to the printer.
Continue to prompt the user for additional
options until a request to exit is made.

HAZARD: printer file names

You must use the correct file name, in the definition of **PRINTNAME** according to the requirements of your C compiler. In this example, "prn" is used. Refer to Appendix A and your compiler's documentation for additional details.

Here is the **EPSET** program:

```
#include <stdio.h>

#define PRINTNAME       "prn"
#define TRUE            1
#define PutPrinter(Ch)  putc(Ch,ListFile)

main()
```

145

```
{        /* main */
int          CurChar ;
FILE         *ListFile ;

/* Open the printer as a file.
 */
if (!(ListFile = fopen(PRINTNAME,"w"))) {
    printf("Can't open printer.") ;
    exit(0) ;
}

while (TRUE) {
    /* Write the menu.
     */
    printf(
"\n\n\t >>>>>>> EPSET - MX80 PRINTER CONFIGURATOR <<<<<<<<\n\n") ;
    printf(
"\t:----------< SELECT ONE OPTION AT A TIME >----------:\n\n");
    printf(
"\t  (Characters Per Inch - CPI)\n") ;
    printf(
"\t    1 - 80 Columns.... 10 CPI with Single-Strike(SS)\n");
    printf(
"\t    2 - 80 Columns.... 10 CPI with Double-Strike(DS)\n");
    printf(
"\t    3 - 80 Columns.... 10 CPI with Emphasized Strike\n");
    printf(
"\t    4 - 80 Columns.... 10 CPI with DS and Emphasized\n");
    printf(
"\t    5 - 132 Columns... 16.5 CPI with Single-Strike\n");
    printf(
"\t    6 - 132 Columns... 16.5 CPI with Double-Strike\n\n");
    printf(
"\t  (Line Spacing - LPI)\n");
    printf(
"\t    a - Very Tight Spacing......... Lines Touching\n");
    printf(
"\t    b - Tight Spacing............. 8 LPI\n");
    printf(
"\t    c - Single Spacing............ 6 LPI\n");
    printf(
"\t    d - One and One-Half Spacing... 4.5 LPI\n");
    printf(
"\t    e - Double Spacing............ 3 LPI\n\n");

    printf(
"\t    x - exit this Program\n\n");
    printf(
"\t:-------------< ENTER DESIRED FUNCTION >-------------:");

    /* Get the user's response from the keyboard.
     */
    scanf("%1s",&CurChar) ;

    /* Transmit the appropriate codes.
     */
    switch(CurChar) {
        case '1':
            PutPrinter(18) ; PutPrinter(27) ; PutPrinter(65) ;
            PutPrinter(12) ; PutPrinter(27) ; PutPrinter(70) ;
            PutPrinter(27) ; PutPrinter(72) ;
            break ;
```

```
case '2':
    PutPrinter(18)  ;  PutPrinter(27)  ;  PutPrinter(65)  ;
    PutPrinter(12)  ;  PutPrinter(27)  ;  PutPrinter(70)  ;
    PutPrinter(27)  ;  PutPrinter(71)  ;
    break ;

case '3':
    PutPrinter(18)  ;  PutPrinter(27)  ;  PutPrinter(65)  ;
    PutPrinter(12)  ;  PutPrinter(27)  ;  PutPrinter(69)  ;
    PutPrinter(27)  ;  PutPrinter(73)  ;
    break ;

case '4':
    PutPrinter(18)  ;  PutPrinter(27)  ;  PutPrinter(65)  ;
    PutPrinter(12)  ;  PutPrinter(27)  ;  PutPrinter(69)  ;
    PutPrinter(27)  ;  PutPrinter(71)  ;
    break ;

case '5':
    PutPrinter(15)  ;  PutPrinter(27)  ;  PutPrinter(65)  ;
    PutPrinter(12)  ;  PutPrinter(27)  ;  PutPrinter(70)  ;
    PutPrinter(27)  ;  PutPrinter(72)  ;
    break ;

case '6':
    PutPrinter(15)  ;  PutPrinter(27)  ;  PutPrinter(65)  ;
    PutPrinter(12)  ;  PutPrinter(27)  ;  PutPrinter(70)  ;
    PutPrinter(27)  ;  PutPrinter(71)  ;
    break ;

case 'a':
    PutPrinter(27)  ;  PutPrinter(49)  ;
    break ;

case 'b':
    PutPrinter(27)  ;  PutPrinter(48)  ;
    break ;

case 'c':
    PutPrinter(27)  ;  PutPrinter(65)  ;  PutPrinter(140)  ;
    PutPrinter(27)  ;  PutPrinter(50)  ;
    break ;

case 'd':
    PutPrinter(27)  ;  PutPrinter(65)  ;  PutPrinter(146)  ;
    PutPrinter(27)  ;  PutPrinter(50)  ;
    break ;

case 'e':
    PutPrinter(27)  ;  PutPrinter(65)  ;  PutPrinter(152)  ;
    PutPrinter(27)  ;  PutPrinter(50)  ;
    break ;

case 'x':
    exit(0) ;

default:
    printf(
"\t            +++ INVALID OPTION +++\n");
    break ;
}

/* Ring the bell to show transmission is complete.
 */
```

CPT-K

```
        PutPrinter(7) ;

        /* Ensure that the commands are sent to the
         * printer immediately by flushing the buffer.
         */
        fflush(ListFile) ;
    }
}       /* main */
```

ANATOMY: code macros

The **#define** directive has been used often in this book's programs to define constants as expressive names. The **#define** directive can also be used to create a code macro.

PutPrinter appears to be a function used in **EPSET**. It is passed in a single argument which is the code to be sent to the printer. Imagine that this is the function:

```
VOID PutPrinter(Code)
int      Code ;
{    /* PutPrinter */
   putc(Code,ListFile) ;
}    /* PutPrinter */
```

The function is a simple, single statement used in place of **putc** to avoid the repeated use of the name **ListFile** in the call to **putc.**

Instead of coding this function, a code macro can be used:

```
#define PutPrinter(Code)        putc(Code,ListFile)
```

Notice the spacing. No white space is allowed within the macro name **PutPrinter(Code).** The macro name stops when the first white space character appears.

As the **C** compiler's preprocessor makes its pass through the program, it searches for **PutPrinter** and finds the first occurrence:

```
case '1' :
    PutPrinter(18) ; PutPrinter(27) ; PutPrinter(65) ;
```

Instead of calling **PutPrinter** (which doesn't exist in the program as a function), the compiler takes the definition and replaces **PutPrinter** with the definition of the macro. This is called "expanding the macro." As the macro is expanded, the program is actually rewritten, using the macro definition:

```
    case '1' :
        putc(18,ListFile) ; PutPrinter(27) ; PutPrinter(65) ;

    PutPrinter(18) ;             original code
                 |
                 |
                 v
    PutPrinter(Code) ==> putc(Code,ListFile)
   18 replaces Code in the definition
                 |
                 |
                 v
    putc(18,ListFile) ;          after expansion
```

Note what happens: The macro defines new **C** code which replaces the original code in the program. Wherever the macro name and argument list appear, the **C** compiler uses the definition to expand the macro into its final form. The single parameter in the function definition is replaced by the source code in the parameter call to the macro. After complete expansion, the sample code looks like this:

```
case '1':
     putc(18,ListFile) ;  putc(27,ListFile) ;  putc(65,ListFile) ;
```

The compiler then treats these three statements as if they had been originally coded this way. The code macro "rewrites" the program as we go.

Be aware of the difference between macros and function calls. A function call invokes a new function that appears once in the program. A macro causes the expansion to happen every time the macro appears, and modifies the source code. Macros are most appropriate for replacing short, simple functions that are frequently called. For these short functions, the use of a macro reduces the time taken in calling a function. Depending on the compiler, this calling time can be considerable. Repeated use of macros can make the program larger, because every time the macro is used, it expands into more code.

Many **C** facilities are really code macros, not functions. In most **C** compilers, **getc** is a macro that calls lower-level input routines which are never seen. **getc**'s definition is in **stdio.h**, which explains why **stdio.h** must be included whenever **getc** is used. The character test and case translation functions such as **tolower** and **isdigit** are defined in **ctype.h**.

A function for **isdigit** is written:

```
int isdigit(Ch)
char      Ch ;
{    /* isdigit */
   return((Ch >= '0' && Ch <= '9') ? TRUE : FALSE) ;
}    /* isdigit */
```

Or, as a macro it is:

```
#define isdigit(Ch) ((Ch >= '0' && Ch <= '9') ? TRUE : FALSE)
```

Every time **isdigit(Ch)** occurs in the program, the **C** compiler replaces it with the definition **((Ch >= '0' && Ch <= '9') ? TRUE : FALSE)**.

Using the macro, how would the compiler expand this statement?

```
if (isdigit(Char)) {
   . . .
                 }
```

The macro **isdigit** is replaced by its definition, substituting the macro definition placeholder **Ch** with **Char**:

```
if (((Char >= '0' && Char <= '9') ? TRUE : FALSE)) {
   . . .
}
```

Code macros may be defined with as many parameters as are needed. Code macros are usually short, with one or two parameters.

ANATOMY: opening devices

Most devices (such as printers and displays) are treated as files by C programs. The printer is opened as a file:

```
/* Open the printer. */
if (!(ListFile = fopen(PRINTNAME,"w"))) {
    printf("Can't open printer.") ;
    exit(0) ;
}
```

In this example program, **PRINTNAME** is "**prn**". A special filename string represents the printer. Because this filename is specific to the compiler, consult the documentation for details about how to access devices attached to your computer. The printer is opened for writing, of course. A peripheral device usually can support either reading or writing, but not both. Obviously, the printer is not opened for reading.

ANATOMY: fflush

Some C compilers store several characters in memory before writing them to the destination file. This is called *buffering*. In this application, buffering the control codes can be a problem: configuration codes are written to the printer and nothing seems to happen. An ASCII BEL (7 decimal) code is sent to the printer to make it sound its bell, giving audible proof something has happened. Note: not all printers have bells, buzzers or other sounders. The Epson MX80 does have a sounder.

When the codes have been sent to the printer, the buffer is flushed to the file with the system function **fflush**:

```
fflush(ListFile) ;
```

fflush sends all characters stored in any buffers to the file. **fflush** takes a single argument: a pointer to a file opened using **fopen**. Any open file can be flushed at any time. However, it is not usually necessary to flush files. All files in a program are automatically flushed when the program ends. **EPSET** uses **fflush** to immediately send the control codes to the printer without waiting for the buffer to be sent at a later time. **fflush** is also used in programs where program or system failure causes loss of critical data stored in a buffer. The important files are flushed to write the data to their destination.

10

TXTRDR1: Quantitative Analysis of Text

Writers often know specifically or have a reasonable estimate of the length of the text they intend to prepare. The length may be dependent on the number of words or the number of lines. Obviously, manual counts are time consuming, tedious, and subject to human error. Time taken to do such counts reduces the amount of time available for the creative process. However, the computer itself, properly programmed, can relieve the writer of the negative aspects of word and line counting and, at the same time, produce highly accurate results.

TXTRDR1 is a program designed to read text files that have been created with text editors or word processors, then display statistics about the text. The program's objective is described as:

> Read a text file indicated by the user
> on the command line. Count the number
> of lines, words, sentences, and characters
> contained in the file. Give statistics for
> the average number of characters per word
> and the average number of words per sentence.

How is Counting Done?

Counting characters seems simple: merely read character by character from the file until the end-of-file is reached. Increment a character counter for each character, including newlines and spaces, that is read. However, writers usually want to see only a count of printable, visible characters. The **TXTRDR1** program is deliberately designed to count only the printable, or non-whitespace, characters.

The number of newlines can be used as the line-counter. If the input document has extra blank lines for page formatting, this algorithm fails. It is simple, though, and works for most cases.

But how are sentences counted? The easiest way is to count characters that normally end sentences: periods, question marks, and exclamation points. However, if the text contains decimal points in tables of numbers, this will give an inaccurate sentence count. Errors introduced by this compromise should be small in most documents. A sentence is defined as a sequence of characters ending in a special punctuation mark. Doing a more accurate analysis of the document to determine sentences requires more complex code.

How are words counted? Here is a definition for a word:

A sequence of characters that starts with
a printable character and ends with a white
space character: a space, a tab, or a newline.

This, too, may give an erroneous count because numbers will be counted as words. Again, the error should be small. The definition is the key to coding a word counter: look for a printable character and set a flag to show the start of a word. Count the word, and don't count any more words until the end of the current word is found. When the next white space character is found, reset the flag and search for the start of the next word.

Problems with Word Processors

Many word processing programs for microcomputers insert special characters into the text to signal a special action to the word processor. Unfortunately, these characters may get in the way of the counting process. Let's take an example.

WordStar, a popular word processor for microcomputers, flags the last character of each word and every newline in the middle of a paragraph. To understand the flags we must understand how characters are stored.

On most microcomputers (and most minicomputers) a character is a sequence of eight bits:

```
|_|_|_|_|_|_|_|_|
 7 6 5 4 3 2 1 0
```

The bits are numbered from right to left and start with zero.

A normal ASCII character is stored in bits zero through six. Every character corresponds to a number between zero and 127. Normally, bit seven is zero.

WordStar sets bit seven to one (high or on) to flag a character as special. These high bits must be stripped before processing because the **C** character class functions will not work correctly if these bits are allowed to remain turned on, or high. A mask, and a new operation called **bitwise and** is needed:

```
1 0 1 1 1 0 0 1
|_|_|_|_|_|_|_|_|    original character
7 6 5 4 3 2 1 0

0 1 1 1 1 1 1 1
|_|_|_|_|_|_|_|_|    mask: 7F hexadecimal
7 6 5 4 3 2 1 0
       |
       |
       V
       &  -- the C 'bitwise and' operator
       |
       |
       V
0 0 1 1 1 0 0 1
|_|_|_|_|_|_|_|_|    character after masking
7 6 5 4 3 2 1 0
```

The **bitwise and** operator compares each bit in two characters, integers, or longs.
If the bit is *one* in both, it returns a *one*. If the bit is *zero* in either, it returns a *zero*.
The mask has all bits set to *one* except bit *seven*. This sets the seventh bit to *zero*.
The 'bitwise and' operator is a single ampersand **&**. It is used as all **C** arithmetic
operators: the operator appears between the original character and the mask. For
example, the **C** code to 'bitwise and' the character variable **Ch** with the hexadecimal
mask **7F** is:

```
Ch = Ch & 0x7F ;
```

When a Newline is Not a Newline

Microcomputers store newlines in text files as two characters, not one. A **newline**
is a sequence of an **ASCII CR** (carriage return) and an **ASCII LF** (linefeed). Many
minicomputer systems, including UNIX systems, use only an **ASCII LF** to end lines.
In **C** programs, the **newline** symbol **\n** is used to mean an **ASCII LF**. When reading
a text file, most microcomputer **C** compilers automatically translate these characters
into a single character, a newline.

When **WordStar** turns the high bit on in a CR-LF sequence, microcomputer **C**
compilers get confused and don't do the correct translation. The translation must
be deliberately incorporated into the program's code. After the high bit in each
character has been zeroed, the program must check for an **ASCII CR**. If it is found,
the next character is read. If the next character is an **ASCII LF**, a **newline** is recogniz-
ed. The **ASCII CR** is discarded and the **ASCII LF** becomes the **newline**. If the
next character is not an **ASCII LF**, the character is put back to be read again.

Pseudocode

The program's flow is described in pseudo-code:

> Open the input file.
> while the condition is not end-of-file,
>   read each character. {
>   assign the character to CurChar.

```
    if CurChar is a CR,
        read the next character
        if the next character is a LF,
            throw away the CR and assign
            a newline to CurChar
        else
        ·   put back the second character and
            leave CurChar alone

    if CurChar is not a white space character
        count it as a character

    if CurChar is an end-of-sentence mark
        count a new sentence

    if CurChar is a newline
        count a newline

    if CurChar is a white space character
        set InWord to FALSE
    else
        if InWord is FALSE
            start a new word by setting InWord
            TRUE. Count the word.
}
print statistics
```

TXTRDR1 Source Code

The program below uses initializers to set the starting values of variables. Some microcomputer **C** compilers do not have initializers, or place restrictions on their use. If your compiler does not accept the initializers in this program, simply replace them with assignment statements following the variable declarations.

```c
#include <stdio.h>

#define CR      0X0D
#define BOOL    int
#define FALSE   0
#define LF      0X0A
#define MASK    0x7F
#define TRUE    1

main(argc,argv)
int     argc ;
char    *argv[] ;
{       /* main */
    int         CurChar ;
    FILE        *InFile ;
    BOOL        InWord = FALSE ;
    int         NumChars = 0 ;
    int         NumLines = 0 ;
    int         NumSent = 0 ;
```

```
int           NumWords = 0 ;
char          Temp ;

/* Print an error-message if the command line is
 * incomplete.
 */
if (argc < 2) {
    printf("\tYou Didn't Enter A File Name!\n") ;
    printf("\tProper Use: TXTRDR1 filename <CR>\n") ;
    exit(0) ;
}
/* Attempt to open the file.  Print an error-message
 * if the file cannot be found on the disk.
 */
if (!(InFile = fopen(argv[1],"r"))) {
    printf("\tNo Such File On The Disk!\n") ;
    printf("\tProper Use: TXTRDR1 filename <CR>\n") ;
    exit(0) ;
}

/* Read the file a character at a time until
 * end-of-file is reached
 */
while ((CurChar = getc(InFile)) != EOF) {
    /* Strip the high bit.  This is important for
     * files created by many microcomputer word-processing
     * programs such as WordStar.
     */
    CurChar &= MASK ;

    /* Do special processing for WordStar files: check
     * for WordStar's unusual end-of-line characters.
     * WordStar end-of-line characters are 8D 0A, not 0D 0A.
     * These cause the run-time newline-translation routines
     * of microcomputer C compilers to see two characters
     * instead of just a newline.
     *
     * Scan two characters in succession.  If the character
     * following an 0D (CR) is an 0A (LF), a newline has been found.
     * Throw a character away and continue.  Otherwise, put
     * back the character for the next read.
     */
    if (CurChar == CR) {
        if ((Temp = getc(InFile)) == LF)
            /* This is a real end-of-line; throw-away CR.
             */
            CurChar = '\n' ;
        else
            /* Not a sequence; put back the character.
             */
            ungetc(Temp,InFile) ;
    }

    /* Count non-whitespace characters.
     */
    if (!isspace(CurChar))
        NumChars++ ;

    /* Count sentences by counting sentence-ending
     * punctuation marks.
     */
    if (CurChar == '.' || CurChar == '!' || CurChar == '?')
        NumSent++ ;
```

```
    )  count lines by counting newlines,
    */
    if (CurChar == '\n')
        NumLines++ ;

    /* Count words by looking for movement from a
     * non-word to a word.  A word begins with a
     * non-whitespace character, and ends with the
     * next whitespace character.
     */
    if (isspace(CurChar))
        InWord = FALSE ;
    else
        if (!InWord) {
            InWord = TRUE ;
            NumWords++ ;
        }
}

/* Report statistics.
 */
printf("\n\n\n\n\n\n\n\n\n\n\n") ;
printf("\t\tDATA FOR FILE:   %s\n",argv[1]) ;
printf("\t\t-------------------------------\n") ;
printf("\t\t\t\tLINE COUNT: %d\n",NumLines) ;
printf("\t\t\t\tWORD COUNT: %d\n",NumWords) ;

printf("\t\t\t\tAVERAGE CHARACTERS/WORD: %4.1f\n",
    (float)NumChars/(float)NumWords) ;
printf("\t\t\t\tSENTENCE COUNT: %d\n",NumSent) ;
printf("\t\t\t\tAVERAGE WORDS/SENTENCE: %4.1f\n",
    (float)NumWords/(float)NumSent) ;

}  /* main */

BOOL    isspace(Ch)
char    Ch ;
/* isspace returns TRUE if Ch is a space, a tab, or a newline.
 */
{       /* isspace */
  return((Ch == ' ' || Ch == '\t' || Ch == '\n') ? TRUE : FALSE) ;
}       /* isspace */
```

ANATOMY: initializers

C lets the starting values of variables be set when we come into a function in the same line in which the variable is declared. This is called an *initializer*:

```
int         NumWords = 0 ;
```

NumWords is declared as **int** and, at the same time, is assigned an initial value of 0. The assignment happens when the **main** function is entered. If an initializer is used in a function, the value of the variable is reinitialized each time the function is entered.

Variables of any type can be initialized. Some examples of initializers are:

```
int         NumChars = 0 ;
char        CurChar = ' ' ;
int         SmallArray[3] = {0,1,2} ;
char        *String = "This is a string" ;
```

NumChars is identified as an integer and set to zero at the same time. In the same way, **CurChar** is assigned the value of a space. Character and numeric initializers can be used freely.

SmallArray is an array of three elements. Each element of the array can be initialized by putting the values inside curly brackets and separating the values with commas. If there are fewer values than elements in the array, the remaining elements are set to zero. It is an error to have more values than elements in an array. If an initial value appears more than once in an array initializer, it must be explicitly repeated each time. There is no way to repeat initial values.

The last example shows how string variables can be initialized. A character pointer is declared and set equal to the quoted string value. C allocates space for the string, zero terminates it, and sets the pointer to point to the first character. This is a convenient way to set up string variables that do not change during the program. C reserves only enough space for the string that is initialized; if another string is appended to it, other variables in the program may be destroyed.

ANATOMY: read until end-of-file

Text files are read, using **fgets,** until there are no more lines. When the end-of-file is reached, **fgets** returns a zero.

TXTRDR1 reads characters with **getc.** When end-of-file is found, **getc** returns **EOF,** a constant defined in **stdio.h.** **EOF** can only be stored in an integer variable. To see **EOF,** the results of **getc** must always be assigned to an integer variable.

The following **while** statement reads characters and tests for **EOF** simultaneously:

```
while ((CurChar = getc(InFile)) != EOF) {
```

First, read from **InFile,** assign the character to the **CurChar,** and then test for **EOF.** When end-of-file is found, the loop is immediately exited.

ANATOMY: hexadecimal notation with
'bitwise and'
and
'bitwise or'

C provides the 'bitwise and' operator, for example, to strip the word processor flags from a character:

```
CurChar &= 0x7F
```

As mentioned above, the single apmersand **&** is the **bitwise and** operator. This combination **bitwise and** and assign operator is similar to the combinations of operators previously described. This statement takes the current value of **CurChar,** does the bitwise and operation as described above, and assigns the result back to **CurChar.**

C enables free movement between decimal and hexadecimal notation for numbers. Decimal numbers are entered as one normally would. Hexadecimal numbers begin with the special characters **0x** or **0X.** In this example, **0x7F** is the hexadecimal number **7F** (127 decimal). Upper or lowercase letters from **A** through **F** may be used in hexadecimal numbers.

C also provides the **bitwise or** operator. The **bitwise or** operator sets the bit to *one* in the result, if either of the corresponding bits in the two operators is *one.* For example:

```
1 0 1 1 1 0 0 1
|_|_|_|_|_|_|_|_|    original character
7 6 5 4 3 2 1 0

0 1 0 0 0 0 0 0
|_|_|_|_|_|_|_|_|    40 hexadecimal
7 6 5 4 3 2 1 0
        |
        |
        |
        v

        |  -- the C 'bitwise and' operator

        |
        |
        v
1 1 1 1 1 0 0 1
|_|_|_|_|_|_|_|_|    character after masking
7 6 5 4 3 2 1 0
```

A single vertical stroke | (a "stick") means **bitwise or.** For example:

```
char I,J,K ;

I = J | K ;
```

DISCUSSION: newline translation

Translating **newlines** presents an interesting problem in C programming:

After the high bit in each character is set
to zero, test for an **ASCII CR**. If it is found,
the next character is read. If the next character
is an **ASCII LF**, a newline has been found. Throw
away the characters and return a newline.
If the next character is not an **ASCII LF**,
the character is put back to be read again.

Translated into **C** code, this becomes:

```
#define CR        0x0D
#define LF        0x0A

if (CurChar == CR) {
    if ((Temp = getc(InFile)) == LF)
        /* This is a real end-of-line; throw away CR.
         */
        CurChar = '\n' ;
    else
        /* Not a sequence; put back the character.
```

```
    */
    ungetc(Temp,InFile) ;
}
```

0x0D and **0x0A** are the hexadecimal codes for **ASCII CR** and **ASCII LF,** respectively.

Next, the character is tested to determine if it is an **ASCII CR.** If it is, the next character is read and checked against an **ASCII LF.** If it is an **ASCII LF,** the **ASCII CR** is thrown away and **CurChar** is set equal to **ASCII LF,** a **newline.** Otherwise, the character is put back with **ungetc,** to be read again later.

ANATOMY: ungetc

Often it is necessary to read ahead of the current place in a file to see what's coming so a decision can be made on what action to take. If it is determined the next character is not needed, it must be processed later. **C** provides a convenient way to put back a character with **ungetc** so it can be read later using the normal **C** input functions.

ungetc is called with the character to be put back. Also, the file pointer is open for reading:

```
ungetc(Temp,InFile)
```

This puts **Temp** back into **InFile.** The next time **InFile** is read, the value of **Temp** is read again.

A caution about **ungetc:** only one character can be put back. Strange errors will happen if attempts are made to put back several characters.

DISCUSSION: counting words

The design for the word counter was:

Search for a printable character and set
a flag to identify the start of a word.
Count the word, and don't count any more
words until the end of the current word
is identified. When the next white-space
character is reached, the flag is reset and
the start of the next word is sought.

The **C** code for word counting is:

```
BOOL    InWord ;

if (isspace(CurChar))
    InWord = FALSE ;
else
    if (!InWord) {
        InWord = TRUE ;
        NumWords++ ;
    }
```

InWord is declared as **BOOL**, which is defined as **int**. **BOOL** is used to mean this variable is either **TRUE** or **FALSE**. The name **BOOL** comes from George Boole, an important figure in symbolic logic. The **BOOL** definition is used often in **C** programs as a commenting technique.

Assume that **CurChar** is a white-space character. **InWord** is set to **FALSE** and reading continues. When a non-white-space character is read, a test is made to determine if **InWord** is **FALSE**. It is, in this instance, so it is set to **TRUE** and **NumWords** is incremented. The first character in a word has just been read. The search for characters continues while there are characters in the word. When the white space character ending word is found, **InWord** is reset to **FALSE**. The process is repeated when the next character that starts a word is found.

DISCUSSION: statistics

Study the use of casts in the statistics section of the program. The variables are **ints**. If they are divided directly, the remainder is truncated. First these **ints** are cast to **floats,** then divided and assigned to a **float** variable.

A Sample Run of TXTRDR1

Using this chapter as input, **TXTRDR1** gives this output:

```
DATA FOR FILE:  chap10
-----------------------------------
               LINE COUNT: 580
               WORD COUNT: 3068
               AVERAGE CHARACTERS/WORD:   4.7
               SENTENCE COUNT: 193
               AVERAGE WORDS/SENTENCE: 15.9
```

11

TXTRDR2 and TXTRDR3: Qualitative Analysis Of Text

Source code was given in the previous chapter for deriving data that serve useful purposes in quantifying text files. It is also useful to qualify the merits of the text. Within certain pragmatic limits, it is possible to write code that examines a text file and displays a variety of measures-of-merit about the readability of the content.

TXTRDR2 is an extension of **TXTRDR1** that incorporates additional code for qualitative evaluation of text files. While the method used to evaluate the text may indeed be challengeable when considered in the context of the universe of written matter, the program is useful in comparing the relative "readability" qualities of the separate works of an individual author.

How is Readability Determined?

Several studies have been made in search of methods or techniques for testing reading matter for readability. *Readability* is both: (1) ease of reading, and (2) human interest. A well-known study to produce a definitive formula for calculating readability of text is described in *The Art of Readable Writing* by Rudolf Flesch, Harper & Row, 1974.

Flesch developed an algorithm or mathematical construction which attempts to determine readability from the number of words, average sentence length, syllable count, personal words, and personal sentences used in the text being measured. The data were collected manually; this was before the general availability of computers.

The score for reading ease (how easy is a segment of text to read), is arrived at by factoring the average sentence length and the number of syllables per 100 words, adding them together, and subtracting this new number from a fixed reference.

Rules of syllabification of English words are complex. Rather than demand that the computer make a direct count, **TXTRDR2** reads a text file and estimates the number of syllables by referencing the number of vowels per hundred words. Since every syllable must have at least one vowel, an approximate syllable count is made

161

in this relatively uncomplicated way, Syllables may have more than one vowel; therefore, by empirical test methods, it is estimated that the number of syllables in a text are represented by 86% of the number of vowels counted.

Counting the number of words and the number of sentences is accomplished by source code taken from **TXTRDR1**. Thus, the average number of words per sentence can be readily calculated.

How is the Human Interest Level Determined?

Flesch concluded the score for human interest can be derived by counting and factoring the number of personal words (names and personal pronouns) and the number of personal sentences used in the text matter. The two factored counts are added together to arrive at the human interest score. Such calculations for readability and human interest are simple tasks for a microcomputer program that has been properly coded.

TXTRDR2 essentially follows Rudolf Flesch's method with some liberties taken by the program's authors to adapt it for use with microcomputers and the **C** programming language. Again, the value of **TXTRDR2** is in its ability to provide relative reference points for comparing the various writings of a single author. Although it may be used for the purpose, it is not intended to compare one author with another, nor is it intended to replace or act as a substitute for human judgement of the qualities of literature.

Searching for Personal Words

TXTRDR2 reads each word in the text or document being examined and compares each word with a master list of personal pronouns (the personal words). Searching through the list to find a match is an important problem in computer science. The first approach reveals a simple solution to this specific problem. To match a word somewhere in a list, the program starts its search at the beginning of the list. If a match is found, we count the word as a personal word. The program then continues, examining the next item in the list. The process continues until either a match is found or the master list in the program is exhausted. The process of beginning at the top and looking at each item in turn is called a *linear search*. The linear search strategy is the simplest method. Unfortunately, it is a rather slow process.

TXTRDR2 Strategy

The program opens a text file or document called from the command line. Error checking is provided. **TXTRDR2** reads this file and stores the personal words in an array of character strings.

As **TXTRDR2** reads each character from the document, it saves the characters that form a word. **TXTRDR2** begins saving characters in a character string when a word is found. When the word ends, it stops saving characters and calls a function that searches for this word in the master personal word list. The function returns **TRUE** if the word is found in the master list.

TXTRDR2 Source Code

The task is complex and, as a result, **TXTRDR2** is a relatively long program. To improve the comprehension of this program, one function at a time is presented and studied. Here are the declarations preceding **main**:

```
/*****************************************************************/
/*                      include files                          */
/*****************************************************************/
#include <stdio.h>

/*****************************************************************/
/*                      definitions                            */
/*****************************************************************/
#define BOOL          int
#define CR            0x0D
#define EQUALS        0
#define FALSE         0
#define LF            0x0A
#define MAXNUMWORDS   127
#define MAXSTRLEN     255
#define MAXWORDLEN    255
#define PFILENAME     "persword"
#define TRUE          1
#define VOID          int

/*****************************************************************/
/*                      code macros                            */
/*****************************************************************/
#define   min(a,b)    ((a > b) ? b : a)
#define   max(a,b)    ((a < b) ? b : a)

/*****************************************************************/
/*                      global variables                       */
/*****************************************************************/
int     NumRead ;
/* Number of words read into the PersWords array.
 */

char    PersWords[MAXNUMWORDS][MAXWORDLEN] ;
/* Repository of personal words.
 */
```

Most of the **#define** compiler directives are the same as in **TXTRDR1**. A constant, **MAXWORDLEN**, has been added and is the longest word to be stored in the program.

Following the **#define** section, two variables, **NumRead** and **PersWords** are declared. These variables hold the number of personal words to be read from the master text file and the personal words themselves. In other examples of code in this book, we have not declared variables outside a function. These are called *global variables*, and need special consideration.

Up to this point, each of the programs has declared variables inside the functions where each of the variables is used. Recall these variables are only known inside

CPT-L

the function where they are declared. This gives some protection against inadvertently changing the value of an important variable by executing another section of code. Parameters have been used to pass the values of variables into functions. Other than these parameters, no function knows about the other variables in the program. It is as though there is a set of boxes with clearly defined **IN** and **OUT** doors. The only way to pass information into any of the boxes is to use parameters.

ANATOMY: global variables

Sometimes a program needs an important variable to be known in all functions. Explicitly passing the variable becomes a problem, because it is needed in every parameter list for every function in the program. For these variables, **C** provides the concept of global variables. A global variable is declared outside a function body, usually at the beginning of a program. A global variable is known inside every function in the program by the same name.

Global variables are subject to side effects that occur when a variable is changed inadvertently in one part of the program in a way that destroys its usefulness to the rest of the program. Bugs owing to side effects are hard to trace. It is better to avoid the problem by using global variables only where they simplify the program.

FUNCTION: main

TXTRDR2's **main** function borrows heavily from **TXTRDR1**. The major additions are in saving characters into words and in calculating and reporting the final statistics.

```
main(argc,argv)
int      argc;
char     *argv[] ;
{
    int      CurChar ;
    char     CurWord[MAXWORDLEN] ;
    float    HndrdWrds = 0.0 ;
    FILE     *InFile ;
    float    InterestIndex = 0.0 ;
    BOOL     InWord = FALSE ;
    int      NumChars = 0 ;
    int      NumLines = 0 ;
    int      NumPersSent = 0 ;
    int      NumPersWords = 0 ;
    int      NumSent = 0 ;
    int      NumSyllables = 0 ;
    int      NumVowels = 0 ;
    int      NumWords = 0 ;
    float    PerslWrdsPerHndrd = 0.0 ;
    float    ReadIndex = 0.0 ;
    float    SylPerHndrdWrds = 0.0 ;
    char     Temp ;
    char     *WorkingChar ;

    NumRead = SetupPersWords() ;
```

```
/* If the command line is incomplete
 * or incorrect, print an error message.
 */
if (argc < 2) {
    printf("\n\tYou didn't enter a filename.\n") ;
    printf("\tProper entry: TXTRDR2 filename <CR>\n\n") ;
    exit(0) ;
}

/* Open the file and print an error message
 * if the file cannot be found.
 */
if (!(InFile = fopen(argv[1],"r"))) {
    printf("\n\tNo such file on the disk!\n") ;
    printf("\tProper entry: TXTRDR2 filename <CR>\n\n") ;
    exit(0) ;
}

printf("\nEach Pword: is a personal-word found in: %s\n\n",
    argv[1]) ;
WorkingChar = CurWord ;
while ((CurChar = getc(InFile)) != EOF) {

    /* Strip the high bit for word processors.
     */
    CurChar &= 0x7f ;

    /* Do special end-of-line processing
     * for word processors.
     */
    if (CurChar == CR) {
        if ((Temp = getc(InFile)) == LF)
            /* This is a real end-of-line.
             * Throw away CR.
             */
            CurChar = '\n' ;
        else
            /* Not a sequence; put back the character.
             */
            ungetc(Temp,InFile) ;
    }

    /* Count non-whitespace characters.
     */
    if (isspace(CurChar) == FALSE)
        NumChars++ ;
    /* Count sentences by counting sentence-ending
     * punctuation marks.
     */
    if (CurChar == '.' || CurChar == '!' || CurChar == '?')
        NumSent++ ;

    /* Count lines by counting newlines.
     */
    if (CurChar == '\n')
        NumLines++ ;

    /* Count words by looking for movement from
     * a non-word to a word.  A word begins with a
     * non-whitespace character, and ends with the
     * next whitespace character.
     */
    if (isspace(CurChar) == TRUE)
        InWord = FALSE ;
    else if (!InWord) {
        InWord = TRUE ;
        NumWords++ ;
```

```
            *WorkingChar++ = CurChar ;
        }
        else {
            *WorkingChar++ = CurChar ;
        }

        /* Simulate syllable-count by counting vowels.
         */
        if (isvowel(CurChar) == TRUE)
            NumVowels++ ;

        /* Check all words to see if they are personal words.
         * Count personal words.  Check a word whenever InWord
         * is FALSE, meaning we've finished with a word.
         */
        if (!InWord) {
            /* Terminate the current word. */
            *WorkingChar = '\0' ;
            if (isperslwrd(CurWord)) {
                printf("Pword: %s\t",CurWord) ;
                NumPersWords++ ;
            }
            /* After the word has been examined, discard it and
             * reset the pointer to the beginning of the buffer.
             */
            WorkingChar = CurWord ;
        }
}

/* Report statistics.         */
printf("\n\n\n\n\n") ;
printf("\tTXTRDR2 - Analysis of Text-File: %s\n",argv[1]) ;
printf("\t-------------------------------------------------\n") ;
printf("\tLine count: %d\n",NumLines) ;
printf("\tWord count: %d\n",NumWords) ;
printf("\tAverage characters/word: %5.2f\n",
    (float)NumChars / (float)NumWords) ;
printf("\tSentence count: %d\n",NumSent) ;
printf("\tAverage words/sentence: %5.2f\n",
    (float)NumWords / (float)NumSent) ;
HndrdWrds = (float)NumWords * 0.01 ;

PerslWrdsPerHndrd = (float)NumPersWords / HndrdWrds ;

/* NOTE: Syllables are estimated to be
 * 86% of the vowel count.
 */

NumSyllables = (float)NumVowels * 0.86 ;
SylPerHndrdWrds = (float)NumSyllables / HndrdWrds ;

/* NOTE: Personal sentences are estimated to be
 * 65% of the personal word count.
 */
NumPersSent = (float)NumPersWords * 0.65 ;

printf("\t===============================") ;
printf("\t===============================\n") ;

ReadIndex = 215 - ((NumPersSent * 1.015) +
    (SylPerHndrdWrds * 0.846)) ;
ReadIndex = max(ReadIndex,0) ;
ReadIndex = min(ReadIndex,100) ;
printf("\tReading-ease level:      %5.2f",ReadIndex) ;
```

```
InterestIndex = (PerslWrdsPerHndrd * 3.635) +
    ((((float)NumPersSent / (float)NumSent) * 100) * 0.314) ;
InterestIndex = max(InterestIndex,0) ;
InterestIndex = min(InterestIndex,100) ;
printf("\tHuman-interest scale:   %5.2f\n",InterestIndex) ;

printf("\t=============================") ;
printf("\t=============================\n") ;

printf("\t 0-30  Very difficult          0-10  Dull\n") ;
printf("\t30-50  Difficult              10-20  Mildly interesting\n")
printf("\t50-60  Fairly difficult       20-40  Interesting\n") ;
printf("\t60-70  Standard difficulty    40-60  Very Interesting\n") ;
printf("\t70-80  Fairly easy            60-100 Dramatic\n") ;
printf("\t80-90  Easy\n") ;
printf("\t90-100 Very Easy") ;
    /* main */
}
```

main calls **SetupPersWords** to read the text file containing the master personal word list. **SetupPersWords** returns the number of words it read, which is stored in **NumRead**. Neither of the two global variables, **NumRead** and **PersWords**, changes throughout the remainder of the program.

The **while** loop that reads characters from **InFile** does the same actions it did in **TXTRDR1**. Recall **InWord** is **TRUE** whenever a word is being read. The code that counts words to save characters is augmented inside a word at the same time:

```
if (isspace(CurChar) == TRUE)
    InWord = FALSE ;
else if (!InWord) {
    InWord = TRUE ;
    NumWords++ ;
    *WorkingChar++ = CurChar ;
}
else {
    *WorkingChar++ = CurChar ;
}
```

If **CurChar** is not a white space character, check to see if **InWord** is **TRUE** or **FALSE**. If it is **FALSE**, a word is beginning. As before, count the word by incrementing **NumWords**, and set **InWord** to **TRUE**. We begin saving characters by assigning **CurChar** to *****WorkingChar**. **WorkingChar** is initialized at the beginning of the loop to point to the beginning of **CurWord**, a character string **MAXWORDLEN** characters long. After storing the first character, **WorkingChar** is moved to point to the next character in the sequence.

If **InWord** is **FALSE**, the program is outside a word. A word may have just finished and **CurWord** now contains the last word read. The program may also be in a sequence of white space characters, and **CurWord** contains nothing. In either case this code is executed:

```
if (!InWord) {
    /* Terminate the current word. */
    *WorkingChar = '\0' ;
    if (isperslwrd(CurWord)) {
        printf("Pword: %s\t",CurWord) ;
        NumPersWords++ ;
    }
```

```
            /* After the word has been examined, discard it and
             * reset the pointer to the beginning of the buffer.
             */
            WorkingChar = CurWord ;
        }
```

The current word ends by setting ***WorkingChar** to the null character. Since the pointer **WorkingChar** always points to the *next* character to be filled in **Cur-Word**, this code properly terminates the word. Then **isperslwrd** is called, which returns **TRUE** if **CurWord** is a personal word. **CurWord** is passed to **isperslwrd** because **CurWord** points to the beginning of the word.

If a personal word is found, **NumPersWords** is incremented. In any case, **WorkingChar** is reset to point to the beginning of **CurWord**. When the program begins to save characters in the next word, **WorkingChar** is pointing at the correct spot.

The calculation section of **TXTRDR1** is expanded. **ReadIndex** (the reading ease index) and **InterestIndex** (the human interest index) are calculated directly from the counts. Note the use of casts to change integer variables to floats before some critical calculations.

Counting Vowels Using isvowel

The vowel counter is part of the large **while** loop:

```
            /* Simulate syllable-count by counting vowels.
             */
            if (isvowel(CurChar) == TRUE)
                NumVowels++ ;
```

FUNCTION: isvowel

Vowels are counted with the help of an additional function, **isvowel**, which returns **TRUE** if its parameter is a vowel:

```
            BOOL isvowel(Ch)
            /* isvowel returns TRUE if Ch is a vowel; FALSE otherwise.
             */
            char    Ch ;
            {       /* isvowel */
                Ch = tolower(Ch) ;
                return ((Ch == 'a' || Ch == 'e' || Ch == 'i' || Ch == 'o' ||
                    Ch == 'u' || Ch == 'y') ? TRUE : FALSE) ;
            }       /* isvowel */
```

Reading the Personal Word File

SetUpPersWords reads the personal word master list from a text file and stores each personal word as an element of **PersWords.** The file contains one personal word on a each line. All personal words are in lower case.

```
int     SetupPersWords()
/* SetupPersWords reads personal words from a text file
 * and installs them in the PersWords table.  It returns the
 * number of words read.
 */
{       /* SetupPersWords */
    char        NewWord [MAXSTRLEN] ;
    FILE        *PersFile ;
    int         WordCounter ;
    char        *Working ;

    /* Open the personal word file.
     */
    if (!(PersFile = fopen(PFILENAME,"r"))) {
        printf("Can't find %s\n",PFILENAME) ;
        exit(0) ;
    }

    /* Insert personal words into the table.
     */
    for (WordCounter = 0 ;
                fscanf(PersFile,"%s",PersWords[WordCounter])
                    != EOF ;
                WordCounter++)
        LowerString(PersWords[WordCounter]) ;

    fclose(PersFile) ;
    /* Return the number of words read.
     */
    return (WordCounter) ;
}       /* SetupPersWords */

VOID LowerString(Value)
char    *Value ;
/*  LowerString converts any upper-case letters in  the  string
 * Value to lower-case.
 */
{       /* LowerString */
    for ( ; *Value != '\0' ; Value++)
        *Value = tolower(*Value) ;
}       /* LowerString */
```

Open the text file whose name is stored in the defined constant **PFILENAME** for reading. The **for** loop calls **fscanf** as part of the continuation condition. **fscanf** reads in one string using the **%s** format. The **%s** format causes **fscanf** to skip all white space; only printing characters are included in the string. When **fscanf** finds end-of-file, it returns **EOF** and the loop stops. **WordCounter** is incremented each time through the loop.

As each word is read, it is converted to lower case and copied into the next available slot in **PersWords.** After the entire file is read, **SetupPersWords** returns the number of words read.

FUNCTION: isperslwrd

This function performs the search for personal words. **isperslwrd** returns **TRUE** if **Word,** its formal parameter, is found in **PersWords**, the personal word array:

```
BOOL isperslwrd(Word)
/* isperslwrd returns TRUE if Word is found in the
 * personal word list; FALSE otherwise.
 */
char            *Word ;
{          /* isperslwrd */
    int         WordCounter ;
    char        *Working ;

    LowerString(Word) ;

    /* Search through the table, working from beginning
     * to end, until the word is found, or the search fails.
     */
    for (WordCounter = 0 ; WordCounter < NumRead ; WordCounter++) {
        if (strcmp(PersWords[WordCounter],Word) == EQUALS)
            return (TRUE) ;
    }
    return (FALSE) ;
}          /* isperslwrd */
```

isperslwrd first converts **Word** to lower case, then checks each entry in **PersWords** to see if it equals **Word**. It returns **TRUE** if a match is found. If the entire list is searched without success, it returns **FALSE**.

Optimizing TXTRDR2 for Speed

TXTRDR2 is now complete. However, the program takes 1 minute and 14 seconds when a three thousand word file is analyzed on an IBM Personal Computer. The program, as written, is considered too slow for processing long documents.

Optimizing a program means taking steps either to speed up the program or to reduce the memory storage requirements for the program. **TXTRDR2** must run faster. Optimizing a program in a high level language such as **C** is best done by carefully analyzing the methods used to solve the problem. Often dramatic improvements in speed are possible by picking a better approach to the problem. This final version, **TXTRDR3**, uses a better way to search a list of words for a match.

An Introduction to Hashing

An extremely fast way to find a word in a list of words is called *hashing*. Hashing means "to cut up into pieces," which exactly describes what happens in a *hashing* search.

TXTRDR2 does a linear search of the master word list. It starts at the beginning of the list and continues until the word is found or the end of the list is reached. The original word list is stored in exactly the order we read it in.

The *hashing search technique* first stores the master word list in an unusual order. We take each word and add the values of the ASCII codes of the letters together. The technique called *hashing* produces a nonsense number. Call this number **HashIndex**. The personal word in the master word list is stored in the **HashIndex**-th position in the table. Words are inserted in the table, using the same hashing technique, until all the words are stored. During the search, hashing works as follows.

To search for a word in the master word table, the word is hashed in the same way as when the original word list was stored. Let's say we have just read a word that is present in the list. After hashing, we get a hash index which takes us to the entry in the table where we stored the word originally. If everything is successful, hashing takes only one try to find the word even in a very long list of words.

The most serious problem with hashing methods is called *collision*. Collision occurs when two different words hash to the same hash index. If the hash index number is created by adding up the letters in a word, most documents will have at least two words that give the same hash index.

Much work has been done by computer scientists in resolving the collision problem. If a collision happens, the first hash table index is transformed to a new one through a process called *probing*. The new index created by probing is unique for that word. Otherwise, the probing continues. Every time a collision takes place, one more comparison must be made. The more often collision happens, the slower the search.

As the word table is more completely filled, collision becomes more and more frequent. The hashing algorithm has a maximum number of probes it will try before signaling a fatal error.

To prevent collision, the word table must be longer than the number of words to be stored. This means some memory must be sacrificed for the improved speed.

TXTRDR3 Source Code

TXTRDR3 starts with some declarations in addition to those in **TXTRDR2**:

```
#define HTSIZE          127              /* must be prime */

char    HashTable [HTSIZE][MAXWORDLEN] ;
/* repository of personal words.
 */
```

The global variable **PersWords** is renamed **HashTable** for this program. **HashTable** has space for **HTSIZE** words in it; **HTSIZE** must be prime for the hashing algorithm to work to its best. **NumWords** has been eliminated.

The hashing method used in **TXTRDR3** needs a hash table with a prime number of elements to work effectively. A prime number is not evenly divisible by any number other than one and itself, which makes it suited to the mathematical transformation   used   here.

Changes To main

main changes only slightly in **TXTRDR3**. The call to **SetupPersWords** is replaced with the call:

```
SetupHashTable() ;
```

SetupHashTable reads the personal word file and inserts the words read into the hash table using the hashing technique for proper placement of the words in the table. **SetupHashTable**   returns   nothing.

Setting Up the Hash Table

SetupHashTable uses the new function **InsertWord** to put the word that is read into the hash table at the correct location. **SetupHashTable** is ignorant of the hashing process and never knows the final location of the word within the table.

```
VOID SetupHashTable()
/* SetupHashTable inserts the personal word list into the hash
 * table.  Note the number of words is assumed to be about 70% of
 * HTSIZE.  The words are read from a text file.
 */
{       /* SetupHashTable */
    int       Counter ;
    FILE      *PersFile ;
    char      PersWord [MAXSTRLEN] ;

    /* Set the the first character of each string in the hash
     * table to the null character.
     */
    for (Counter = 0 ; Counter < HTSIZE ; Counter++)
        HashTable[Counter][0] = '\0' ;

    /* Open the personal word file.
     */
    if (!(PersFile = fopen(PFILENAME,"r"))) {
        printf("Can't find %s\n",PFILENAME) ;
        exit(0) ;
    }

    /* Insert personal words into table.
     */
    while (fscanf(PersFile,"%s",PersWord) != 0) {
        LowerString(PersWord) ;
        if (!InsertWord(PersWord)) {
            fprintf(stderr,"Hash table full.") ;
            exit(0) ;
        }
    }
}       /* SetupHashTable */
```

Searching for the Word

isperslwrd uses two hashing functions, **TransformId** and **GenerateNewIndex**, to look through the **HashTable** for **Word**. After converting **Word** to lower case, we get a hash index using **TransformId**. This is assigned to both **InitHTIndex**, the initial hash table index, and to **HTIndex**, the current hash table index. **InitHTIndex** is needed because the probing method requires the initial hash table index to do its work.

After hashing, the program looks at the entry in **HashTable** indexed by **HTIndex**. If the same word is found there, the search is successful, and **TRUE** is returned immediately. If there is no word at that place in the hash table (indicated by a null string at that place in the table), the word is not in the table, and **FALSE** is returned immediately.

If a different word is found in the table, a mismatch occurs. **GenerateNewIndex** gives us a new hash table index from **InitHTIndex** and **ProbeCounter**, the number of times the hash table has been probed. For every new probe, the word stored in the new location in the hash table is checked and returns **TRUE** if the same word is there, or **FALSE** if there is no word stored there. Probing continues if a different word is found.

As the number of elements in the hash table increases, the frequency of collisions rises. A check is done to ensure the search stops if too many collisions happen. In this program, **HTSIZE** / 2 collisions in a row signals an error from the hashing routines.

```
BOOL isperslwrd(Word)
/* isperslwrd returns TRUE if Word is found in the personal word
 * list; FALSE otherwise.
 */
char      *Word ;
{         /* isperslwrd */
     int        HTIndex ;       /* index for word into hash table */
     int        InitHTIndex ;
     int        ProbeCounter ;
     char       *Working ;

     /* If the first character in the word is a NULL, the word
      * has no length; return FALSE.
      */
     if (!*Word)
          return(FALSE) ;

     LowerString(Word) ;

     /* Get hash index. */
     HTIndex = InitHTIndex = TransformId(Word) ;

     /* If the word is in the table, return TRUE! */
     if (strcmp(HashTable[HTIndex],Word) == EQUALS)
          return(TRUE) ;
     /* If the index into the table is to a non-existent word
      * and the word has not been seen before, return FALSE.
      */
     if (*HashTable[HTIndex] == '\0')
          return(FALSE) ; /* No word found. */

     /* If the two words are unequal, a mismatch exists.
      * Continue probing for a while.
      */
     for (ProbeCounter = 0 ; ProbeCounter < (HTSIZE / 2) ;
                  ProbeCounter++) {
          HTIndex = GenerateNewIndex(InitHTIndex,ProbeCounter) ;
          if (strcmp(HashTable[HTIndex],Word) == EQUALS)
               return(TRUE) ;       /* Found it at last! */
          if (*HashTable[HTIndex] == '\0')
               return(FALSE) ;      /* Still no word found. */
     }

     /* If all probing fails, return FALSE */
     return(FALSE) ;
}         /* isperslwrd */
```

HASHING FUNCTIONS: TransformId

The basic hashing function is **TransformId**. It takes a word (or any character string), and returns an initial hash index for the word. The ASCII value of each character in the word is added to the previous total of characters multiplied by a constant factor. The constant factor is a prime number that gives a good mathematical distribution of hash numbers.

```
int TransformId(Word)
char        Word [] ;
/* TransformId converts the identifier into an integer within the
 * index range of HashTable.  A number is generated and reduced
 * modulo HTSIZE.
 */
{       /* TransformId */
    int        Term ;
    int        WordIndex ;

    for (Term = 0,WordIndex = strlen(Word) - 1 ; WordIndex > -1 ;
    WordIndex--)
        Term = (257 * Term) + Word[WordIndex] ;
    Term = (Term < 0) ? -Term : Term ;
    return(Term % HTSIZE) ;
}       /* TransformId */
```

TransformId hashes **Word**. After working through the entire word, we ensure we have a positive number, because overflow may have happened during hashing. Finally, the result of hashing is reduced modulo **HTSIZE**. This reduction ensures that the hash table is within the range zero through **HTSIZE**.

ANATOMY: modulus operator

C defines the **%** as the modulus operator. The modulus operator divides the first operand by the second and returns the *remainder*, not the quotient. As the remainder of a division is always less than the divisor, the modulus function gives an easy way to reduce an integer below a given value.

The modulus operator is defined only for integers and longs.

HASHING FUNCTIONS: GenerateNewIndex

If a collision state exists, the hash table is probed with **GenerateNewIndex**. We pass the original hash table index and the number of times we have probed for this case. **GenerateNewIndex** returns a new hash table index. This new index is then used in the search.

```
int GenerateNewIndex(OriginalKey,ProbeNumber)
int            OriginalKey ;
int            ProbeNumber ;
/* GenerateNewIndex takes the current hash table index
 * and generates a new index for collision resolution.
 */
{       /* GenerateNewIndex */
    return( (OriginalKey + ProbeNumber * ProbeNumber) % HTSIZE) ;
}       /* GenerateNewIndex */
```

HASHING FUNCTIONS: InsertWord

InsertWord inserts a copy of the parameter **Word** into **HashTable**. It calls **Hash** to return a guaranteed collision-resolved hash table index. If the **HashTable** element referred to by hash table index is empty, the word is copied into the table. If the **HashTable** element is already filled, do nothing.

Hash returns a minus one if the hash table is already full. If this happens, return **TRUE**. If the table can accommodate still more entries, return **FALSE**.

```
BOOL InsertWord(Word)
char            *Word ;
/* InsertWord inserts the word into the hash table and returns TRUE.
 * If the end-of-hash table is reached, FALSE is returned.
 */
{       /* InsertWord */
    int         HTIndex ;

    /* Get an index.  If the table is full, return TRUE. */
    if ((HTIndex = Hash(Word)) == -1)
        return(FALSE) ;

    /* Here's an empty slot.  Put the word in place. */
    if (*HashTable[HTIndex] == '\0') {
        strcpy(HashTable[HTIndex],Word) ;
    }
    return(TRUE) ;
}       /* InsertWord */
```

HASHING FUNCTIONS: Hash

Hash returns a hash table index guaranteed to be free of collisions for the word. It gets an initial hash table index using **TransformId**. If the index references an empty slot in **HashTable**, this index is returned. If the slot is already filled, the hash table is probed using **GenerateNewIndex** just as in **isperslwrd**. If the table is probed too many times, a minus one is returned to show an error state.

```
int Hash(Word)
char            *Word ;
/* Hash returns the HTIndex of the Word passed, or an appropriate
 * HTIndex for the word.  If HashTable is full, Hash returns -1.
 */
{       /* Hash */
    int         HTIndex ;
    int         IdLen ;
    int         InitHTIndex ;
    int         ProbeCounter = 0 ;

    if (!(IdLen = strlen(Word)))
        printf("Hash: Word of no length\n") ;

    /* Get the initial hash index for Word.
     */
    HTIndex = InitHTIndex  = TransformId(Word) ;

    /* If the index goes to an empty slot in the hash table, we
     * win immediately!  Do nothing.
     */
```

```
        if (*HashTable[HTIndex] == '\0')
            /* NULL */ ;
        else
            /* Has the word been found already installed?
             */
            if (strcmp(Word,HashTable[HTIndex]) == EQUALS)
                /* DONE: A direct hit! */ ;
            /* A collision!  Generate new indices through probing.
             */
            else
                for (ProbeCounter = 0 ; ProbeCounter < (HTSIZE / 2) ;
                    ProbeCounter++) {
                    HTIndex = GenerateNewIndex(InitHTIndex,ProbeCounter) ;
                    /* An empty slot. */
                    if (*HashTable[HTIndex] == '\0')
                        break ;
                    /* The word is already installed. */
                    else if (strcmp(Word,HashTable[HTIndex]) == EQUALS)
                        break ;
                }
    /* If we probed too many times, the table is full.
     * Signal an error.
     */
    if (ProbeCounter >= (HTSIZE / 2))
        return(-1) ;
    return(HTIndex) ;
}       /* Hash */
```

A Sample Run of TXTRDR3

When given this chapter as input, **TXTRDR3** gave this output:

```
Each Pword: is a personal-word found in: a:chap11ss.ms

Pword: them      Pword: we        Pword: they      Pword: they
Pword: they      Pword: we        Pword: them      Pword: we
Pword: we        Pword: we        Pword: we        Pword: us
Pword: we        Pword: we        Pword: us        Pword: we
Pword: we        Pword: we        Pword: we        Pword: we
Pword: we        Pword: you       Pword: people    Pword: he
Pword: she       Pword: i         Pword: you       Pword: your
Pword: yours     Pword: yourself  Pword: yourselves
Pword: him       Pword: himself   Pword: his       Pword: her
Pword: herself   Pword: hers      Pword: my        Pword: myself
Pword: self      Pword: selves    Pword: mine      Pword: me
Pword: our       Pword: ours      Pword: dr.       Pword: mr.
Pword: mrs.      Pword: ms.       Pword: us        Pword: we
Pword: gentleman     Pword: gentlemen    Pword: miss
Pword: mister    Pword: madame    Pword: myself    Pword: ourselves
Pword: ourself   Pword: they      Pword: them      Pword: their
Pword: theirs    Pword: man       Pword: men       Pword: woman
Pword: women     Pword: wife      Pword: wives     Pword: husband
Pword: husbands  Pword: father    Pword: fathers   Pword: mother
Pword: mothers   Pword: person    Pword: persons   Pword: sister
Pword: sisters   Pword: brother   Pword: lady      Pword: ladies
Pword: son       Pword: sons      Pword: daughter Pword: daughters
```

```
TXTRDR2 - Analysis of Text-File: chap11
----------------------------------------------          --------
Line count: 998
Word count: 5310
Average characters/word:   5.14
Sentence count: 331
Average words/sentence: 16.04
============================          ============================
Reading-ease level:      39.57       Human-interest scale:    11.10
============================          ============================
  0-30   Very difficult               0-10   Dull
 30-50   Difficult                    10-20   Mildly interesting
 50-60   Fairly difficult             20-40   Interesting
 60-70   Standard difficulty          40-60   Very Interesting
 70-80   Fairly easy                  60-100  Dramatic
 80-90   Easy
 90-100  Very Easy
```

Closing Comments

TXTRDR3 took twenty-six seconds to process the same file that **TXTRDR2** took more than ninety seconds to process! It is especially interesting that anything so seemingly complex can be better than the straightforward linear search.

Do not be alarmed if you are uncomfortable with the techniques used in making the hash indices. The methods used above have been developed by professional computer scientists and mathematicians. With the functions developed for **TXTRDR3**, hashing can be used to solve many kinds of searching problems.

Personal Word List

A suggested list of personal words is:

```
people    he         she        i            you
your      yours      yourself   yourselves
him       himself    his        her          herself
hers      my         myself     self         selves
mine      me         our        ours         dr.
mr.       mrs.       ms.        us           we
gentleman gentlemen  miss       mister       madame
myself    ourselves  ourself    they         them
their     theirs     man        men          woman
women     wife       wives      husband      husbands
father    fathers    mother     mothers      person
persons   sister     sisters    brother      brothers
lady      ladies     son        sons         daughter
daughters
```

Of course, personal names may be included in the list.

12

WFREQ: Analysis of Word Frequency

Knowing how often words appear in a document can be important to an author. The special value is in the discovery that certain words such as "I" and "me" may have been undesirably used too frequently. Thus, the author has the opportunity to revise the text, correcting the condition. Starting with some of the code from **TXTRDR3**, a word frequency analyzer is constructed.

The objective is:

Read a text file. Store all newly found
words in a table. Count all words that
occur more than once in a document.
After processing the document, sort
the words in alphabetical order. List all the
words found and the frequency of occurrence.

This program is called **WFREQ**, a contraction of word and frequency.

General Strategy

Sections of the **TXTRDR2** code are used for word-by-word reading of the text file. The same hashing technique as in **TXTRDR3** is used to store the words so the table can be quickly searched for repeated occurrences of words.

The number of times each word occurs must be counted. The easiest way to do this is to change the way data are stored for each word; a count is stored along with the actual word. The word and the count can be grouped together into a logical unit as a data structure.

After the entire file is processed, the words must be sorted in alphabetical order. Just as with hashing, a well-known sorting method called the *shell sort* is used.

A complete list of all words in the document with their frequencies of occurrence is displayed after sorting.

CPT-M

Pseudocode for the **main** function in **WFREQ** follows:

Open files.
while (not end-of-file) {
  Read character-by-character until a complete word
  is read.

  Store the word in the hash table, or increment its
  frequency counter.
}
Sort all the words.
List the words and their frequency.

Let's look in detail at storing the word in the hash table:

Get the hash table index for the word.

if (the word is already stored in that location)
  increment its counter.
else
  store the word and set the counter to one.

C Data Structures

As programs become more complex, time must be dedicated to designing the way
we want to store data. A good design for data storage makes programming tasks
clearer and helps us easily change the code when change is needed. Clear data design
also enables us to know what a program's storage requirements are.

C provides two ways to logically group related information together in a data structure. Arrays are data structures: data having the same base type are grouped together.
For example the declaration **int   Foo   [10] ;** creates an array called **Foo** that stores
ten integers.

This works fine when every item of data has the same base type. In **WFREQ**,
it is necessary to store a word and the number of times it has occurred. These two
items are logically related; they describe a single word, but the base data type of
the two items is different. An array just will not work here. A structure is used.

ANATOMY: structures

C *structures* make it possible to define data structures where the individual data
items are different. For **WFREQ**, each word is described by the word itself and
a count of its frequency of occurrence. The declaration of a structure that stores
these items is:

```
struct WordType {
    char      *Value ;
    int       NumOccur ;
} ;
```

WordType is a structure. All structure declarations begin with the **C** keyword **struct** and the name of the structure. This structure has two fields. A *field* is one data item stored within the structure. Fields are declared after the structure name within curly brackets. In our example, **Value** is a pointer to a character and **NumOccur** is an integer.

The declaration of the structure above is not the same as reserving space for the structure. To declare a variable as a **struct WordType**, write:

```
struct WordType    Word ;
```

Word is a structure having two fields, **Value** and **NumOccur**.

You are not limited to having only one declaration of a given structure in a program. Declare **Word1** and **Word2** as:

```
struct WordType    Word1 ;
struct WordType    Word2 ;
```

Both **Word1** and **Word2** are structures which each have two fields: **Value** and **NumOccur**.

ANATOMY: referring to fields in a structure

Elements in an array are accessed by element number. Fields in a structure are accessed by element name. **C** uses the *dot operator* to reference a field name:

```
Word.NumOccur = 1 ;
```

This statement sets the **NumOccur** field of the **Word** data structure to one. The dot operator is placed between the structure name and the field name. Values can be assigned to fields in a structure by using, on the left side of the assignment operator, the structure name, the dot operator, and the field name. Values in a field are accessed by using the full structure and field name anywhere on the right side of the assignment operator, or in function calls.

ANATOMY: arrays of structures and structures with arrays

As an example, to write a personnel program, a structure such as this one is needed to store basic information:

```
struct EmployeeType {
    char       Name [30] ;
    char       SSN [9] ;
    float      Salary ;
} ;
```

Name is a character array inside **EmployeeType**. If we declare

```
struct EmployeeType FirstOne ;
```

FirstOne.Salary is a floating point number where an employee's salary is stored. **FirstOne.Name** is a character array. It is used as any other character array is. For example, a name can be placed in this field with the statement:

```
strcpy(FirstOne.Name,"Tom") ;
```

The character string **Tom** is copied into **FirstOne.Name.**

If it is necessary to store information on one hundred employees, declare:

```
struct EmployeeType     AllEmployees [100] ;
```

AllEmployees is an array of **EmployeeType** structures. The name of the tenth employee is called **AllEmployees[10].Name**, and the salary of the fiftieth employee is called **Allemployees[50].Salary**. Refer to any element of an array of structures with an index number immediately after the array name, then follow the closing square bracket with the dot operator and the field name.

How To Reserve Storage for Words

How do we know how much space to reserve for words in an arbitrary text file? Assume a file that will never have more than one thousand words. How long is a word? Let's assume a word is always less than twenty characters. Space can be reserved for the thousand words, but the first user that has a text file with long words exceeding the limit will get a surprise! Many words are shorter than twenty characters, of course. Reserving space for twenty characters in each word is terribly wasteful. The size of each word stored could be doubled, but the storage requirement gets larger and larger. Really, we may never know precisely how much space to reserve.

However, **C** provides *dynamic storage allocation* to solve this problem. Dynamic storage allocation reserves space for the words that are read as the program runs.

ANATOMY: reserving space with malloc

The function **malloc** reserves space dynamically as the program runs. **malloc** takes a single argument, the size of the space to be reserved, expressed as the number of characters in the space. It returns a pointer to the new stored region, or zero if no space is available. **C** programs commonly define **NULL** as zero. We then say **malloc** returns **NULL** if no space is available.

Assume we have **CharPtr**, a pointer to a character. Space is reserved for ten characters with the statement:

```
CharPtr = malloc(10) ;
```

malloc now returns a pointer to a new region in memory ten characters long. Remember that all character strings in **C** have a null character as terminator; **CharPtr** points to a region large enough to store a nine-character string plus the terminator.

When calling **malloc**, a check should be made to see if space is successfully reserved. This is done by testing the value of the pointer returned:

```
if ((CharPtr = malloc(10)) == NULL)
    fprintf(stderr,"Out of space.") ;
```

HAZARD: other names for malloc

Some microcomputer **C** libraries refer to **malloc** as **alloc**. The UNIX convention is that **malloc** is the main allocation function. **alloc** in turn calls **malloc** to reserve space. **alloc** then fills the entire space reserved with zeros.

If you use a **C** that lacks **malloc** but has **alloc**, change the words in **WFREQ** from **malloc** to **alloc**.

WFREQ: declarations

The **#include** and **#define** directives, structure declarations, function declarations, and global variable declarations for **WFREQ** are:

```
/*****************************************************************/
/*                      include files                          */
/*****************************************************************/
#include <stdio.h>
#include <ctype.h>

/*****************************************************************/
/*                      definitions                            */
/*****************************************************************/
#define BOOL            int
#define EQUALS          0
#define FALSE           0
#define FIRSTGREATER    1
#define FIRSTLESS       -1
#define HTSIZE          1009    /* must be prime */
#define MAXSTRLEN       255
#define MAXWORDSIZE     20
#define NULL            0
#define TRUE            1
#define VOID            int

/*****************************************************************/
/*                  function declarations                      */
/*****************************************************************/
extern char     *malloc() ;

/*****************************************************************/
/*                  structure declarations                     */
/*****************************************************************/
/* Value is a pointer to the word being stored.
 * NumOccur is a counter of the number of times the
 * word has occurred.
 */
struct WordType {
        char        *Value ;
        int         NumOccur ;
} ;

/*****************************************************************/
/*              global variable declarations                   */
/*****************************************************************/
struct WordType HashTable [HTSIZE] ;
```

malloc is explicitly declared as a function that returns a pointer to a character. **HashTable** is an array of **WordType**. Each word read from the input file is hashed into **HashTable**. **HTSIZE** is 1009 but, because hashing is never completely efficient in the use of space, fewer than 1009 words are stored. Change **HTSIZE** to a larger prime number to store more words, but the storage requirement increases.

WFREQ: main

WFREQ's main function opens files, reads the input file, and inserts words into the hash table. The routine **InsertWord** automatically hashes the word, and either inserts the new word or increments the word counter if the word was seen before. After the file is completely read, **SortBuffer** is called to sort the words alphabetically. Following the sort, all the words are displayed in order. As the words are displayed, the program keeps track of the length of words in the file. At the end of the word list, a table shows the distribution of word sizes in the document.

```
main(argc,argv)
int             argc ;
char            *argv [] ;
{       /* main */
    char        Counter ;
    char        CurWord [MAXSTRLEN] ;
    int         EndOfFile = FALSE ;
    int         EndOfHT = FALSE ;
    int         HTIndex ;
    FILE        *InFile ;
    int         LengthDistn [MAXWORDSIZE] ;
    int         NumWords = 0 ;
    int         PrintLine ;
    int         WordLen ;

    /* Initialize the hash table and the length distribution
     * table.
     */
    for (Counter = 0 ; Counter < MAXWORDSIZE ; Counter++)
        LengthDistn[Counter] = 0 ;
    for (Counter = 0 ; Counter < HTSIZE ; Counter++) {
        HashTable[Counter].Value        = NULL ;
        HashTable[Counter].NumOccur     = 0 ;
    }

    /* Check for a filename on the command line.
     */
    if (argc < 2) {
        printf ("\n\tYou didn't enter a filename!\n") ;
        printf ("\tProper entry:  WFREQ filename <CR>\n") ;
        exit(0) ;
    }

    /* Open the input file.
     */
    if (!(InFile = fopen(argv[1],"r"))) {
        printf ("\n\t%s not on the disk.\n",argv[1]) ;
        printf ("\tProper entry:  WFREQ filename <CR>\n") ;
        exit(0) ;
    }

    /* Read the words and insert them in the hash table.
     */
    while (EndOfFile == FALSE && EndOfHT == FALSE) {
        EndOfFile = GetNextWord(InFile,CurWord) ;
        if (!EndOfFile)
            EndOfHT = InsertWord(CurWord) ;
    }
```

```
/* Sort the words alphabetically.
 */
SortBuffer(HTSIZE) ;

/* Print the results. */
printf("\tNumber of                    Number of\n") ;
printf(
"\tTimes Used:    Actual Word:    Times Used:    Actual Word:\n") ;

printf(
"\t--------------------------    ---------------------------- \n") ;

PrintLine = 0 ;
for (HTIndex = 0 ; HTIndex < HTSIZE ; HTIndex++)
    if (HashTable[HTIndex].Value != '\0') {
        NumWords++ ;

        /* Store the length of each word in a table.
         */
        if ((WordLen = strlen(HashTable[HTIndex].Value))
                < MAXWORDSIZE - 1)
            LengthDistn[WordLen]++ ;
        else
            LengthDistn[MAXWORDSIZE - 1]++ ;
        printf("\t%3d ... %-20s",HashTable[HTIndex].NumOccur,
        HashTable[HTIndex].Value) ;

        /* Terminate line if second entry on this line.
         */
        if (PrintLine)
            printf("\n") ;

        /* Flip-flop the PrintLine flag.
         */
        PrintLine = (PrintLine == 0) ? 1 : 0 ;
    }

/* Print the length distribution.
 */
printf("\n\n\n\t\t   NumChars:    NumWords:\n") ;
printf("\t\t   ---------    ---------\n") ;
for (WordLen = 1 ; WordLen < MAXWORDSIZE ; WordLen++)
    printf("\t\t\t  %2d           %3d\n",WordLen,LengthDistn[WordLen]) ;
    /* main */
}
```

Reading Words

main uses the function **GetNextWord** to read a word from the input file and store it in a character array. A word is defined as beginning with an alphabetic character. Characters continue to be added to the word until a non-alphabetic character is found. **GetNextWord** returns **TRUE** if end-of-file is encountered; **FALSE** otherwise.

```
BOOL GetNextWord(WhichFile,Word)
FILE        *WhichFile ;
char        *Word ;
/* GetNextWord reads from WhichFile until a word is completely
 * read, or end-of-file is reached.  If end-of-file is reached,
 * return TRUE; otherwise FALSE.
 */
{       /* GetNextWord */
    int        CurChar ;
```

```
/* Continue reading characters until either end-of-file
 * is reached, or an alphabetic character is found,
 */
while ((CurChar = GetCStripped(WhichFile)) != EOF)
    if (isalpha(CurChar))
        break ;

/* Put characters into Word while we have alphabetic
 * characters and end-of-file hasn't been reached.
 */
do {
    if (!isalpha(CurChar))
        break ;
    *Word++ = toupper(CurChar) ;
}
while ((CurChar = GetCStripped(WhichFile)) != EOF) ;

/* Terminate the word.
 */
*Word = '\0' ;
return ((CurChar == EOF) ? TRUE : FALSE) ;
}       /* GetNextWord */
```

GetNextWord uses **GetCStripped** to read characters from the input file. **GetC-Stripped** returns the character read masked with **0X7F** to remove microcomputer word processor codes. If end-of-file is encountered, **GetCStripped** returns **EOF** directly.

```
int GetCStripped(WhichFile)
FILE            *WhichFile ;
/* GetCStripped returns the next character from WhichFile.  If the
 * character is an not end-of-file, strip the high-order bit for
 * microcomputer word processors and return it.  Otherwise, return
 * end-of-file.
 */
{       /* GetCStripped */
    int             Temp ;

    if ((Temp = getc(WhichFile)) != EOF)
        return(Temp & 0x7f) ;
    return(EOF) ;
}       /* GetCStripped */
```

Inserting and Counting Words

main calls **InsertWord** to store words read from the input file into the hash table.

```
BOOL InsertWord(Word)
char            *Word ;
/* InsertWord inserts the word into the hash table if the
 * word is new.  If the word is previously known, it increments
 * the NumOccur field for that word.  It then returns FALSE.
 * If the end-of-hash table is reached, TRUE is returned.
 */
{       /* InsertWord */
    int             HTIndex ;
```

```
        HTIndex = Hash(Word) ;
        if (HTIndex == -1)
            return(TRUE) ;
        if (HashTable[HTIndex].Value == NULL) {
            HashTable[HTIndex].NumOccur = 1 ;
            HashTable[HTIndex].Value   = Copy(Word) ;
        }
        else
            HashTable[HTIndex].NumOccur++ ;
        return(FALSE) ;
    }       /* InsertWord */
```

After hashing the word, check if a word has been stored in
HashTable[HTIndex].Value—a pointer to the character string where words are
stored. If the pointer is **NULL**, no character string is yet stored there. Copy **Word**,
the new word, into this character string and set the **NumOccur** field to one.

If a non-**NULL** pointer is in the **Value** field, the word is already known. Rather
than install the word a second time, increment the word counter.

InsertWord uses **Copy** to reserve space for a new word and copy the word into
this new space.

```
char *Copy(OldString)
char     *OldString ;
/* Copy makes a copy of OldString and returns the
 * address of the copy.
 */
{       /* Copy */
    char         *NewString ;

    /* Allocate a string able to hold the length of the
     * string plus one for the terminator.
     */
    NewString = malloc(strlen(OldString) + 1) ;

    /* Copy the string and return a pointer to it.
     */
    strcpy(NewString,OldString) ;
    return (NewString) ;
}       /* Copy */
```

OldString is the string to be copied. Note how the number of characters to reserve
using **malloc** is determined: take the length of the string and add one for the null
terminator. A call to **strcpy** copies **OldString** into **NewString**, and then returns
the pointer that **malloc** returned.

Hashing Words

Words are hashed into **HashTable** using a small variation of the **TXTRDR2** hash
code.

```
int Hash(Word)
char            *Word ;
/* Hash returns the HTIndex of the Word passed, or an appropriate
 * HTIndex for the word.  If HashTable is full, Hash returns -1.
 */
```

```
{          /* Hash */
    int         HTIndex ;
    int         IdLen ;
    int         InitHTIndex ;
    int         ProbeCounter = 0 ;

    IdLen = strlen(Word) ;
    if (IdLen == 0)
        printf("Hash: Word of no length\n") ;
    HTIndex = InitHTIndex = TransformId(Word) ;

    if (HashTable[HTIndex].Value == NULL)
        ; /* NULL - We've got it. */
    else            /* have we found the correct index? */
        if (strcmp(Word,HashTable[HTIndex].Value) == EQUALS)
            ; /* DONE: A direct hit! */
        else    /* Collision - generate new indices */
            for (ProbeCounter = 0 ; ProbeCounter < (HTSIZE / 2) ;
            ProbeCounter++) {
                HTIndex = GenerateNewIndex(InitHTIndex,ProbeCounter) ;
                if (HashTable[HTIndex].Value == NULL)
                    break ;         /* We've got it ! */
                else if (strcmp(Word,HashTable[HTIndex].Value)
                == EQUALS)
                    break ;         /* We've got it ! */
            }
    if (ProbeCounter >= (HTSIZE / 2))
        return(-1) ;
    return(HTIndex) ;
}          /* Hash */
```

The only significant change from TXTRDR2 is in the **strcmp** calls to compare **Word**, the new word being hashed, with the **Value** field of a particular element of **HashTable**.

```
int GenerateNewIndex(OriginalKey,ProbeNumber)
int     OriginalKey ;
int     ProbeNumber ;

/* GenerateNewIndex takes the current hash table index and
 * generates a new index for collision resolution.
 */
{          /* GenerateNewIndex */
    return ((OriginalKey + ProbeNumber * ProbeNumber) % HTSIZE) ;
}          /* GenerateNewIndex */

int TransformId(Word)
char        Word [] ;
/* TransformId converts the identifier into an integer within the
 * index range of HashTable.
 */
{          /* TransformId */
    int         Term ;
    int         WordIndex ;

    Term = 0 ;
    for (WordIndex = strlen(Word) - 1 ; WordIndex > -1 ;
            WordIndex--)
        Term = (257 * Term) + Word[WordIndex] ;
    Term = (Term < 0) ? -Term : Term ;
    return (Term % HTSIZE) ;
}          /* TransformId */
```

Sorting

Sorting items into some order is a tremendously important operation in computing.
Years of theoretical work have brought several fast sorting techniques to light. The
most straightforward way of sorting is called the *bubble sort*. In a bubble sort, two
adjacent items in a table are compared. If the second item should appear ahead of
the first item in the final sorted order, the two are exchanged. This diagram shows
how it works:

```
Original table
      ----
    |bb  |  <----
    |----|          |----- compare 'bb' and 'aa'.
    |aa  |  <----         'aa' should come first.
    |----|
    |cc  |
      ----
After the exchange:
      ----
    |aa  |
    |----|
    |bb  |
    |----|
    |cc  |
      ----
```

In the bubble sort, this compare-and-exchange process continues until the entire table
is sorted.

   While bubble sorting is easy to understand, it is the slowest sort available. Let's
sort the sequence:

```
----------------------------------
|aa   |cc   |bb   |cc   |aa   |cc   |
----------------------------------
```

The first two elements are compared. They are already in the right order, so nothing
happens. The second and third elements are then compared. They are out of order,
so the values are exchanged:

```
----------------------------------
|aa   |cc   |bb   |cc   |aa   |cc   |
----------------------------------
         |       |
          \     /
          /     \
         |       |
         v       v
----------------------------------
|aa   |bb   |cc   |cc   |aa   |cc   |
----------------------------------
```

'cc' and 'cc', the third and fourth elements, are already equal. Now 'cc' and 'aa'
are compared. Again a swap happens:

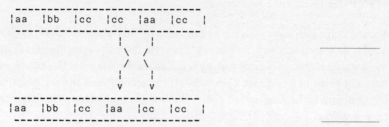

The sort reaches the end of the list. It now starts over, correcting any still unsorted elements. Unfortunately, to move the 'aa' near the end of the list to the beginning takes many passes. Ordering a radically unsorted list with a bubble sort is slow.

The *Shell sort* makes comparisons between far-away elements in the list first. Using the same example, the list has six elements. The gap between the comparisons is set to half the list's length. Elements separated by a gap of three are first compared:

```
-----------------------------------
¦aa  ¦cc  ¦bb  ¦cc  ¦aa  ¦cc  ¦
-----------------------------------
 ¦             ¦
 -----------------
       Reorder?
```

These two are OK. Go on to the next:

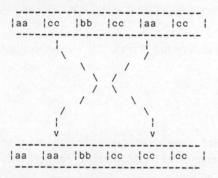

The wayward 'aa' at the end of the list is moved to the head in a single operation!

On the next pass, the size of the gap is decreased by half, and the sort continues. The gap gets progressively smaller, until the sort compares adjacent elements, just like a bubble sort. This bubble sort at the end fixes local disorder, but it runs much faster because the great disorders have already been eliminated.

Why is such a strange method faster than the bubble sort? Many lists have great disorder in them. Elements that should appear near the beginning are at the end, and vice versa. The bubble sort takes much time to move an element from one end of the list to the other, because it moves an element and its next nearest neighbor. The Shell sort, however, gets rid of these distant sorting problems first, leaving the bubble sort to take care of disordering between close neighbors.

```
VOID SortBuffer(SortNumber)
int             SortNumber ;
/* SortBuffer sorts the words in HashTable in alphabetical order
 * using a Shell sort.
 */
{       /* SortBuffer */
    int         BaseCounter ;
    int         CurCounter ;
    int         CurGapCounter ;
    int         Gap ;
    int         LastInBuf ;
    char        *Temp ;
    int         TempNum ;

    LastInBuf = SortNumber ;
    /* Loop through all Gaps, starting with a gap that is half
     * size of the list.  Each time reduce the size of the gap by
     * dividing by two.
     */
    for (Gap = LastInBuf / 2 ; Gap > 0 ; Gap /= 2)

        /* BaseCounter moves between the Gap-th element and
         * the last element in the list.  The sort using the
         * current Gap runs until I is the LastInBuf-th element
         * in the list.
         */
        for (BaseCounter = Gap ; BaseCounter < LastInBuf ; BaseCounter++)

            /* For an BaseCounter we compare the CurCounter-th and the
             * CurGapCounter-th elements in the list.  CurCounter and
             * CurGapCounter are always separated by Gap.
             */
            for (CurCounter = BaseCounter - Gap ; CurCounter >= 0 ;
                     CurCounter -= Gap) {
                CurGapCounter = CurCounter + Gap ;

                /* If the two elements compare correctly, stop.
                 */
                if (NameCompare(CurCounter,CurGapCounter) < EQUALS)
                    break ;
                /* Otherwise, exchange the elements.
                 */
                Temp = HashTable[CurCounter].Value ;
                HashTable[CurCounter].Value =
                        HashTable[CurGapCounter].Value ;
                HashTable[CurGapCounter].Value =
                        Temp ;

                TempNum =
                        HashTable[CurCounter].NumOccur ;
                HashTable[CurCounter].NumOccur =
                        HashTable[CurGapCounter].NumOccur ;
                HashTable[CurGapCounter].NumOccur =
                        TempNum ;
            }
}       /* SortBuffer */
```

The series of tight loops make **SortBuffer** initially hard to read. The outermost loop controls **Gap**, the distance between values that are compared. With a **Gap** value, **BaseCounter** begins with the **Gap**-th element and moves to the end.

For every **BaseCounter** value, a **CurCounter** and a **CurGapCounter** value are generated. **CurCounter** starts at the beginning of the list; **CurGapCounter** is **Gap** elements later. If the comparison function **NameCompare** returns that the **CurCounter**-th and the **CurGapCounter**-th elements are out of order, they are exchanged.

SortBuffer uses **NameCompare** to make the actual comparisons.

```
int NameCompare(First,Second)
int      First ;
int      Second ;
/* NameCompare compares the two entries in HashTable referenced
 * by the indices First and Second.  It returns FIRSTLESS if
 * First < Second;   EQUALS if they equal;
 * FIRSTGREATER if First > Second.
 */
{        /* NameCompare */
    /* If the first entry has no value, the first is less.
     */
    if (HashTable[First].Value == NULL)
        return(FIRSTLESS) ;

    /* Then if the second has no value, the first is greater.
     */
    if (HashTable[Second].Value == NULL)
        return(FIRSTGREATER) ;

    /* Otherwise return the comparison from strcmp.
     */
    return (strcmp(HashTable[First].Value,HashTable[Second].Value)) ;

}        /* NameCompare */
```

A Sample Run of WFREQ

Using this chapter as input, **WFREQ** gives the following output. Only a portion of the word table is reproduced here.

```
Number of                          Number of
Times Used:     Actual Word:       Times Used:     Actual Word:
----------------------------       ----------------------------
94 ... A                           23 ... AA
 1 ... ABLE                         1 ... ABOVE
 3 ... ACCESSED                     1 ... ACTERS
 4 ... ACTUAL                       1 ... ADD
 1 ... ADDED                        1 ... ADDRESS
 2 ... ADJACENT                     9 ... AFTER
 1 ... AGAIN                        1 ... AHEAD
 8 ... ALL                          4 ... ALLEMPLOYEES
 5 ... ALLOC                        1 ... ALLOCATE
 3 ... ALLOCATION                   1 ... ALONG
 4 ... ALPHABETIC                   3 ... ALPHABETICAL
 2 ... ALPHABETICALLY               5 ... ALREADY
 1 ... ALSO                         2 ... ALWAYS
20 ... AN                           1 ... ANALYSIS
 1 ... ANALYZER                     4 ... ANATOMY
54 ... AND                          3 ... ANY
```

```
NumChars:     NumWords:
---------     ---------
       1            12
       2            33
       3            53
       4           130
       5           112
       6            83
       7            92
       8            66
       9            64
      10            34
      11            30
      12            11
      13             4
      14             1
      15             0
      16             1
      17             0
      18             0
      19             0
```

XREF: C Program Cross Reference Listing

As **C** programs get larger, it becomes increasingly difficult to keep track of where specific names are used. A standard tool in software development is the *cross reference listing* in which a list of names used in the program is made in sorted order along with the line numbers where the names are used. **XREF**, the program discussed in this chapter, fills this need.

XREF's objective is:

> Read a file containing (syntactically correct) **C** source code. Make a listing of the code, adding line numbers. Store all names used in the program in a hash table. Each time a name is read, store the current line number along with the name. After the entire file is read, sort the names in alphabetical order and print the names and the line numbers associated with each of the names.

XREF: pseudocode

XREF has three main tasks: (1) Store the **C** names and line numbers in a hash table. (2) Sort the names alphabetically. (3) Print a table of the names and the line numbers in the program where each name is used.

Names used in a programming language are generically termed *tokens*. In **XREF**, a token is any **C** identifier—a sequence of letters and digits. A token begins with a letter and contains the letters and digits which follow it. It ends when a character that is neither a letter nor a digit appears. The underscore character __ is considered a letter.

Pseudocode for **XREF** follows:

Open Input file.
while (there's another token--CurToken)
　　Store CurToken in the hash table.

Sort the tokens.
Print the cross-reference listing.

Storing the Line Numbers

WFREQ uses a hash table to store words read from the input text file. With minor changes, this same code serves to store the incoming **C** tokens.

Storing the line numbers is a different matter. **WFREQ** simply counts the number of times a word appears in the file. **XREF** must store a line number every time a token appears in the file. How can this number be known in advance?

The answer is that the number of line numbers to store can never be known in advance. **XREF** uses a flexible method called list processing to store these line numbers.

An Introduction to List Processing

List processing is a general technique that stores and arbitrarily processes large lists of information. The amount of information to be stored is never known in advance and, indeed, can change dynamically during the program's execution. Some languages, such as **LISP** (for **LISt** Processing), are entirely devoted to list processing. These languages give powerful basic functions that make list processing easy.

C provides all the language constructions needed to do list processing, but the functions required must be written for the application. Consider a list of information:

```
Alice
Sue
Betty
Mark
end-of-list
```

Lists contain arbitrary information. The lists that **XREF** uses are called *linear lists*. Linear lists are well described by the King in *Alice's Adventures in Wonderland*: "[They] Begin at the beginning, and go on till you come to the end: then stop." Sounds silly? All linear list processing is based on this property.

A diagram representing how **C** stores this list is:

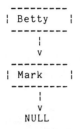

Each block containing a name is called a *node*. A linear list is made of nodes linked together by links leading from one node to the next. The list ends with a special indicator usually called **NULL** in **C** programs. **NULL** is a defined name having the value zero.

XREF represents all line numbers as linear lists, where each node in the list contains a line number and a link to the next number. The last number in the list is linked to **NULL**.

Links between nodes are pointers in **C**. Each node contains both its value and a pointer to the next node in the list. A data structure for the line number node is:

```
struct rType {
      int          Reference ;   /* line number */
      struct rType *Link ;       /* link to next reference */
} ;
```

The **Reference** field of the **rType** structure holds the line number for this node; the **Link** field is a pointer to a **rType** structure.

For example, tokens in a sample **C** source file appear on lines three, five, and nine. A linear list of **rType** structures representing these source file line numbers is:

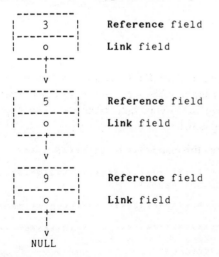

XREF builds these lists as it reads the input file.

Hash Table Data Structures

WFREQ's hash table stored the word being counted and the number of times the word occurred. **XREF**'s hash table must store the token and a pointer to the beginning of the line number list for that word. Given the definition for the **rType** data structure above, a definition for the hash table data structure is:

```
struct tType {
    char            *Value ;
    struct rType    *OccurList ;
} ;
```

The **Value** field is a pointer to the token's name and **OccurList** is a pointer to the beginning of the line number list for the token.

XREF: declarations

The include files, definitions, data structure declarations, and global variable declarations for **XREF** follow:

```
/**********************************************************************/
/*                          include files                           */
/**********************************************************************/
#include <stdio.h>
#include <ctype.h>

/**********************************************************************/
/*                          definitions                             */
/**********************************************************************/
#define BOOL            int
#define DQUOTE          '"'
#define EQUALS          0
#define FALSE           0
#define FIRSTGREATER    1
#define FIRSTLESS       -1
#define HTSIZE          1009    /* must be prime */
#define MAXSTRLEN       255
#define MAXWORDSIZE     20
#define NULL            0
#define SLASH           '/'
#define SQUOTE          '\''
#define STAR            '*'
#define TRUE            1
#define VOID            int

/**********************************************************************/
/*                          code macros                             */
/**********************************************************************/
#define PutBack(Ch)     {PutBackChar = Ch; }

/**********************************************************************/
/*                          typedefs                                */
/**********************************************************************/
/* Reference is the line number where the name occurs.
 * Link is a pointer to the next reference for this name.
 */
```

```
typedef struct rType {
    int          Reference ;
    struct rType *Link ;
}
RefType,*RefPtr ;

/* Value is the name of the token considered.
 * OccurList is a pointer to the beginning of the line
 * number list.
 */
typedef struct tType {
    char         *Value ;
    RefPtr       OccurList ;
}
TokenType,*TokenPtr ;

/*******************************************************************/
/*                    external functions                          */
/*******************************************************************/
extern char     *malloc() ;
extern RefPtr   MakeOccurrence() ;

/*******************************************************************/
/*                    global variables                            */
/*******************************************************************/
int          CurLineNo = 1 ;           /* Line being read. */
TokenType    HashTable [HTSIZE] ;
int          PutBackChar = '\0' ;      /* Character put back after
                                        * input.
                                        */
```

Note the global variables declared: **CurLineNo** is the number of the line currently being read. **HashTable** stores all the tokens and line numbers. **PutBackChar** stores a character put back by use of the code macro **PutBack**. This special put-back mechanism solves a nasty problem discussed below.

ANATOMY: typedef

Often it is inconvenient to continually repeat the full name of a structure in declarations. For example, the first definition of the hash table data structures above is:

```
struct rType {
    int          Reference ;
    struct rType *Link ;
} ;

struct tType {
    char         *Value ;
    struct rType *OccurList ;
} ;
```

A function that returns a pointer to an **rType** data structure is declared as:

```
extern struct rType *MakeOccurrence() ;
```

C provides a shorthand for naming a type created in the program with the **typedef** construction.

A type is named using the **typedef** keyword in a declaration:

```
typedef struct rType {
    int         Reference ;
    struct rType *Link ;
}
RefType,*RefPtr ;

typedef struct tType {
    char        *Value ;
    RefPtr      OccurList ;
}
TokenType,*TokenPtr ;
```

The first declaration defines the type **RefType** as **struct rType**. From this point in the program, the names **struct rType** and **RefType** are equivalent. In the same declaration the type **RefPtr** is defined. **RefPtr** is a pointer to a **struct rType**; hence the star appearing immediately before the name **RefPtr**. The second declaration defines **TokenType** and **TokenPtr**. Note the declaration is made using a previously defined **typedef**: **RefPtr**.

In the first declaration, the field **Link** is declared as **struct rType ***—a pointer to **struct rType**. Why not declare it as a **RefPtr** and simplify the construction? **typedef**s can only be used after they have been defined. This means that using **RefPtr** before its definition two lines later causes an error.

XREF: main

XREF's **main** function closely parallels its pseudocode:

```
main(argc,argv)
int     argc ;
char    *argv[] ;
{       /* main */
    int     Counter ;
    char    CurToken [MAXSTRLEN] ;
    FILE    *InFile ;

    if (!(InFile = fopen(argv[1],"r"))) {
        fprintf(stderr,"Can't open input file %s.\n",argv[1]) ;
        exit(0) ;
    }

    /* Initialize the hash table.
     */
    for (Counter = 0 ; Counter < HTSIZE ; Counter++) {
        HashTable[Counter].Value = NULL ;
        HashTable[Counter].OccurList = NULL ;
    }

    /* Write the first line number to the output stream.
     */
    printf("\n%4d    ",CurLineNo) ;

    /* Read and store each token.
     */
    while (GetNxtToken(CurToken,InFile)) {
        if (InsertToken(CurToken)) {
            fprintf(stderr,"Hash table size exceeded.\n") ;
            break ;
        }
    }
    printf("   End-of-file.\n\n") ;
```

```
      /* Sort the tokens alphabetically.
       */
      SortTokens(HTSIZE) ;

      PrintTable() ;
}         /* main */
```

The input file is opened and the hash table initialized to zero using the **setmem** function. The line number and some spaces are written to **stdout**; how the source listing with line numbers is made is discussed below. A token is read with **GetNxt-Token**. If a token is available, **InsertToken** is called to store it in the hash table. When all tokens have been read, end-of-file is reached and the **while** loop stops. The token list is sorted by **SortTokens**, and the final table is written by **PrintTable**.

Reading the Tokens

GetNxtToken returns the next token. Remember the definition of a token: a sequence of letters and digits that begins with a letter. A letter is an upper or lower case letter or an underscore.

```
BOOL  GetNxtToken(Buffer,InputFile)
char     *Buffer ;
FILE     *InputFile ;
/* GetNxtToken returns in Buffer the next valid C token in the
 * program.
 */
{         /* GetNxtToken */
    int          CurChar ;

    /* Read characters from InputFile until starting letter is
     * found.  Stop when find a valid letter or end-of-file.
     */
    while (!IsStartingLetter(CurChar = GetNxtChar(InputFile)) &&
    CurChar != EOF)
        ;

    /* Insert the first character.
     */
    *Buffer++ = CurChar ;

    /* Read and accumulate characters in Buffer while they are
     * valid letters for a token.
     */
    while (IsTokenLetter(CurChar = GetNxtChar(InputFile)) &&
            CurChar != EOF)
       *Buffer++ = CurChar ;

    /* Put back the last character we read.
     */
    if (CurChar != EOF)
        PutBack(CurChar) ;

    /* Terminate the token.
     */
    *Buffer = '\0' ;

    /* Return end-of-file status.
     */
    return ((CurChar == EOF) ? FALSE : TRUE) ;
}         /* GetNxtToken */
```

GetNxtToken begins by reading characters until it reads a valid starting letter. It places this letter in **Buffer**, and continues reading and storing characters in **Buffer** until a character is read that cannot appear inside a token. It puts back this character, and returns the token read in **Buffer** and the end-of-file status.

GetNxtToken uses two letter classification functions:

```
BOOL IsStartingLetter(Ch)
char    Ch ;
/* IsStartingLetter returns TRUE if Ch is a valid character to
 * begin a C token.
 */
{       /* IsStartingLetter */
    return ((isalpha(Ch) || Ch == '_') ? TRUE : FALSE) ;
}       /* IsStartingLetter */

BOOL IsTokenLetter(Ch)
char    Ch ;
/* IsTokenLetter returns TRUE if Ch is a valid character inside a C
 * token.
 */
{       /* IsTokenLetter */
    return ((isalpha(Ch) || isdigit(Ch) || Ch == '_')
            ? TRUE : FALSE) ;
}       /* IsTokenLetter */
```

Any program that reads programming language source code must handle comments. Comments in **C** are dropped by the compiler. Likewise, **XREF** must not consider any tokens that appear inside a comment. While the **C** compiler does use information inside a quoted string, this information is not treated in the same way as **C** identifiers. As **XREF** reads the input file it must discard both comments and quoted strings.

This problem can be troublesome. **GetNxtChar** returns the next character read from **InputFile** that is neither inside a comment nor inside a quoted string.

```
int GetNxtChar(InputFile)
FILE    *InputFile ;
/* GetNxtChar returns the next non-comment an non-string
 * character from InputFile.
 *
 * A least one character is read from InputFile.  If
 * the character could start a comment the next character
 * is checked. If the slash-star of a comment
 * is read the reading of characters continues until the end
 * of the comment is found.  If a single or  double quote
 * is read the reading of characters continues until
 * the closing mark is found.  When end-of-file is encountered
 * EOF is returned.  GetNxtChar therefore never returns
 * characters inside comments or quotes.
 */
{       /* GetNxtChar */
    int         CheckChar ;
    int         NewChar ;
    int         TempChar ;

    /* If end-of-file is found, return immediately.
     */
    if ((NewChar = GetRawChar(InputFile)) == EOF)
        return(EOF) ;
```

```
/* If a single or double quote is found, process the string.
 */
if (NewChar == SQUOTE || NewChar == DQUOTE) {
    CheckChar = NewChar ;
    /* Continue reaing until the matching quote character
     * is found.
     */
    while ((NewChar = GetRawChar(InputFile)) != CheckChar &&
            NewChar != EOF) ;
    /* The terminating character has now been read.
     * Read one more and return it.
     */
    NewChar = GetRawChar(InputFile) ;
}

/* Next handle comment processing.  If SLASH is read,
 * check to see if the next character is a STAR.  If it is,
 * continue reading until the matching STAR-SLASh is found.
 */
else if (NewChar == SLASH) {
        if ((TempChar = GetRawChar(InputFile)) != STAR) {
            /* Not a comment; put back the character.
             */
            PutBack(TempChar) ;
        }
        else
            /* Here's a comment.  Search for the end.
             */
            while (TRUE) {
                /* Read characters until a STAR is found.
                 */
                while ((NewChar = GetRawChar(InputFile)) != STAR &&
                        NewChar != EOF) ;

                if ((NewChar = GetRawChar(InputFile)) == SLASH) {
                    /* The end of the comment is found.
                     */
                    NewChar = GetRawChar(InputFile) ;
                    break ;
                }
                else
                    /* Not end of comment.  Put the character back.
                     */
                    PutBack(NewChar) ;
                /* If end-of-file has been found, stop processing.
                 */
                if (NewChar == EOF)
                    break ;
            }
    }
    return (NewChar) ;
}          /* GetNxtChar */
```

GetNxtChar returns immediately if end-of-file is read. Otherwise it checks for the beginning of a quoted string or a comment. Quoted strings begin with a double quote; quoted character constants begin with a single quote. If **NewChar**, the character just read, is either of these quotes, **GetNxtChar** continues reading until it finds a matching one. It then reads the character following the ending quote and returns it.

If a slash is read, **GetNxtChar** reads another character to see if a star follows, beginning a comment. If it does not, the second character is put back by **PutBack**.

If it does, an inner loop reads characters until end-of-file is reached, or a star is read. If a star is read, the next character is read and checked to see if it is a slash, ending the comment.

GetNxtChar reads characters by calling **GetRawChar**.

```
int     GetRawChar(InputFile)
FILE    *InputFile ;
/* GetRawChar reads the next character from InputFile and
 * returns it.  If a newline is read, it increments CurLineNo.
 * If end-of-file is read, it returns EOF.
 */
{       /* GetRawChar */
    int         NextChar ;
    /* Check PutBackChar to see if the next character has
     * already been read.  If so, process it and set PutBackChar
     * to the null character.
     */
    if (PutBackChar != '\0') {
        NextChar = PutBackChar ;
        PutBackChar = '\0';
    }
    else {
        /* Echo the character read to the output stream.
         * If a newline is read, increment the line count.
         */
        if ((NextChar = getc(InputFile)) == '\n')
            printf("\n%4d    ",++CurLineNo) ;
        else
            putchar(NextChar) ;
    }

    if (NextChar == EOF)
        return (EOF) ;

    return (NextChar) ;
}       /* GetRawChar */
```

GetRawChar handles several problems. It checks **PutBackChar** to see if a character has been put-back. If so, **GetRawChar** returns that character immediately.

XREF produces a listing of the program by line number. **GetRawChar** echoes the characters it reads to **stdout**. Whenever a newline is read, it increments **CurLineNo**, counting the line, and it writes the new line number to **stdout** for the listing.

The special character put-back mechanism becomes clear now. **GetRawChar** echoes all the characters it reads to **stdout**. If characters were simply put back with **ungetc**, these characters would be written to **stdout** twice: once when read, and once when read again after being put-back with **ungetc**. The put-back mechanism internal to **XREF** solves this problem: characters are read and echoed only once.

Token Hashing and List Building

main calls **InsertToken** after each token is read. **InsertToken** handles storing new tokens and saving line numbers in a line number occurrence list.

```
BOOL InsertToken(Token)
char          *Token ;
/* InsertToken inserts the token into the hash table if it is
 * new.  If the token is previously known, it adds the line
 * number to the occurrence list. It then returns FALSE.
 * If the end-of-hash table is reached, TRUE is returned.
 */
{         /* InsertToken */
    int        HTIndex ;

    HTIndex = Hash(Token) ;
    if (HTIndex == -1)
        return (TRUE) ;

    if (HashTable[HTIndex].Value == NULL) {
        HashTable[HTIndex].Value = Copy(Token) ;
        HashTable[HTIndex].OccurList = MakeOccurrence() ;
    }
    else
        AddOccurrence(HashTable[HTIndex].OccurList) ;

    return (FALSE) ;
}         /* InsertToken */
```

InsertToken calls **Hash** to return the index into **HashTable** for **Token**. If the **Value** field for this hash table entry has no string inserted, **InsertToken** calls **Copy** to make a copy of the token, and it calls **MakeOccurrence** to start the line number list. If the **Value** field for the token is already filled, **InsertToken** calls **AddOccurrence** to add a new line number to the line number list for this token.

For example, **main** calls **InsertToken** with the token **foo** for the first time. **CurLineNo** is fifteen. After returning, the hash table entry for **while** looks as follows:

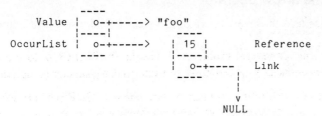

The **Value** field now points to a copy of the token **while**. **OccurList** points to the first node of the line number list. The **Reference** field of this node has the value fifteen; the **Link** field is **NULL**, meaning end-of-list.

MakeOccurrence creates the first line number list node. It returns a **RefPtr**—a pointer to the new line number node created. **InsertToken** stores this pointer for future use.

```
RefPtr MakeOccurrence()
/* MakeOccurrence creates the first entry of the line occurrence
 * list.  It creates the next node in the list and inserts CurLineN
 * It then sets Link to NULL in preparation for the next entry.
 */
{         /* MakeOccurrence */
    RefPtr        NewNode ;

    if ((NewNode = (RefPtr)malloc(sizeof(RefType))) == NULL) {
        fprintf("Out of memory in MakeOccurrence.") ;
        exit(0) ;
    }
```

```
        NewNode->Reference = CurLineNo ;
        NewNode->Link = (RefPtr)NULL ;

        return (NewNode) ;
}          /* MakeOccurrence */
```

MakeOccurrence allocates enough space to store a **RefType**. It then stores **CurLineNo** in the **Reference** field and sets the **Link** field to point to **NULL**. Note the use of casts in the call to **malloc. malloc** returns a pointer to a character. **NewPtr** is a **RefPtr**. The cast makes the pointer types match.

ANATOMY: sizeof

Counting how many characters of information to reserve to store a data structure can be painful. Even worse, if the data structure changes size, all the **malloc** calls must be changed. **C** supplies a shorthand called **sizeof** that lets the compiler automatically insert the current correct size of a data structure, array, or type:

```
        if ((NewNode = (RefPtr)malloc(sizeof(RefType))) == NULL) {
```

malloc's single argument is the number of characters of storage to reserve. **sizeof(RefType)** asks the compiler to insert the current size of **RefType**. If **RefType** should change in size, the compiler makes all necessary corrections.

sizeof accepts variable names or types as its argument. The types are either **C** defined types like float or user-defined types.

ANATOMY: the arrow operator

MakeOccurrence uses the arrow operator to access a field inside a structure:

```
        NewNode->Reference = CurLineNo ;
        NewNode->Link = (RefPtr)NULL ;
```

NewNode is a **RefPtr**—a pointer to a **RefType**. Recall that a **RefType** has two fields: a **Reference** field and a **Link** field. Using the **NewNode** pointer, the arrow operator refers to any field within the structure to which **NewNode** points:

```
                          ----
    NewNode ------->|      |     NewNode->Reference
                    |------|
                    |      |     NewNode->Link
                          ----
```

The arrow operator is used on the left side of an assignment operator to assign new values to the indicated field. On the right side of an assignment statement, the arrow operator accesses the current value stored in the field.

Adding to the End of a List

Now the list for **foo** is started. If another **foo** token is read, **InsertToken** calls **Add-Occurrence** to add the token to the end of the list.

```
VOID AddOccurrence(HeadPtr)
RefPtr    HeadPtr ;
/* AddOccurrence adds a new line occurrence to the
 * end of the list that HeadPtr begins.
 */
{        /* AddOccurrence */
    RefPtr        CurPtr ;
    RefPtr        NewPtr ;

    /* Find the end of the list by starting at the beginning
     * and advancing through the list until we find the end.
     */
    for (CurPtr = HeadPtr ; CurPtr->Link != NULL ;
            CurPtr = CurPtr->Link)
        ;

    CurPtr->Link = NewPtr = (RefPtr)malloc(sizeof(RefType)) ;
    if (NewPtr == NULL) {
        fprintf("Out of memory in AddOccurrence.") ;
        exit(0) ;
    }   NewPtr->Reference = CurLineNo ;
    NewPtr->Link = (RefPtr)NULL ;
}        /* AddOccurrence */
```

AddOccurrence must first find the end of the list. Remember that a linear list begins at the beginning, then goes on until it ends. The first **for** loop advances through the list until the end is found.

For example, **HeadPtr** points to the head of a list having three nodes:

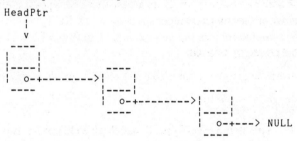

The **for** loop sets **CurPtr** to equal **HeadPtr**, so it also points to the beginning of the list.

The loop continuation condition, **CurPtr->Link != NULL,** is true (**CurPtr->Link** points to the next node), and the loop increment action is done. But what a strange action! **CurPtr** is set to the current value of **CurPtr->Link**. This diagram shows what is happening:

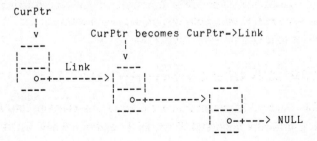

CurPtr ->Link points to the next node on the list. **CurPtr** is set to be this pointer. When the loop again executes, **CurPtr** points to the second of the three nodes:

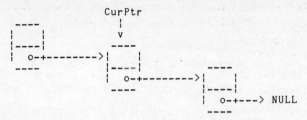

CurPtr->Link is not **NULL**, so the increment action advances **CurPtr** to the next node in the list:

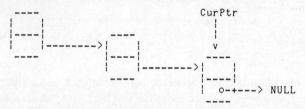

This time, **CurPtr->Link** is **NULL**, and the loop stops. **CurPtr** now points to the last node in the list.

   AddOccurrence now calls **malloc** to reserve space for a new **RefType**—the next node on the list. When **malloc** returns the new pointer, **CurPtr->Link** is set to point to the new node:

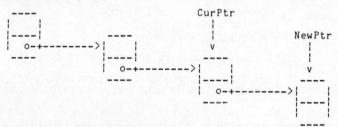

The list is now one longer than it was before. **NewPtr->Link** is set to **NULL**, and the reference field filled in. The final picture is:

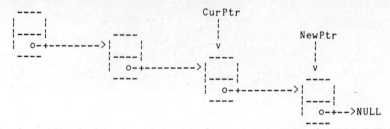

The ending **NULL** is critically important. It marks the end of the new list.

Sorting

SortTokens sorts the hash table entries in alphabetical order by token value. With only a simple change to the **WFREQ** sort, the code now reads:

```
VOID SortTokens(SortNumber)
int            SortNumber ;
/* SortTokens sorts the tokens into alphabetical order
 * using a Shell sort.
 */
{       /* SortTokens */
    TokenType    Exchange ;
    int          BaseCounter ;
    int          CurCounter ;
    int          CurGapCounter ;
    int          Gap ;
    int          LastInBuf ;

    LastInBuf = SortNumber ;
    /* Look through all Gaps starting with a gap half the
     * size of the list.  Each time reduce the size of the gap by
     * dividing by two.
     */
    for (Gap = LastInBuf / 2 ; Gap > 0 ; Gap /= 2)

        /* BaseCounter moves between the Gap-th element and
         * the last element in the list.  The sort using the
         * current Gap runs until I is the LastInBuf-th element
         * in the list.
         */
        for (BaseCounter = Gap ; BaseCounter < LastInBuf ; BaseCounter+-

            /* For an BaseCounter we compare the CurCounter-th and the
             * CurGapCounter-th elements in the list.  CurCounter and
             * CurGapCounter are always separated by Gap. */
            for (CurCounter = BaseCounter - Gap ; CurCounter >= 0 ;
                        CurCounter -= Gap) {
                CurGapCounter = CurCounter + Gap ;

                /* If the two elements compare correctly, stop.
                 */
                if (NameCompare(CurCounter,CurGapCounter) < EQUALS)
                    break ;

                /* Otherwise, exchange the elements.
                 */
                Exchange.Value =
                        HashTable[CurCounter].Value ;
                Exchange.OccurList =
                        HashTable[CurCounter].OccurList ;
                HashTable[CurCounter].Value =
                        HashTable[CurGapCounter].Value ;
                HashTable[CurCounter].OccurList =
                        HashTable[CurGapCounter].OccurList ;
                HashTable[CurGapCounter].Value =
                        Exchange.Value ;
                HashTable[CurGapCounter].OccurList =
                        Exchange.OccurList ;
            }
}       /* SortTokens */
```

The change from **WFREQ** is in the exchange of values: the data structure field names are changed. **NameCompare** is unchanged from **WFREQ**.

Printing the Cross Reference Table

PrintTable prints the cross reference table. Each new token begins on a new line. After **PrintTable** writes the name of the token, it runs down the list of line numbers, writing the numbers as it goes:

```
VOID PrintTable()
/* Printable prints the list of identifiers and line occurrences.
 */
{       /* PrintTable */
    RefPtr      ListPtr ;
    int         NumOnLine ;
    int         TokenCounter ;

    for (TokenCounter = 0 ; TokenCounter < HTSIZE ;
            TokenCounter++) {
        if (HashTable[TokenCounter].Value) {
            printf("\n%-20s    ",HashTable[TokenCounter].Value) ;
            for (ListPtr = HashTable[TokenCounter].OccurList,
            NumOnLine = 0 ; ListPtr != NULL ;
            ListPtr = ListPtr->Link,NumOnLine++) {
                if (NumOnLine == 10) {
                    printf("\n                            ") ;
                    NumOnLine = 0 ;
                }
                printf("%3d  ",ListPtr->Reference) ;
            }
        }
    }
    printf("\n") ;
}       /* PrintTable */
```

The internal **for** loop that writes the line numbers needs some explanation. **ListPtr** is set to point to the first number in the list. While **ListPtr** does not point to **NULL**, it points to a valid **RefType** node. If **NumOnLine**, the number printed on the current line, does not exceed ten, the new number is printed. The **for** loop increment action moves **ListPtr** to point to the next node in the list. The code exactly parallels **AddOccurrence**.

If ten items have been written on the current line, a newline and some spaces are written to neatly format the output.

Miscellaneous Routines

Many of **WFREQ**'s routines are used again in **XREF**. They are **Copy**, **GenerateNewIndex**, **Hash**, **NameCompare**, and **TransformId**. Refer to the code in Chapter 12.

A Sample Run of XREF

When **XREF** is run with its own source code as input, the following output is produced:

```
 1    /***********************************************************/
 2    /*                     include files                     */
 3    /***********************************************************/
 4    #include <stdio.h>
 5    #include <ctype.h>
 6
 7    /***********************************************************/
 8    /*                     definitions                       */
 9    /***********************************************************/
10    #define BOOL            int
11    #define DQUOTE          '"'
12    #define EQUALS          0
13    #define FALSE           0
14    #define FIRSTGREATER    1
15    #define FIRSTLESS       -1
16    #define HTSIZE          1009      /* must be prime */
17    #define MAXSTRLEN       255
18    #define MAXWORDSIZE     20
19    #define NULL            0
20    #define SLASH           '/'
21    #define SQUOTE          '\''
22    #define STAR            '*'
23    #define TRUE            1
24    #define VOID            int
25
26    /***********************************************************/
27    /*                     code macros                       */
28    /***********************************************************/
29    #define PutBack(Ch)     {PutBackChar = Ch; }
30
31    /***********************************************************/
32    /*                     typedefs                          */
33    /***********************************************************/
34    typedef struct rType {
35          int             Reference ;     /* line number */
36          struct rType *Link ;            /* link to next reference */
37    }
38    RefType,*RefPtr ;
39
40    typedef struct tType {
41          char            *Value ;        /* pointer to token */
42          RefPtr          OccurList ;     /* line number list */
43    }
44    TokenType,*TokenPtr ;
45
46    /***********************************************************/
47    /*                     external functions                */
48    /***********************************************************/
49    extern char     *malloc() ;
50    extern RefPtr   MakeOccurrence() ;
51
52
53    /***********************************************************/
54    /*                     global variables                  */
55    /***********************************************************/
56    int             CurLineNo = 1 ;         /* Line being read. */
57    TokenType       HashTable [HTSIZE] ;
58    int             PutBackChar = '\0' ;    /* Character put back
59                                               after input. */
60
61    main(argc,argv)
62    int     argc ;
63    char    *argv[] ;
64    {       /* main */
65          int       Counter ;
```

CPT-O

```
66        char        CurToken [MAXSTRLEN] ;
67        FILE        *InFile ;
68
69        if (!(InFile = fopen(argv[1],"r"))) {
70            fprintf(stderr,"Can't open input file %s.\n",argv[1]) ;
71            exit(0) ;
72        }
73
74        /* Initialize the hash table.
75         */
76        for (Counter = 0 ; Counter < HTSIZE ; Counter++) {
77            HashTable[Counter].Value = NULL ;
78            HashTable[Counter].OccurList = NULL ;
79        }
80
81        /* Write the first line number to the output stream.
82         */
83        printf("\n%4d    ",CurLineNo) ;
84
85        /* Read and store each token.
86         */
87        while (GetNxtToken(CurToken,InFile)) {
88            if (InsertToken(CurToken)) {
89                fprintf(stderr,"Hash table size exceeded.\n") ;
90                break ;
91            }
92        }
93        printf("   End-of-file.\n\n") ;
94
95        /* Sort the tokens alphabetically.
96         */
97        SortTokens(HTSIZE) ;
98
99        PrintTable() ;
100    }       /* main */
101
102    VOID AddOccurrence(HeadPtr)
103    RefPtr  HeadPtr ;
104    /* AddOccurrence adds a new line occurrence to the
105     * end of the list that HeadPtr begins.
106     */
107    {       /* AddOccurrence */
108        RefPtr      CurPtr ;
109        RefPtr      NewPtr ;
110
111        /* Find the end of the list by starting at
112         * the beginning and advancing through the list
113         * until we find the end.  * /
114        for (CurPtr = HeadPtr ; CurPtr->Link != NULL ;
115                    CurPtr = CurPtr->Link)
116            ;
117
118        CurPtr->Link = NewPtr = (RefPtr)malloc(sizeof(RefType)) ;
119        if (NewPtr == NULL) {
120            fprintf("Out of memory in AddOccurrence.") ;
121            exit(0) ;
122        }   NewPtr->Reference = CurLineNo ;
123        NewPtr->Link = (RefPtr)NULL ;
124    }       /* AddOccurrence */
125
126    char *Copy(OldString)
127    char    *OldString ;
128    /* Copy makes a copy of OldString and returns the
129     * address of the copy.
```

```
30      */
31      {       /* Copy */
32          char        *NewString ;
33
34          /* Allocate a string able to hold the length of the
35           * string plus one for the terminator.
36           */
37          NewString = malloc(strlen(OldString) + 1) ;
38
39          /* Copy the string and return a pointer to it.
40           */
41          strcpy(NewString,OldString) ;
42          return (NewString) ;
43      }       /* Copy */
44
45      int GenerateNewIndex(OriginalKey,ProbeNumber)
46      int     OriginalKey ;
47      int     ProbeNumber ;
48
49      /* GenerateNewIndex takes the current hash table index and
50       * generates a new index for collision resolution.
51       */
52      {       /* GenerateNewIndex */
53          return ((OriginalKey + ProbeNumber * ProbeNumber) % HTSIZE) ;
54      }       /* GenerateNewIndex */
55
56      int GetNxtChar(InputFile)
57      FILE    *InputFile ;
58      /* GetNxtChar returns the next non-comment
59       * a non-string character from InputFile.
60       *
61       * A least one character is read from InputFile.  If
62       * the character could start a comment the next character
63       * is checked. If the slash-star of a comment
64       * is read the reading of characters continues until the end
65       * of the comment is found.  If a single or  double quote
66       * is read the reading of characters continues until
67       * the closing mark is found.  When end-of-file is encountered
68       * EOF is returned.  GetNxtChar therefore never returns
69       * characters inside comments or quotes.
70       */
71      {       /* GetNxtChar */
72          int         CheckChar ;
73          int         NewChar ;
74          int         TempChar ;
75
76          /* If end-of-file is found, return immediately.
77           */
78          if ((NewChar = GetRawChar(InputFile)) == EOF)
79              return(EOF) ;
80
81          /* If a single or double quote is found, process the string.
82           */
83          if (NewChar == SQUOTE || NewChar == DQUOTE) {
84              CheckChar = NewChar ;
85              /* Continue reaing until the matching quote character
86               * is found.
87               */
88              while ((NewChar = GetRawChar(InputFile)) != CheckChar &&
89                      NewChar != EOF) ;
90              /* The terminating character has now been read.
91               * Read one more and return it.
92               */
93              NewChar = GetRawChar(InputFile) ;
```

```
194            }
195
196            /* Next handle comment processing.  If SLASH is read,
197             * check to see if the next character is a STAR.  If it is,
198             * continue reading until the matching STAR-SLASh is found.
199             */
200            else if (NewChar == SLASH) {
201                if ((TempChar = GetRawChar(InputFile)) != STAR) {
202                    /* Not a comment; put back the character.
203                     */
204                    PutBack(TempChar) ;
205                }
206                else
207                    /* Here's a comment.  Search for the end.
208                     */
209                    while (TRUE) {
210                        /* Read characters until a STAR is found.
211                         */
212                        while ((NewChar = GetRawChar(InputFile)) != STAR &&
213                            NewChar != EOF) ;
214
215                        if ((NewChar = GetRawChar(InputFile)) == SLASH) {
216                            /* The end of the comment is found.
217                             */
218                            NewChar = GetRawChar(InputFile) ;
219                            break ;
220                        }
221                        else
222                            /* Not end of comment.  Put the character back.
223                             */
224                            PutBack(NewChar) ;
225                        /* If end-of-file has been found, stop processing.
226                         */
227                        if (NewChar == EOF)
228                            break ;
229                    }
230            }
231        return (NewChar) ;
232    }          /* GetNxtChar */
233
234    BOOL GetNxtToken(Buffer,InputFile)
235    char     *Buffer ;
236    FILE     *InputFile ;
237    /* GetNxtToken returns in Buffer the next valid C token in the
238    program. */
239    {          /* GetNxtToken */
240        int        CurChar ;
241
242        /* Read characters from InputFile until starting letter is
243         * found.  Stop when find a valid letter or end-of-file.
244         */
245        while (!IsStartingLetter(CurChar = GetNxtChar(InputFile)) &&
246        CurChar != EOF)
247            ;
248
249        /* Insert the first character.
250         */
251        *Buffer++ = CurChar ;
252
253        /* Read and accumulate characters in Buffer while they are
254         * valid letters for a token.
255         */
256        while (IsTokenLetter(CurChar = GetNxtChar(InputFile)) &&
257                    CurChar != EOF)
```

```
258              *Buffer++ = CurChar ;
259
260          /* Put back the last character we read.
261           */
262          if (CurChar != EOF)
263              PutBack(CurChar) ;
264
265          /* Terminate the token.
266           */
267          *Buffer = '\0' ;
268
269          /* Return end-of-file status.
270           */
271          return ((CurChar == EOF) ? FALSE : TRUE) ;
272      }        /* GetNxtToken */
273
274      int      GetRawChar(InputFile)
275      FILE     *InputFile ;
276      /* GetRawChar reads the next character from InputFile and
277       * returns it.  If a newline is read, it increments
278       * CurLineNo.  If end-of-file is read, it returns EOF.
279       */
280      {        /* GetRawChar */
281          int          NextChar ;
282        /* Check PutBackChar to see if the next character has
283         * already been read.  If so, process it and set PutBackChar
284         * to the null character.
285         */
286          if (PutBackChar != '\0') {
287              NextChar = PutBackChar ;
288              PutBackChar = '\0';
289          }
290          else {
291              /* Echo the character read to the output stream.
292               * If a newline is read, increment the line count.
293               */
294              if ((NextChar = getc(InputFile)) == '\n')
295                  printf("\n%4d    ",++CurLineNo) ;
296              else
297                  putchar(NextChar) ;
298          }
299
300          if (NextChar == EOF)
301              return (EOF) ;
302
303          return (NextChar) ;
304      }        /* GetRawChar */
305
306      int Hash(Word)
307      char              *Word ;
308      /* Hash returns the HTIndex of the Word passed, or an
309       * appropriate HTIndex for the word.  If HashTable is
310       * full, Hash returns -1 */
311      {        /* Hash */
312          int          HTIndex ;
313          int          IdLen ;
314          int          InitHTIndex ;
315          int          ProbeCounter = 0 ;
316
317          IdLen = strlen(Word) ;
318          if (IdLen == 0)
319              printf("Hash: Word of no length\n") ;
320          HTIndex = InitHTIndex = TransformId(Word) ;
321
```

```
322            if (HashTable[HTIndex].Value == NULL)
323                ; /* NULL - We've got it. */
324            else            /* have we found the correct index? */
325                if (strcmp(Word,HashTable[HTIndex].Value) == EQUALS)
326                    ; /* DONE: A direct hit! */
327                else    /* Collision - generate new indices */
328                    for (ProbeCounter = 0 ; ProbeCounter < (HTSIZE / 2) ;
329                         ProbeCounter++) {
330                        HTIndex = GenerateNewIndex(InitHTIndex,ProbeCounter) ;
331                        if (HashTable[HTIndex].Value == NULL)
332                            break ;        /* We've got it ! */
333                        else if (strcmp(Word,HashTable[HTIndex].Value)
334                            == EQUALS)
335                            break ;        /* We've got it ! */
336                    }
337            if (ProbeCounter >= (HTSIZE / 2))
338                return(-1) ;
339            return(HTIndex) ;
340        }        /* Hash */
341
342    BOOL InsertToken(Token)
343    char            *Token ;
344    /* InsertToken inserts the token into the hash table if it is
345     * new.  If the token is previously known, it adds the line
346     * number to the occurrence list. It then returns FALSE.
347     * If the end-of-hash table is reached, TRUE is returned.
348     */
349        {        /* InsertToken */
350        int            HTIndex ;
351
352        HTIndex = Hash(Token) ;
353        if (HTIndex == -1)
354            return (TRUE) ;
355
356        if (HashTable[HTIndex].Value == NULL) {
357            HashTable[HTIndex].Value = Copy(Token) ;
358            HashTable[HTIndex].OccurList = MakeOccurrence() ;
359        }
360        else
361            AddOccurrence(HashTable[HTIndex].OccurList) ;
362
363        return (FALSE) ;
364        }        /* InsertToken */
365
366    BOOL IsStartingLetter(Ch)
367    char    Ch ;
368    /* IsStartingLetter returns TRUE if Ch is a valid character
369     * to begin a C token.
370     */
371        {        /* IsStartingLetter */
372        return ((isalpha(Ch) || Ch == '_') ? TRUE : FALSE) ;
373        }        /* IsStartingLetter */
374
375    BOOL IsTokenLetter(Ch)
376    char    Ch ;
377    /* IsTokenLetter returns TRUE if Ch is a valid character
378     * inside a C token.
379     */
380        {        /* IsTokenLetter */
381     return ((isalpha(Ch) || isdigit(Ch) || Ch == '_') ? TRUE : FALSE) ;
382        }        /* IsTokenLetter */
383
384    RefPtr MakeOccurrence()
385    /* MakeOccurrence creates the first entry of the line occurrence
```

```
386      * list.  It creates the next node in the list, inserts CurLineNo
387      * and sets Link to NULL in preparation for the next entry.
388      */
389      {        /* MakeOccurrence */
390         RefPtr       NewNode ;
391
392         if ((NewNode = (RefPtr)malloc(sizeof(RefType))) == NULL) {
393             fprintf("Out of memory in MakeOccurrence.") ;
394             exit(0) ;
395         }
396         NewNode->Reference = CurLineNo ;
397         NewNode->Link = (RefPtr)NULL ;
398
399         return (NewNode) ;
400      }        /* MakeOccurrence */
401
402      int NameCompare(First,Second)
403      int      First ;
404      int      Second ;
405      /* NameCompare compares the two entries in HashTable referenced
406       * by the indices First and Second.  It returns FIRSTLESS if
407       * First < Second;   EQUALS if they equal;
408       * FIRSTGREATER if First > Second.
409       */
410      {        /* NameCompare */
411         /* If the first entry has no value, the first is less.
412          */
413         if (HashTable[First].Value == NULL)
414             return(FIRSTLESS) ;
415
416         /* Then if the second has no value, the first is greater.
417          */
418         if (HashTable[Second].Value == NULL)
419             return(FIRSTGREATER) ;
420
421         /* Otherwise return the comparison from strcmp.
422          */
423       return (strcmp(HashTable[First].Value,HashTable[Second].Value)) ;
424      }        /* NameCompare */
425
426      VOID PrintTable()
427      /* Printable prints the list of identifiers and line occurrences.
428       */
429      {        /* PrintTable */
430         RefPtr       ListPtr ;
431         int          NumOnLine ;
432         int          TokenCounter ;
433
434         for (TokenCounter = 0 ; TokenCounter < HTSIZE ;
435                 TokenCounter++) {
436             if (HashTable[TokenCounter].Value) {
437                 printf("\n%-20s    ",HashTable[TokenCounter].Value) ;
438                 for (ListPtr = HashTable[TokenCounter].OccurList,
439                 NumOnLine = 0 ; ListPtr != NULL ;
440                 ListPtr = ListPtr->Link,NumOnLine++) {
441                     if (NumOnLine == 10) {
442                         printf("\n                                    ") ;
443                         NumOnLine = 0 ;
444                     }
445                     printf("%3d  ",ListPtr->Reference) ;
446                 }
447             }
448         }
449         printf("\n") ;
```

```
450        }        /* PrintTable */
451
452     VOID SortTokens(SortNumber)
453     int             SortNumber ;
454     /* SortTokens sorts the tokens into alphabetical order
455      * using a Shell sort.
456      */
457     {        /* SortTokens */
458        TokenType    Exchange ;
459        int          BaseCounter ;
460        int          CurCounter ;
461        int          CurGapCounter ;
462        int          Gap ;
463        int          LastInBuf ;
464
465        LastInBuf = SortNumber ;
466        /* Look through all Gaps starting with a gap half the
467         * size of the list.  Each time reduce the size of the
468         * gap by dividing by two.
469         */
470     for (Gap = LastInBuf / 2 ; Gap > 0 ; Gap /= 2)
471
472           /* BaseCounter moves between the Gap-th element and
473            * the last element in the list.  The sort using the
474            * current Gap runs until I is the LastInBuf-th
475            * element in the list.
476            */
477     for (BaseCounter = Gap ; BaseCounter < LastInBuf ; BaseCounter++)
478
479              /* For an BaseCounter we compare the CurCounter-th and
480               * the CurGapCounter-th elements in the list.  CurCounter
481               * and CurGapCounter are always separated by Gap. */
482     for (CurCounter = BaseCounter - Gap ; CurCounter >= 0 ;
483              CurCounter -= Gap) {
484        CurGapCounter = CurCounter + Gap ;
485
486        /* If the two elements compare correctly, stop.
487         */
488              if (NameCompare(CurCounter,CurGapCounter) < EQUALS)
489                 break ;
490
491              /* Otherwise, exchange the elements.
492               */
493              Exchange.Value =
494                    HashTable[CurCounter].Value ;
495              Exchange.OccurList =
496                    HashTable[CurCounter].OccurList ;
497              HashTable[CurCounter].Value =
498                    HashTable[CurGapCounter].Value ;
499              HashTable[CurCounter].OccurList =
500                    HashTable[CurGapCounter].OccurList ;
501              HashTable[CurGapCounter].Value =
502                    Exchange.Value ;
503              HashTable[CurGapCounter].OccurList =
504                    Exchange.OccurList ;
505              }
506        }        /* SortTokens */
507
508     int TransformId(Word)
509     char            Word [] ;
510     /* TransformId converts the identifier into an integer
511      * within the index range of HashTable.
512      */
513     {        /* TransformId */
```

```
514          int      Term ;
515          int      WordIndex ;
516
517          Term = 0 ;
518          for (WordIndex = strlen(Word) - 1 ; WordIndex > -1 ;
519                     WordIndex--)
520             Term = ( 257 * Term) + Word[WordIndex] ;
521          Term = (Term < 0) ? -Term : Term ;
522          return (Term % HTSIZE) ;
523       }        /* TransformId */
524
525       End-of-file.
```

AddOccurrence	102	361							
BOOL	10	234	342	366	375				
BaseCounter	459	477	477	477	482				
Buffer	234	235	251	258	267				
Ch	29	29	366	367	372	372	375	376	381	381
	381								
CheckChar	172	184	188						
Copy	126	357							
Counter	65	76	76	76	77	78			
CurChar	240	245	246	251	256	257	258	262	263	271
CurCounter	460	482	482	483	484	488	494	496	497	499
CurGapCounter	461	484	488	498	500	501	503			
CurLineNo	56	83	122	295	396				
CurPtr	108	114	114	115	115	118			
CurToken	66	87	88						
DQUOTE	11	183							
EOF	178	179	189	213	227	246	257	262	271	300
	301								
EQUALS	12	325	334	488					
Exchange	458	493	495	502	504				
FALSE	13	271	363	372	381				
FILE	67	157	236	275					
FIRSTGREATER	14	419							
FIRSTLESS	15	414							
First	402	403	413	423					
Gap	462	470	470	470	477	482	483	484		
GenerateNewIndex	145	330							
GetNxtChar	156	245	256						
GetNxtToken	87	234							
GetRawChar	178	188	193	201	212	215	218	274		
HTIndex	312	320	322	325	330	331	333	339	350	352
	353	356	357	358	361				
HTSIZE	16	57	76	97	153	328	337	434	522	
Hash	306	352							
HashTable	57	77	78	322	325	331	333	356	357	358
	361	413	418	423	423	436	437	438	494	496
	497	498	499	500	501	503			
HeadPtr	102	103	114						
IdLen	313	317	318						
InFile	67	69	87						
InitHTIndex	314	320	330						
InputFile	156	157	178	188	193	201	212	215	218	234
	236	245	256	274	275	294			
InsertToken	88	342							
IsStartingLetter	245	366							
IsTokenLetter	256	375							
LastInBuf	463	465	470	477					
Link	36	114	115	118	123	397	440		
ListPtr	430	438	439	440	440	445			
MAXSTRLEN	17	66							

Symbol	References
MAXWORDSIZE	18
MakeOccurrence	50 358 384
NULL	19 77 78 114 119 123 322 331 356 392 397 413 418 439
NameCompare	402 488
NewChar	173 178 183 183 184 188 189 193 200 212 213 215 218 224 227 231
NewNode	390 392 396 397 399
NewPtr	109 118 119 122 123
NewString	132 137 141 142
NextChar	281 287 294 297 300 303
NumOnLine	431 439 440 441 443
OccurList	42 78 358 361 438 495 496 499 500 503 504
OldString	126 127 137 141
OriginalKey	145 146 153
PrintTable	99 426
ProbeCounter	315 328 328 329 330 337
ProbeNumber	145 147 153 153
PutBack	29 204 224 263
PutBackChar	29 58 286 287 288
RefPtr	38 42 50 103 108 109 118 123 384 390 392 397 430
RefType	38 118 392
Reference	35 122 396 445
SLASH	20 200 215
SQUOTE	21 183
STAR	22 201 212
Second	402 404 418 423
SortNumber	452 453 465
SortTokens	97 452
TRUE	23 209 271 354 372 381
TempChar	174 201 204
Term	514 517 520 520 521 521 521 521 522
Token	342 343 352 357
TokenCounter	432 434 434 435 436 437 438
TokenPtr	44
TokenType	44 57 458
TransformId	320 508
VOID	24 102 426 452
Value	41 77 322 325 331 333 356 357 413 418 423 423 436 437 493 494 497 498 501 502
Word	306 307 317 320 325 333 508 509 518 520
WordIndex	515 518 518 519 520
argc	61 62
argv	61 63 69 70
break	90 219 228 332 335 489
char	41 49 63 66 126 127 132 235 307 343 367 376 509
ctype	5
define	10 11 12 13 14 15 16 17 18 19 20 21 22 23 24 29
else	200 207 222 290 297 324 327 333 361
exit	71 121 394
extern	49 50
fopen	69
for	76 114 328 434 438 470 477 482 518
fprintf	70 89 120 393
getc	294
h	4 5
if	69 88 119 178 183 200 201 215 227 262 286 294 300 318 322 325 331 333 337 353 356 392 413 418 436 441 488
include	4 5

nt	11	25	35	56	58	62	65	145	146	147

nt   11   25   35   56   58   62   65 145 146 147
            156 172 173 174 240 274 281 306 312 313
            314 315 350 402 403 404 431 432 453 459
            460 461 462 463 508 514 515
salpha   372 381
sdigit   381
ain   61
alloc   49 118 137 392
rintf   83   93 295 319 437 442 445 449
utchar   297
Type   34   36
eturn   142 153 179 231 271 301 303 338 339 354
            363 372 381 399 414 419 423 522
izeof   118 392
tderr   70   89
tdio   4
trcmp   325 333 423
trcpy   141
trlen   137 317 518
truct   34   36   40
Type   40
ypedef   34   40
hile   87 188 209 212 245 256

A Problem for You to Solve

XREF has a problem handling quoted strings containing a quote mark immediately preceded by a backslash. The backslash character is used to make a quote mark a literal character and not the end of a string. For example:

```
"He said, \"Hi!\""
```

is read as the literal character string

```
He said, "Hi!"
```

The combination \" is a literal double quote in the string.

A simple change in **XREF** solves this problem. Find where the character input and scanning needs to be changed, and fix it.

14

CALLS: C Program Call Chart Generator

Large **C** programs have many functions each calling the other, often in ways that can be difficult to trace. A call chart generator is a software tool for large-program development. It generates a list of all the functions in a program in an indented style to show the calling hierarchy within the program. This chapter presents source code and discusses a specific call chart generator named **CALLS**. An example of a call chart is:

```
GetNextToken
        IsStartingLetter
                isalpha
        GetNextChar
                GetRawChar
                        getc
                        printf
                        putchar[external]
        PutBack
```

GetNextToken calls **IsStartingLetter** and **GetNextChar**. **GetNextChar** in turn calls **GetRawChar**, which calls **getc**, **printf**, and so on.

The objective is:

Read a **C** source file.
List a call chart to **stdout**.
Let the user specify the
function with which to
begin the chart.

CALLS: strategy and definitions

A call chart is a diagram where every function called within a function is listed. The listing of functions-calling-functions continues until all calls made in the program are described. The process can be described as:

• Find a function.

223

- Scan for all function calls within this function.
- Store them in a list.

CALLS must scan for function calls. It must determine where a function call or definition is made in a program. A simple way to define a function call or definition is:

A function is called or defined whenever
the next character following a **C** identifier
is a left parenthesis.

This definition is surprisingly simple to code. However, problems do arise from this simple definition. Several **C** keywords, such as **for**, **if**, and **return**, have the same syntax as a function call: an identifier (here, the keyword) followed by a left parenthesis. Another problem is that code macro calls are treated as function calls.

The first problem is solved by hashing the **C** keywords which look like function calls into an identifier hash table. Every potential function read from the input file is checked in the hash table and all **C** keywords eliminated. The second problem is difficult to solve, and is ignored in this simple program.

CALLS must also know where the code for a function begins and ends. As you know, a function begins with its name; code within a function begins with a left curly bracket and continues until a matching right curly bracket is read.

CALLS: definitions

CALLS's include files and definitions follow:

```
/*********************************************************************/
/*                        include files                           */
/*********************************************************************/
#include <stdio.h>
#include <ctype.h>

/*********************************************************************/
/*                        definitions                             */
/*********************************************************************/
#define BLANK             ' '       /* ASCII blank character */
#define BOOL              int
#define DEFINED           1         /* result of FindNextFunction */
#define DEFINING          0         /* result of FindNextFunction */
#define EOFCHAR           26        /* end-of-file character */
#define EOL               '\n'      /* ASCII end-of-line character */
#define EOS               '\0'      /* end-of-string marker */
#define FALSE             0
#define HASHTABLEFULLFLAG -1        /* Indicates hash table overflow */
#define HTSIZE            1009      /* Must be a prime number */
#define MAXDEPTH          25        /* Maximum recursive-calling depth */
#define MAXFILENAME       100       /* Maximum length of a file name */
#define MAXSYMLENGTH      20        /* Maximum significant characters
                                     * in a symbol.
                                     */
#define PAPERWIDTH        132       /* Default output page width */
#define TABSIZE           8         /* Default output indentation size */
#define TRUE              1
#define USAGE             "calls file [function...]"
#define VOID              int
```

There are several definitions to note. **PAPERWIDTH** and **TABSIZE** are parameters used to format the final listing. To fit the listing to a printer, change these definitions. The maximum number of characters stored for any identifier in **CALLS** is **MAXSYMLENGTH**. Twenty characters is a large symbol, but if memory is not a problem and twenty characters is too small, increase **MAXSYMLENGTH**. Also note **EOS** and **EOL**; the end of string and end of line characters are defined to be a null character and a newline, respectively.

CALLS: code macros

CALLS uses more intricate code macros than those used in previous programs. They are:

```
/***********************************************************************/
/*                         code macros                               */
/***********************************************************************/
#define assert(expr)     if (!(expr))\
{fprintf("Assertion %s failed\n","expr") ; exit(0) ;}
#define GenericMalloc(t)  ((t *) malloc(sizeof(t)))
#define GenerateNewIndex(x,y)   (((x+y*y)%HTSIZE)+1)
#define GenericNULL(t)    ((t *) 0)
#define StrEq(a,b)        (strcmp((a),(b))==0)
```

ANATOMY: the macro continuation character

The definition of a code macro can be longer than will comfortably fit on one line. **assert**'s definition is long, but is split over two lines. The first definition line ends with a single backslash. The next line is appended to the previous line, making the complete definition.

Most compilers have a limit on the number of characters possible in a macro definition. When combined, all macro definition continuation lines must form a line shorter than this limit.

Checking for What Should Never Happen

Every programmer says some condition will never happen in the lifetime of a program. Usually this statement accompanies writing code that opens the program for disaster if the impossible should occur.

The **assert** macro is a convenient way to check for a condition that should never happen. In the midst of critical code, **assert** is used:

```
VOID BackUp ()
/* Pops an item from the active stack.    */
{     /* BackUp */
    assert (MaxActiveIndex > 0) ;
    ActiveList[MaxActiveIndex--] = NULL ;
}     /* BackUp */
```

When **BackUp** is called, **MaxActiveIndex** must be greater than zero. After expansion, **BackUp** looks like this:

```
VOID BackUp ()
/* Pops an item from the active stack.        */
{    /* BackUp */
    if (!(MaxActiveIndex > 0)) {
        fprintf("Assertion %s failed\n",
        "MaxActiveIndex > 0") ; exit(0) ;
    }
    ;
    ActiveList[MaxActiveIndex--] = NULL ;
}    /* BackUp */
```

assert's argument is a condition. In the definition, it is placed into an **if** statement that checks to see if the condition failed. If the **assert** fails, the **fprintf** statement prints the bad news, and the program stops.

The replacement works like this:

```
assert (MaxActiveList > 0) ;
        ------------------
              ¦
              v
assert (expr) ==>  if (!(expr)) {
    fprintf("Assertion %s failed\n","expr") ;
    exit(0) ;}
```

expr is used twice in the definition, so it is replaced twice:

```
assert (MaxActiveList > 0) ;
        ------------------
              ¦---------------------------------
              v                                ¦
if (!(MaxActiveList > 0)) {                    v
    fprintf("Assertion %s failed\n","MaxActiveList > 0") ;
    exit(0) ;}
```

Note how flexibly the code macro works here. The first replacement causes the expression to be directly replaced in the **if** condition clause. But in the **fprintf**, the replacement is within double quotes; the resulting code behaves like a string!

Solving a Cast Problem

malloc returns a pointer to a character string. Often, though, the space reserved is for a data structure. Although **C** compilers do not require it, a cast should be used to change the type of the pointer.

Using casts constantly in a program can be messy. Two code macros, **Generic-Malloc** and **GenericNULL**, solve the problem. When allocating space for a data structure, **CALLS** uses **GenericMalloc**:

```
if (!(NamePtr = GenericMalloc(NameType)))
```

The definition for **GenericMalloc** calls for two substitutions, one in a cast the other in a **sizeof** clause. After expansion, the code reads:

```
if (!(NamePtr = (NameType *)malloc(sizeof(NameType))))
```

The macro uses **sizeof** to determine how much space to reserve and a cast to change the type of the pointer.

Similarly, **GenericNull** changes the type of **NULL** to match the pointer:

```
LastNamePtr = GenericNULL(NameType) ;
```

After expansion, this reads:

```
LastNamePtr = (NameType *)NULL ;
```

Using these macros, correct use of casts is easy.

CALLS: typedefs

CALLS uses two types of data structures:

```
/***********************************************************************/
/*                          typedefs                                   */
/***********************************************************************/
/* NameDefinition is the NameType for this instance.
 * NextCallee is the next instance called.
 */
typedef struct iType {
    struct nType        *NameDefinition ;
    struct iType        *NextCallee ;
}
InstanceType,*InstPtrType ;

/* FunctionName is the unique function name.
 * CallCount is the number of times the function is called.
 * FirstLineNumber is the line when first printed.
 * FirstCallee is a pointer to an InstanceType describing the first
 *        all for this function.
 * NextNamePtr is the next function NameType in the list.
 */
typedef struct nType {
    char                FunctionName [MAXSYMLENGTH] ;
    int                 CallCount ;
    int                 FirstLineNumber ;
    InstPtrType         FirstCallee ;
    struct nType        *NextNamePtr ;
}
NameType,*NamePtrType ;
```

Data Structures and Program Data Flow

NameType contains information on each function in the program. The name, number of times called, and where first printed in the listing are all stored. Additionally, **NameType** stores two pointers: a pointer to the next **NameType** (**NextNamePtr**), and a pointer (**FirstCallee**) to the first function called by this function.

Each time a function is called, an **InstanceType** is stored to represent the information. An **InstanceType** stores a pointer to a **NameType** describing the function called (**NameDefinition**), and a pointer to the next function called in the chain (**NextCallee**). This diagram illustrates the data structure linkage:

```
¦    ¦ NameType data structure
¦----¦    ----
¦  o-+---->¦    ¦ InstanceType data structure
¦----¦    ¦----¦    ----
¦    ¦    ¦  o-+---->¦    ¦ InstanceType data structure
 ----     ----    ¦----¦    ----
  ¦         ¦  o-+--->NULL
  ¦              ----
  v
next NameType data structure
```

The **NameType** data structures store the basic information about the function. A **NameType** data structure is created for every function in the program. An **InstanceType** data structure is created for every function called by the function under consideration. These **InstanceType**s are linked into a linear list.

When a function is called, an **InstanceType** data structure is created describing it. Each of these **InstanceType**s are linked to the **NameType** data structure where the basic function is described. This second level of linkage is not shown in this diagram.

The call chart is printed from this data structure. Starting from any one function (a specific **NameType**), all the functions called by the function are described by **InstanceType**s linked to it. Printing the call chart is done by following the list of **InstanceType**s linked to a **NameType**.

In turn, a function called by another function may itself call several functions. When a called function is printed, all the functions called by it are printed beneath it, indented one level. These functions are printed by following the list of **Instance-Type**s for this called function. The entire call chart is printed by following all possible paths in the network of nodes and links. Printing the chart sounds complicated, but a powerful programming technique called *recursion* solves the problem swiftly. Recursion is discussed below as the routine **Output** is described.

CALLS: external functions

Several functions in **CALLS** need special declarations as they return pointers to data structures. These declarations solve typing problems.

```
/*********************************************************************/
/*                      external functions                         */
/*********************************************************************/
extern NamePtrType FindNameEntry() ;
extern NamePtrType LookFor() ;
extern char *malloc() ;
```

CALLS: global variables

CALLS uses these global variables:

```
/*********************************************************************/
/*                      global variables                           */
/*********************************************************************/
NamePtrType ActiveList [MAXDEPTH] ;
/* Used by Output to avoid infinite recursion.
 */
```

```
int       BracketCount = 0 ;
/* Keeps track of the nesting of brackets.  A function found when
 * BracketCount is 0 must be its DEFINING occurrence, since function
 * invocations must always appear within some block of code.
 */
FILE      *FilePtr ;                /* Input file pointer */
char      *HashTable [HTSIZE] ;
int       LineCount = 0 ;

int       MaxActiveIndex = 0 ;
/* Indexes ActiveList from 0 to MAXDEPTH.
 */

NamePtrType NameListHead = GenericNULL(NameType) ;
FILE      *OutFile ;

int       TabsPerPage = (PAPERWIDTH-MAXSYMLENGTH)/TABSIZE ;
/* Default number of tabs per page.
 */

BOOL      Terse = TRUE ;
```

As the comment says, **BracketCount** counts the nesting of brackets. When **BracketCount** is zero, the first function seen must be the definition of the function, because function definitions must appear outside of other functions.

CALLS: main

CALLS's main function is described in pseudocode as:

Insert **C** keywords in the hash table.
Open files.
while (Getting another function is successful)
    if (The call DEFINES the function)
        Put the function in the function list.
    else
        Put the call in the instance list.

Print the call chart.

The code follows:

```
VOID main(argc, argv)
int       argc ;
char      *argv [] ;
{       /* main */
      int         ActListIndex ;
      int         ArgIndex = 1 ;
      char        Identifier[MAXSYMLENGTH] ;
      NamePtrType CallerPtr ;
      char        *FileName ;
      int         FunctionUse ;
      int         HTIndex ;
      NamePtrType NamePtr ;

      /* Initialize the hash table.
       */
      for (HTIndex = 0 ; (HTIndex < HTSIZE) ; HTIndex++)
            HashTable[HTIndex] = GenericNULL(char) ;
```

```
/* The following are keywords that look like
 * function calls in C.
 */
InsertWord("for") ;
InsertWord("if") ;
InsertWord("return") ;
InsertWord("sizeof") ;
InsertWord("switch") ;
InsertWord("while") ;

/* Initialize the active list.
 */
for (ActListIndex = 0 ; (ActListIndex < MAXDEPTH) ; )
    ActiveList[ActListIndex++] = GenericNULL(NameType) ;

/* There must be at least one command-line option.
 */
if (argc < 2) {
    printf("USAGE: %s\n",USAGE) ;
    exit(0) ;
}

/* Determine the input file and open it.
 */
if (ArgIndex < argc) {

    /* Extract the filename from the command line.
     */
    strcpy(FileName,argv[ArgIndex++]) ;

    if (!(FilePtr = fopen(FileName,"r")))
        Error("Specified file cannot be opened",TRUE) ;
}

/* Parse the input stream and build the appropriate tables.
 */
CallerPtr = GenericNULL(NameType) ;
while ((FunctionUse =
            FindNextFunction(Identifier,CallerPtr)) != EOF)
    if (FunctionUse == DEFINING)
        CallerPtr = FindNameEntry(Identifier) ;
    else
        NewOccurrence(Identifier,CallerPtr) ;

/* If there are any command line arguments, they are the names
 * of the functions from which to begin the call charts.
 */
if (ArgIndex < argc) {
    do {
        if (NamePtr = LookFor(argv[ArgIndex])) {
            Output(NamePtr,0) ;
            printf("\n\n") ;
        }
        else
            Error(
        "Starting function from command line not found",FALSE)
    }
    while ((++ArgIndex) < argc) ;
}
else {
    /* Print beginning with "main", if there is one.
     */
    if (NamePtr = LookFor("main")) {
        Output(NamePtr,0) ;
```

```
                printf("\n\n") ;
                NamePtr->CallCount = 1 ;
                /* Don't print "main" again later.
                */
        }

        /* Now print all functions not called by
         * anyone else.
         */
        for (NamePtr = NameListHead ; NamePtr ;
                     NamePtr = NamePtr->NextNamePtr)
            if (NamePtr->CallCount == 0) {
                Output(NamePtr,0) ;
                printf("\n\n") ;
            }

        /* Finally, print any mutually recursive functions.
        */
        for (NamePtr = NameListHead ; NamePtr ;
                     NamePtr = NamePtr->NextNamePtr)
            if (NamePtr->FirstLineNumber == 0) {
                Output(NamePtr,0) ;
                printf("\n\n") ;
            }
    }
}       /* main */
```

main follows its pseudocode closely. The problem-causing **C** keywords are first put in the hash table with **InsertWord**. (This hashing is similar to **WFREQ** and **XREF**.) Once the input file is open, the real processing loop begins. It calls **Find-NextFunction** repeatedly. If **BracketCount** is zero when a function is found, it is outside any other function's body. This condition is called the function's defining occurence. If the current occurrence is the defining occurrence, **main** calls **Find-NameEntry** to create a **NameType** for the function. If the occurrence is not a defining occurrence, **main** calls **NewOccurrence** to create a **InstanceType** for this occurrence. These two functions build the data structure and maintain the pointer network described above.

After the input file is read, the call chart is printed. The print code in **main** is described later while discussing the routine **Output**.

Finding Functions

main calls **FindNextFunction** to return the next function from the input file. Recall a function is defined as a **C** identifier immediately followed by a left parenthesis. The following pseudocode describes this process:

Read a character.
If it starts an identifier, read the
characters making up the name and store them.
Read the next character.
If it is a left parenthesis, this is a function.

Unfortunately, the process is more complex than this. Intervening characters can separate the function name from the left parenthesis. Comments and quoted strings must be ignored; even function names in comments and quoted strings must not be returned.

BracketCount must be incremented every time a left curly bracket is seen, and decremented every time a right curly bracket is seen. Since **FindNextFunction** reads character-by-character from the input file, it is convenient to handle the bracket counting as other characters are scanned.

```
int FindNextFunction(Identifier,CurFunction)
char            *Identifier ;
NamePtrType     CurFunction ;
/* Sets its argument to the name of the next function found
 * in the input stream.  It returns as its value DEFINING if this
 * is the DEFINING occurrence of the function, DEFINED if it is
 * simply an invocation of the function, and EOF if the input
 * stream is exhausted.
 */
{       /* FindNextFunction */
    int         CurChar ;

    while (TRUE) {
        CurChar = getc(FilePtr) ;
        if (IsStartingLetter(CurChar)) {
            ungetc(CurChar,FilePtr) ;
            Scan(Identifier) ;
        }
        else {
            switch (CurChar) {
            case '\t':
            case BLANK:
                /* Skip over white space.
                 */
                break ;

            case EOL:
                /* Skip over preprocessor lines.
                 */
                if ((CurChar = getc(FilePtr)) == '#')
                    while ((CurChar = getc(FilePtr)) != EOL)
                        if (CurChar == '\\')
                            getc(FilePtr) ;   /* Continuation */
                ungetc(CurChar,FilePtr) ;
                break ;

            case '\'':
                /* This doesn't work if the literal
                 * contains a quoted apostrophe (\').
                 */
                Identifier[0] = EOS ;
                /* Skip over character literals.
                 */
                while ((CurChar = getc(FilePtr)) != '\'')
                    if (CurChar == '\\')
                        getc(FilePtr) ;   /* Continuation */
                break ;

            case '\"':
                /* This doesn't work if the literal contains a
                 * quoted quotation mark (\").
                 */
                /* Skip over string literals. */

                while ((CurChar = getc(FilePtr)) != '\"')
                    if (CurChar == '\\')
                        getc(FilePtr) ;   /* Continuation */
                break ;
```

```
case '\\':
    Identifier[0] = EOS ;
    getc(FilePtr) ;
    break ;

case '{':
    BracketCount++ ;
    Identifier[0] = EOS ;
    break ;

case '}':
    BracketCount-- ;
    if (BracketCount < 0)
        Error("Brackets are not properly nested",FALSE) ;
    Identifier[0] = EOS ;
    break ;

case '(':
    if (Identifier[0] == EOS)
        break ;   /* No function name was found. */

    /* Ignore any words occurring in the hash
     * table.
     */
    if (!FindWord(Identifier)) {

        /* Not within the body of a function.
         */
        if (BracketCount == 0)
            return(DEFINING) ;


        else if (!Seen(Identifier,CurFunction))
            return(DEFINED) ;
        /* Ignore multiple occurrences within
         * a function.
         */
    }
    Identifier[0] = EOS ;
    break ;

case EOF:
    return(EOF) ;

case '/':
    if ((CurChar = getc(FilePtr)) == '*') {
        /* Skip over comments.
         */
        while (TRUE) {
            while (getc(FilePtr) != '*') ;
            if ((CurChar = getc(FilePtr)) == '/')
                break ;
            ungetc(CurChar,FilePtr) ;
        }
    }
    else ungetc(CurChar,FilePtr) ;
    break ;

    /* All over characters must delimit
     * identifiers.
     */
```

```
                    default:
                        Identifier[0] = EOS ;
                        break ;

                    } /* switch */
               } /* else */
         } /* while */
     }          /* FindNextFunction */
```

FindNextFunction is a large **while** loop which continues forever. There are two exits from the loop: (1) End-of-file is read. (2) A left parenthesis is read after a **C** identifier. If a character is read that begins a **C** identifier, it is put back and **Scan** called to read the identifier. On returning, the next character is read.

When a character is read that does not follow an identifier, a **switch** statement analyzes the character. White space is ignored. Ends of lines are also ignored; note the special processing for the preprocessor continuation character. Literal characters and quoted strings are dropped. Curly brackets cause **BracketCount** to be incremented and decremented. Comments are discarded.

If a left parenthesis is found and a function name is in **Identifier**, a return is made. It is a defining occurrence if **BracketCount** is zero—the name is not found inside any function body. It is a defined occurrence otherwise; the name is found inside another function's body as a function call.

The code for **Scan** follows:

```
VOID Scan(Token)
char     *Token ;
/* Scans the input stream until a token is found that might
 * be the name of a function.  It returns the atom found.
 */
{          /* Scan */
     int        CurChar ;
     int        StringIndex ;

     for (StringIndex = 0 ;
          CurChar = getc(FilePtr),IsStartingLetter(CurChar) ; ) {
          Token[StringIndex++] = CurChar ;
          if (StringIndex >= MAXSYMLENGTH) {
               StringIndex = MAXSYMLENGTH - 1 ;
               break ;
          }
     }
     assert (StringIndex < MAXSYMLENGTH) ;
     Token[StringIndex] = EOS ;
     ungetc(CurChar,FilePtr) ;
}          /* Scan */
```

Scan reads character-by-character until it finds a character that cannot be inside a **C** identifier. This last character is put back with **ungetc**. Note the use of **assert** to check that the identifier length is within the maximum size permitted. **FindNextFunction** calls **FindWord** to try to find the current name in the hash table of **C** reserved words.

```
BOOL FindWord(Word)
char     *Word ;
/* Looks up an identifier in the hash table and returns TRUE or
 * FALSE to indicate the presence or absence of the identifier.
 */
```

```
{         /* FindWord */
    int       HTIndex = Hash(Word) ;
    if ((HTIndex == HASHTABLEFULLFLAG) ||
                (HashTable[HTIndex] == GenericNULL(char)))
        return(FALSE) ;
    return(TRUE) ;
}         /* FindWord */
```

FindNextFunction also uses **Seen** to ensure a function appears only once on the list of functions called by the current one.

```
BOOL  Seen(CheckID,CurFunction)
char          *CheckID ;
NamePtrType    CurFunction ;
/* Determines if the argument string CheckID has already been
 * seen as an argument function.
 */
{         /* Seen */
    InstPtrType InstPtr ;

    assert (CurFunction != GenericNULL(NameType)) ;

    for (InstPtr = CurFunction->FirstCallee ;
                (InstPtr != GenericNULL(InstanceType)) ;
                InstPtr = InstPtr->NextCallee)
        if (StrEq(CheckID,(InstPtr->NameDefinition)->FunctionName))
            return (TRUE) ;

    return (FALSE) ;
}         /* Seen */
```

Inserting a Defined Name

When **FindNextFunction** returns with a defining occurrence of a name, **main** calls **FindNameEntry** to create an instance of a **NameType** for the new function:

```
NamePtrType FindNameEntry(Name)
char      *Name ;
/* Returns a pointer to the argument name on the list of
 * NameEntries.  If the name is not there, a new NameEntry
 * is created.
 */
{         /* FindNameEntry */
    NamePtrType LastNamePtr = NULL ;
    NamePtrType NamePtr ;
    NamePtrType NewNamePtr ;
    int         StrTest ;

    /* Search for the name in the current list of known, defined
     * functions.  Since the names are inserted in sorted order,
     * stop when we have passed the new name in the list.
     */
    for (NamePtr = NameListHead ;
                NamePtr != NULL &&
                (StrTest = strcmp(Name,NamePtr->FunctionName)) >= 0 ;
                LastNamePtr = NamePtr,
                NamePtr = NamePtr->NextNamePtr)
        if (StrTest == 0)
            return(NamePtr) ;

    /* Name was not found, so add it.
     */
    NewNamePtr = AllocNameEntry() ;
    strcpy(NewNamePtr->FunctionName,Name) ;
```

```
/* Link the new name entry into the appropriate place
 * in the chain.
 */
NewNamePtr->NextNamePtr = NamePtr ;
if (!LastNamePtr)
    NameListHead = NewNamePtr ;
else
    LastNamePtr->NextNamePtr = NewNamePtr ;

return (NewNamePtr) ;
}       /* FindNameEntry */
```

The global pointer variable **NameListHead** points to the beginning of a list of all known functions defined in the input program. The entries in the list are always kept in alphabetical order by a special node creation and insertion technique. The first **for** loop in **NameListHead** begins at the head of this list and works forward until it finds the place where the function name should appear. If it already exists, **FindNameEntry** returns a pointer to that node. If it does not exist, **FindNameEntry** creates a new node and inserts it in the list at the correct point. Not all aspects of list insertion and maintenance are covered here, but the following explanation covers how **FindNameEntry** does its work. For example, **NameListHead** points to a list of three **NameType** nodes:

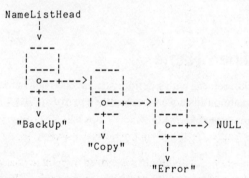

The first node describes the function **BackUp** and has a pointer to its name. The second and third nodes describe **Copy** and **Error**.

In this example, the next function to be inserted is **Create**. **FindNameEntry**'s formal parameter **Name** is the string "Create". **NamePtr** is set to **NameListHead**, and **LastNamePtr** is set to **NULL**.

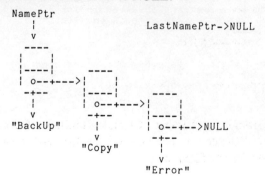

The continuation condition is tested: **NamePtr** is not **NULL**. The result of **strcmp** of **Name** (''Create'') with **NamePtr->FunctionName** (''BackUp'') is greater than or equal to zero. **StrTest**, the result of this comparison, is greater than zero, because ''Create'' is greater than ''BackUp''. Recall that **strcmp** returns a number greater than or equal to zero if the first string is greater than or equal to the second string.

Both conditions are fulfilled, so the loop body is executed. It is an **if** statement. **StrTest** is not zero, so the body of the **if** is not done. Next, the increment actions are taken. **LastNamePtr** is set to where **NamePtr** currently points, and **NamePtr** is moved to point to **NamePtr->NextNamePtr**. The diagram now is:

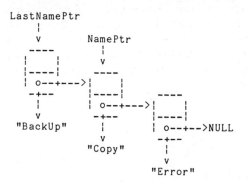

Again the continuation condition is tested. **NamePtr** is still not **NULL**, and, once more, the **strcmp** comparison of ''Create'' and ''Copy'' is a number greater than one. **StrTest** is again not zero, so the **if** statement is not executed.

The increment happens again: **LastNamePtr** is moved to point to where **NamePtr** now points, and **NamePtr** is moved to the next node in the chain. The diagram is:

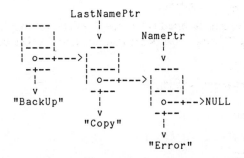

This time the continuation condition fails because ''Create'' is less than ''Error'' (**NamePtr->FunctionName**). ''Create'' is not now on the list, and a new **NameType** must be made and properly filled in.

A call to AllocNameEntry returns a new **NameType**; **NewNamePtr** now contains the new pointer. "Create" is copied into **NewNamePtr->** **FunctionName**. The new node is inserted into the list at the correct point: **NewNamePtr** is set to point where **NamePtr** currently points. If **LastNamePtr** is not **NULL**, **LastNamePtr-> NextNamePtr** is set to point to **NewNamePtr**. The diagram now is:

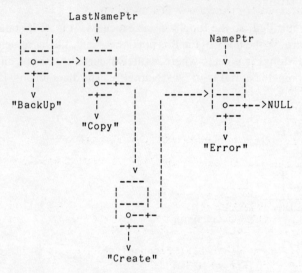

In this way, the **NameType** nodes describing the functions are always kept in alphabetical order.

FindNameEntry's code is deceptively short. The function handles all possible problems in list insertion. Run through several examples. Insert a new node at the beginning and end of the list. Try inserting a function that already exists. The code handles all these cases correctly.

FindNameEntry calls **AllocNameEntry** to create a new instance of a **NameType**.

```
NamePtrType AllocNameEntry()
/* Allocate storage for a NameEntry.
 */
{       /* AllocNameEntry */
    NamePtrType NamePtr ;

    if (!(NamePtr = GenericMalloc(NameType)))
        Error("Ran out of memory",TRUE) ;

    /* Initialize the new entry.
     */
    NamePtr->FunctionName[0]    = EOS ;
    NamePtr->CallCount          = 0 ;
    NamePtr->FirstLineNumber    = 0 ;
    NamePtr->FirstCallee        = GenericNULL(InstanceType) ;
    NamePtr->NextNamePtr        = GenericNULL(NameType) ;

    return (NamePtr) ;
}       /* AllocNameEntry */
```

AllocNameEntry uses **GenericMalloc** to create the new data space. It then initializes the new entry to zeros, and sets all pointers to **NULL**.

Creating an Instance of a Function Call

If the appearance of a function use in a program is not the first defining occurrence, **main** calls **NewOccurrence** to create a new **InstanceType**:

```
VOID NewOccurrence(Name,CallerPtr)
char           *Name ;
NamePtrType    CallerPtr ;
/* Creates an InstanceEntry for a function use.
 */
{        /* NewOccurrence */
    InstPtrType InstPtr ;
    NamePtrType NamePtr ;
    InstPtrType NewInstPtr ;

    assert (CallerPtr != GenericNULL(NameType)) ;

    /* Create the new instance and link it with a NameType
     * describing it.
     */
    InstPtr = CallerPtr->FirstCallee ;
    NamePtr = FindNameEntry(Name) ;
    NewInstPtr = AllocInstanceEntry() ;
    NewInstPtr->NameDefinition = NamePtr ;

    if (InstPtr != GenericNULL(InstanceType)) {
        /* Run down the callee chain until a NULL link is found.
         */
        for ( ; (InstPtr->NextCallee != GenericNULL(InstanceType))
                      InstPtr = InstPtr->NextCallee)
            ; /* No body */

        /* Now add the new instance to the callee chain.
         */
        InstPtr->NextCallee = NewInstPtr ;
    }
    else
        CallerPtr->FirstCallee = NewInstPtr ;

    /* Increment the callee's call count.
     */
    (NamePtr->CallCount)++ ;
}        /* NewOccurrence */
```

Consider again how **main** calls **NewOccurrence:**

```
/* Parse the input stream and build the appropriate tables.
 */
CallerPtr = GenericNULL(NameType) ;
while ((FunctionUse =
             FindNextFunction(Identifier,CallerPtr)) != EOF)
    if (FunctionUse == DEFINING)
        CallerPtr = FindNameEntry(Identifier) ;
    else
        NewOccurrence(Identifier,CallerPtr) ;
```

At the beginning, **main** sets **CallerPtr** to **NULL**. When a defining use of a function is found, **CallerPtr** is reset by a call to **FindNameEntry**. Until another defining instance is found, **CallerPtr** points to the **NameType** describing the function being currently defined.

When **main** calls **NewOccurrence**, it passes this pointer leading to the description for the function being defined. **NewOccurrence** first validates this pointer (the formal parameter **CallerPtr**) to ensure it is not **NULL**. It then sets **InstPtr** to point to the beginning of the function list called by the current function (**CallerPtr->FirstCallee**). It calls **FindNameEntry** to return a pointer to a **NameType** instance describing the called function. It then calls **AllocInstanceEntry** to create a new **InstanceType** to represent this call.

For example, suppose the function **Copy** calls the function **malloc**. This diagram represents the resulting data structure:

The **if** statement checks whether **InstPtr** is **NULL**; this means the new **Instance-Type** is the first one on the list. If not, it moves **InstPtr** down the linked list until it points to the next to last **InstanceType** on the list. This movement works just as in the previous example.

Now the grand data structure linkage: The new **InstanceType** node is added to the end of the list of called functions. This node itself points to the **NameType** node describing the function called:

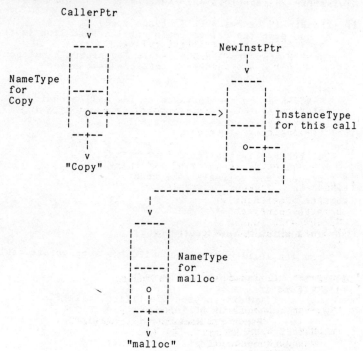

After setting up these links, **NewOccurrence** increments the number of times this function is called.

NewOccurrence calls **AllocInstanceEntry** to create an **InstanceEntry**:

```
InstPtrType AllocInstanceEntry()
/* Allocate storage for an InstanceEntry.
 */
{        /* AllocInstanceEntry */
    InstPtrType InstPtr ;

    if (!(InstPtr = GenericMalloc(InstanceType)))
        Error("Ran out of memory",TRUE) ;

    InstPtr->NameDefinition = GenericNULL(NameType) ;
    InstPtr->NextCallee     = GenericNULL(InstanceType) ;

    return(InstPtr) ;
}        /* AllocInstanceEntry */
```

AllocInstanceEntry creates a new **InstanceEntry** and sets both of the pointers within the data structure to **NULL**.

Printing The CALL Chart

main directs the call chart output with this code:

```
/* If there are any command line arguments, they are the names
 * of the functions from which to begin the call charts.
 */
if (ArgIndex < argc) {
    do {
        if (NamePtr = LookFor(argv[ArgIndex])) {
            Output(NamePtr,0) ;
            printf("\n\n") ;
        }
        else
            Error(
             "Starting function from command line not found",FALSE) ;
    }
    while ((++ArgIndex) < argc) ;
}
else {
    /* Print beginning with "main", if there is one.
     */
    if (NamePtr = LookFor("main")) {
        Output(NamePtr,0) ;
        printf("\n\n") ;
        NamePtr->CallCount = 1 ;
        /* Don't print "main" again later.
         */
    }

    /* Now print all functions not called by
     * anyone else.
     */
    for (NamePtr = NameListHead ; NamePtr ;
                NamePtr = NamePtr->NextNamePtr)
        if (NamePtr->CallCount == 0) {
            Output(NamePtr,0) ;
            printf("\n\n") ;
        }
```

```
/* Finally, print any mutually recursive functions.
 */
for (NamePtr = NameListHead ; NamePtr ;
             NamePtr = NamePtr->NextNamePtr)
    if (NamePtr->FirstLineNumber == 0) {
        Output(NamePtr,0) ;
        printf("\n\n") ;
    }
```

The first **if** tests whether there are additional command line arguments. These are assumed to be names of functions whose call charts are to be printed. This option is handy when a listing of all calls in a program file is long and only one function is of interest.

If there are additional command line arguments, a **do/while** loop scans through them, printing a call chart for each one. **LookFor** is called to search through the list of known functions for the requested name and return a pointer to its **NameType** entry. If this pointer is not **NULL**, **main** calls **Output** with this pointer to write the call chart. The loop continues until it exhausts all command line arguments.

If there are no additional command line arguments, **CALLS** assumes that the entire call chart is to be written, starting from the input program's **main** function, if there is one. **CALLS**'s **main** function calls **LookFor** and searches for a **main** function in the input file. If there is one, it calls **Output** to write the call chart.

After the first part of the call chart is written, a scan is made through all the **NameType** entries, searching for functions never called by anyone. These are printed. Then a scan is made for mutually recursive functions (definition below).

The output scheme depends on one feature of the data structure: all the **NameType** nodes in the system are linked together in a linear list. **NameListHead** points to the head of the list. Starting from **NameListHead**, all the functions in the input file are easily scanned.

LookFor searches through all the **NameType** nodes to find one that describes the function whose name **LookFor** receives as a parameter:

```
NamePtrType LookFor(Name)
char    *Name ;
/* Looks for its argument name on the list of NameEntries.
 * If found, it returns a pointer to the entry; otherwise,
 * it returns NULL.
 */
{       /* LookFor */
    NamePtrType NamePtr ;

    for (NamePtr = NameListHead ;
                (NamePtr != GenericNULL(NameType)) ;
                NamePtr = NamePtr->NextNamePtr)
        if (StrEq(Name,NamePtr->FunctionName))
            return (NamePtr) ;
    return (GenericNULL(NameType)) ;
}       /* LookFor */
```

LookFor sets **NamePtr** to **NameListHead**. It then scans through the entire list of known functions until it is finds a **NameType** whose **FunctionName** field is the same as the function name passed to **LookFor**. The code macro **StrEq** defines a special form of **strcmp** that checks only for string equality.

An Elegant Solution To Printing The Chart: Output

main calls **Output** passing a pointer to the **NameType** describing the function to print. It also passes a zero for the second parameter, the formal parameter **Cur-Tab**. **CurTab** is the current indentation level.

Output prints the name of the function pointed to by its formal parameter **NamePtr**. It prints the name indented to match the function's calling depth within the program. But this function may call other functions. These functions called by the function pointed to by **NamePtr** must be printed below the current function's name and at an indentation level one greater than the current level.

How to handle this chain of calls? What needs to happen in printing the call chart is:

Print the function name.
For any functions called by this
function, print them at an indentation
level one greater than the current one.

The functions called by the function under consideration are all on a list pointed to by the **FirstCallee** field in the **NameType** node describing the function. The elaborate scheme for building the data structures ensures this happy state.

The problem is how to repeatedly print the next function on the list, then follow all its called functions? **CALLS** uses a powerful technique called recursion to solve the problem. *Recursion* happens when a function calls itself.

How does recursion help here? Every time a function calls yet another function, **Output** calls itself with a pointer to the next function. In the call, **Output** increases the indentation level. Thus when **Output** prints the new function, it is printed with a greater indentation level than the current one.

Here is the code:

```
VOID Output(NamePtr,CurTab)
NamePtrType     NamePtr ;
int             CurTab ;
/* A recursive routine that prints one tab for each level of
 * nesting, then the name of the function called, followed by the
 * next function called at the same level.  In doing this, it
 * invokes itself to output the names of the functions called by
 * the current function.  It maintains an active list of functions
 * currently being output by the different levels of recursion,
 * and if it finds itself asked to output one which is already
 * active, it terminates, marking that call with an asterisk.
 */
{       /* Output */
    InstPtrType InstPtr ;
    int         LoopCount ;
    int         NumOfTabs = CurTab ;
    BOOL        PageOverflow ;
    int         TabCount ;
```

CPT-Q

```
LineCount++ ;
printf("\n%4d",LineCount) ;
if (!(MakeActive(NamePtr)))
    printf("*") ;  /* Calls nested too deep. */
else {
    for (TabCount = 0 ; (NumOfTabs > TabsPerPage) ; TabCount++)
        NumOfTabs -= TabsPerPage ;
    for (LoopCount = 0 ; (LoopCount < TabCount) ; LoopCount++)
        printf("<") ;
    printf(" ") ;
    for (LoopCount = 0 ; (LoopCount < NumOfTabs) ; LoopCount++)
        printf("\t") ;

    if (IsActive(NamePtr))  /* recursive call */
        printf("%s [recursive]",NamePtr->FunctionName) ;
    else {
        InstPtr = NamePtr->FirstCallee ;
        if (InstPtr != GenericNULL(InstanceType)) {
            printf("%s",NamePtr->FunctionName) ;
            if (!Terse || (NamePtr->FirstLineNumber == 0)) {
                CurTab++ ;
                if (NamePtr->FirstLineNumber == 0)
                    NamePtr->FirstLineNumber = LineCount ;
                if ((CurTab > TabsPerPage) &&
                        (CurTab%TabsPerPage == 1) &&
                        (InstPtr->NextCallee
                            != GenericNULL(InstanceType))) {
                    printf(
    "\n- - - - - - - - - - - - - - - - - - - - - - - -") ;
                    printf(" - - - - - - - - -") ;
                    PageOverflow = TRUE ;
                }
                else PageOverflow = FALSE ;

                for ( ; (InstPtr != GenericNULL(InstanceType)) ;
                            InstPtr = InstPtr->NextCallee)
                    Output(InstPtr->NameDefinition,CurTab) ;
                if (PageOverflow) {
                    printf(
    "\n- - - - - - - - - - - - - - - - - - - - - - - -") ;
                    printf(" - - - - - - - - -") ;
                    PageOverflow = FALSE ;
                }
            }
            else if (InstPtr != GenericNULL(InstanceType))
                printf(" ... [see line %d]",NamePtr->FirstLineNumber) ;
        }
        else printf("%s",NamePtr->FunctionName) ;
            /* library, external, or macro call */
    }
    BackUp() ;
    if (NamePtr->FirstLineNumber == 0)
        NamePtr->FirstLineNumber = LineCount ;
}
}    /* Output */
```

Output first calls **MakeActive** to place the current function on the active list. A function is active when it is being printed. Marking a function as active is essential if a function should call itself. (**CALLS** must handle programs with recursive functions.) **MakeActive** also does a check to see if the calling depth is inordinately great. If the depth of calling exceeds the defined constant **MAXDEPTH**, **MakeActive**

returns **FALSE**, and **Output** stops calling itself. This safety net prevents recursive functions from calling themselves infinitely many times should an error in building the data structure occur.

```
BOOL MakeActive(CurNameEntry)
NamePtrType      CurNameEntry ;
/* Puts a pointer to the argument NameEntry into the ActiveList.
 * FALSE  is  returned  if the function fails because  the
 * function nesting is too deep; otherwise TRUE is returned.
 */
{       /* MakeActive */
    if (MaxActiveIndex < MAXDEPTH) {
        ActiveList[MaxActiveIndex++] = CurNameEntry ;
        return (TRUE) ;
    }
    else return (FALSE) ;
}       /* MakeActive */
```

Output next runs three **for** loops which keep track of the number of tab stops on a page. A program with great function calling depth causes the indentation to go off the page. **CALLS** marks these cases so the call chart is always consistent. The third loop prints the correct number of tab characters to the output.

Now **Output** prints the function name. If the function is recursive, it is already on the active list, having been put there by a previous call to **Output**. Rather than print it again, **Output** prints the message **[recursive]**, and returns. **Output** calls **IsActive** to see if a function is on the active list:

```
BOOL IsActive(CurNameEntry)
NamePtrType      CurNameEntry ;
/* Checks if its argument is already on the active list.   */
{       /* IsActive */
    int ActListIndex ;

    for (ActListIndex = 0 ; (ActListIndex < MaxActiveIndex-1) ;
                ActListIndex++)
        if (CurNameEntry == ActiveList[ActListIndex])
                return (TRUE) ;
    return(FALSE) ;
}       /* IsActive */
```

Back to **Output**. The first **if** statement after the call to **IsActive** checks if the current function has any calls within its definition. Otherwise, the following **if** statement contains code to adjust the number of tab stops to indent the next function call. This adjustment takes into account the maximum number of tab stops on a page. If an overflow happens, a line of dashes is printed.

Now comes the recursion. For every function on the list pointed to by the current function's **NextCallee** pointer, a call is made to **Output**. Recall **CurTab** has already been adjusted in the preceding code to account for the extra nesting.

If a function uses no functions in its body, its name is printed near the end of **Output**. No additional calls to **Output** are made.

After the name has been printed, **BackUp** is called to remove the function from the list of active functions:

```
VOID BackUp ()
/* Pops an item from the active list.
 */
{         /* BackUp */
    assert (MaxActiveIndex > 0) ;
    ActiveList[MaxActiveIndex--] = NULL ;
}         /* BackUp */
```

Miscellaneous Functions

CALLS uses some functions from previous chapters. One new function **Error** prints
an error message and stops the program if the error is severe. The functions listed
below control the hashing of C reserved words and string copying, as well as **Error**.

```
char    *Copy(OldString)
char    *OldString ;
/* Copy makes a copy of OldString and returns the address of
 * the copy.
 */
{         /* Copy */
    char        *NewString ;
    char        *ReturnPtr ;

    /* Allocate a string able to hold the length
     * of the string plus one for the terminator.
     */
    ReturnPtr = NewString = malloc(strlen(OldString) + 1) ;

    /* Copy the string and return a pointer to it.
     */
    while (*NewString++ = *OldString++) ;
    return(ReturnPtr) ;
}         /* Copy */

VOID Error(Message, AbortFlag)
/* Reports any errors detected.
 */
char    *Message ;
BOOL    AbortFlag ;
{         /* Error */
    fprintf(stderr,"\n*** calls: %s. ***\n",Message) ;
    if (AbortFlag)
        exit(0) ;
}         /* Error */
int Hash(Word)
char    *Word ;
/* Generates a unique hash table index for the argument
 * identifier.  The value of HASHTABLEFULLFLAG is returned
 * if the hash table overflows.
 */
{         /* Hash */
    int        HTIndex ;
    int        InitHTIndex ;
    int        ProbeCounter    = 0 ;

    HTIndex = InitHTIndex = TransformId(Word) ;
    assert (strlen(Word) > 0) ;

    if (HashTable[HTIndex] == GenericNULL(char))
        ; /* no-op - We've got it. */

    else            /* Have we found the correct index? */
```

```
    if (StrEq(Word,HashTable[HTIndex]))
        ;  /* DONE: A direct hit! */

    else        /* Collision -- generate indexes */
        for ( ; (ProbeCounter < (HTSIZE/2)) ; ProbeCounter++) {
            HTIndex = GenerateNewIndex(InitHTIndex,ProbeCounter) ;
            if ((HashTable[HTIndex] == GenericNULL(char)) ||
                        StrEq(Word,HashTable[HTIndex]))
                break ; /* We've got it ! */
        }

    if (ProbeCounter >= (HTSIZE/2))
        return(HASHTABLEFULLFLAG) ;
    return(HTIndex) ;
}       /* Hash */

BOOL InsertWord(Word)
char    *Word ;
/* Inserts an identifier into the hash table and returns TRUE.
 * If the hash table overflows, FALSE is returned.
 */
{       /* InsertWord */
    int         HTIndex ;

    if ((HTIndex = Hash(Word)) == HASHTABLEFULLFLAG)
        return(FALSE) ;

    /* Add Word to the hash table if it is not already present.
     */
    if (HashTable[HTIndex] == GenericNULL(char))
        HashTable[HTIndex] = Copy(Word) ;

    return(TRUE) ;
}        /* InsertWord */

BOOL IsStartingLetter(Ch)
char    Ch ;
/* IsStartingLetter returns TRUE if Ch is a valid character to
 * begin a C token.
 */
{       /* IsStartingLetter */
    return ((isalpha(Ch) || Ch == '_') ? TRUE : FALSE) ;
}       /* IsStartingLetter */

int TransformId(Word)
char    Word[] ;
/* Converts an identifier into an integer within the index
 * range of HashTable.  A polynomial is generated and reduced
 * modulo HTSIZE to produce this number.
 */
{       /* TransformId */
    int         Term = 0 ;
    int         WordIndex ;

    for (WordIndex = strlen(Word)-1 ; (WordIndex >= 0) ; WordIndex--)
        Term = (257*Term) + Word[WordIndex] ;

    Term = abs(Term) ;
    return(Term % HTSIZE) ;
}       /* TransformId */
```

A Sample Run of CALLS

When **CALLS** was run with itself as input, the following output was generated:

```
 1  main
 2      GenericNULL
 3      InsertWord
 4              Hash
 5                      TransformId
 6                              strlen
 7                              abs
 8                      assert
 9                      strlen
10                      GenericNULL
11                      StrEq
12                      GenerateNewIndex
13              GenericNULL
14              Copy
15                      malloc
16                      strlen
17      printf
18      exit
19      strcpy
20      fopen
21      Error
22              fprintf
23              exit
24      FindNextFunction
25              getc
26              IsStartingLetter
27                      isalpha
28              ungetc
29              Scan
30                      getc
31                      IsStartingLetter ... [see line 26]
32                      assert
33                      ungetc
34              Error ... [see line 21]
35              FindWord
36                      Hash ... [see line 4]
37                      GenericNULL
38              Seen
39                      assert
40                      GenericNULL
41                      StrEq
42      FindNameEntry
43              strcmp
44              AllocNameEntry
45                      GenericMalloc
46                      Error ... [see line 21]
47                      GenericNULL
48              strcpy
49      NewOccurrence
50              assert
51              GenericNULL
52              FindNameEntry ... [see line 42]
53              AllocInstanceEntry
54                      GenericMalloc
55                      Error ... [see line 21]
56                      GenericNULL
57      LookFor
58              GenericNULL
59              StrEq
60      Output
61              printf
62              MakeActive
63              IsActive
64              GenericNULL
```

```
65              Output [recursive]
66              BackUp
67                      assert
```

This graphic display of a program's structure makes learning an unfamiliar program much easier.

Postlude—There's More To It!

After this book, where next? This book covers most of the **C** language. There are several major topics which have been omitted from the book. These topics are used in larger, more advanced programs than the ones beginning and moderately advanced programmers write. All of them are covered in Kernighan and Ritchie's *The C Programming Language*. Here's a list:

1. **Separate compilation**. Large programs are inconvenient to develop as a single file. **C** allows compilation of small files that are then linked together to form the final executable program. This is called "separate compilation."

   A function in one file can call a function or reference a global variable in another program file. The **C** declaration **extern** is used to make clear such connections between files.

   Separate compilation and linkage methods vary considerably with the compiler and linker used. Refer to the specific compiler and linker documentation for details.

2. **Storage classes**. Variables declared within a **C** function normally appear when the function begins running and are destroyed when the function ends. These variables are termed *automatic*. Global variables persist throughout the life of a program; these variables are termed *static*. The declaration of a variable then implies how the variable is stored; this is called the variable's *storage class*.

   C allows explicit declaration of storage class. There are four storage classes in **C**: (1) **auto**, (2) **static**, (3) **register**, and (4) **extern**. No program in this book needs explicit storage class declaration.

3. **Unions and bit fields**. Unions and bit fields are two additional kinds of data structures. Unions allow varying kinds of data to be stored in a single kind of data structure. Bit fields allow data to be manipulated at the bit level. This is frequently useful when **C** programs must solve hardware-related problems; for example, determining status information from an I/O port. The bit field allows you to reference each individual bit by name.

Appendix A

Getting Started with Microcomputer C Compilers

Microcomputer compilers are often more complicated to use than compilers intended for minicomputers and mainframes. This appendix gives pointers on using **C** on microcomputers. It is divided into three sections, each answering a specific question:

1. What should one look for when reading **C** compiler documentation to compile and link a **C** program?
2. How does one make effective use of a system library function described in a compiler manufacturer's documentation?
3. What level of **C** language support do microcomputer **C** compilers provide? What degree of conversion effort is needed to move **C** code written under UNIX to a microcomputer **C**?

Compiling and Linking

A **C** program must be compiled to create an object module and linked with the system library before the program can be run. The **C** compiler first preprocesses the program by reading all **#include** files and substituting all **#define** compiler directives in the program. It then scans and parses the source code, creating an intermediate form of the program that is used in the last phase of compilation, code generation. The code generator usually writes the object module directly.

C compilers on minicomputers usually have a simple mechanism for compilation and linkage. Under UNIX, to compile and link a program file **foo**, one says:

```
cc foo.c
```

The system automatically determines from the filename's suffix **.c** that the file contains **C** source code. The **C** compiler is first run, followed by the linker.

Unfortunately, most microcomputer **C** compilers are more complicated to use than this. As these compilers change, the method used to compile and link programs also change.

Most C compilers are a series of programs run one after another. Each phase in compilation generates an intermediate file. The last phase generates a relocatable object module. The linker is run after running the last compiler phase.

There are three general ways microcomputer C compilers are run:

1. Some compilers run just like the UNIX compiler. To compile and link a program file named **foo**, enter the command line:

   ```
   cc foo.c
   ```

   Each phase of the compiler is run automatically. If no error messages are detected, the linker is run. The correct system library is included in the link.

   To use a compiler of this type, read the compiler documentation for answers to these questions: What is the command name to enter to compile a program? What options can be specified to change how the compilation is done? Sometimes additional libraries are provided to supply special capabilities, like mathematical or graphics functions. What are the names of these libraries? When are they included in the link, and how are their names specified?

2. Some compilers are split into several programs that are run one after another until the entire set is completed. For example, this is how the compiler split into three parts is run:

   ```
   cc1 foo
   cc2 foo
   cc3 foo
   ```

   To compile **foo**, the three programs **cc1**, **cc2**, and **cc3** are run. **cc3** produces the relocatable object module the linker uses. The three compiler phases each produce different kinds of error messages. All three phases must run to completely diagnose all syntax errors in a program file. Each phase can use one of several options specified on the command line that customize how the program is compiled.

   The linker is run in a separate step:

   ```
   cl foo clib
   ```

   This links the relocatable object module **foo.o** with the system library **clib.cl**.

   To use a compiler run in separate parts, read the compiler documentation looking for answers to these questions: What is the name of each compiler phase? What compiler options does each phase use? What kinds of error messages does each phase produce?

   To use a linker, read the documentation for answers to these questions: What is the name of the linker? What options does it use? What is the system library's name? If there are additional libraries, what are their names and when and how are they used?

3. The last group of compilers compile C source code to assembly language. The assembly code is then assembled to form an object module. As before, the object module is linked with the system library to create the final, executable program.

This class of compiler resembles those in group two described above. For example, these steps compile and link the program **foo**:

```
c foo.c
as foo.asm
ln foo.o libc.lib
```

The first step compiles the file **foo.c** to the assembly language file **foo.asm**. The assembler **as** assembles the **.asm** file, creating the object file **foo.o**. The linker then links **foo.o** with the system library.

To use a compiler-assembler combination, look for answers to these questions: What is the name of each compiler and assembler phase? What options does each step use? If custom assembly language modules must be created for a program, what assembly language does the assembler use?

Making The Job Easier

Running the compiler and link steps over and over again during program development can become tiresome. Fortunately microcomputer operating systems provide a batch execution facility to run the compilation and linkage steps as a single command. Frequently the compiler manufacturer will provide a file of batch execution instructions. If not, read the documentation provided with the operating system. How is the batch job execution facility used? What must happen to stop a batch job should an error occur in an early compilation step? The batch file facility under CP/M and CP/M-86 is called **SUBMIT**.

Reading System Library Documentation

C system functions are usually described succinctly in the system documentation. The standard way of detailing the parameters to pass to a system function is with a function and parameter declaration:

```
FILE        *fopen(name,mode) ;
char        *name ;
char        *mode ;
```

This example describes **fopen**. The first line says **fopen** is a function that returns a **FILE ***: a pointer to a FILE. **fopen** takes two parameters, **name** (the filename to open), and **mode** (the way to open the file).

The next two lines declare the two parameters to the function. **name** and **mode** are a pointer to a character—really a pointer to a character string. Recall in **C** a quoted string constant, the name of a character array, and a character pointer all are passed to a function as a character pointer. Therefore **fopen** can take its parameters in any of these forms.

Before using any new function, consult the documentation to learn what parameters the function requires. When you use the function, ensure it receives the correct number of parameters, and that each parameter matches exactly the declaration in the documentation. If a function returns anything other than an integer, the function should be explicitly declared before use as follows:

```
extern FILE    *fopen();
```

This declares **fopen** as an external function returning a **FILE** *.

Comparing Microcomputer C Compilers

C is a highly portable language. Effectively, there are no dialects of the **C** programming language. This means that software written in **C** can be easily moved from one machine to another. Many of the programs in this book have been moved to machines as diverse as Data General MV/8000 and DEC VAX 11/780 super minicomputers, 8080/Z80 and 8086/8088 microcomputers, and a variety of PC ("personal" or "professional") computers for which **C** compilers have been configured. In each case, the code required little or no change from the listings as they appear in this book.

Having a complete implementation of **C** is essential to develop portable programs. This appendix discusses and, to some extent, evaluates **C** compilers for microcomputers. Foremost in this appendix is an attempted resolution of the portability question: Can a compiler handle large programs developed under UNIX? Can programs developed using these compilers be moved to UNIX later? Issues of performance in specific areas are also considered.

The way the **C** language is defined tends to cloud the issue. The **C** language itself does not define how standard library functions work. This means input and output functions are not defined as part of the language. A compiler can be represented honestly as a full **C** language compiler and not be able to compile and link programs developed under UNIX without considerable revisions to the code. In this appendix, compilation of the full **C** language and UNIX-compatible system library support are both considered critical criteria.

This appendix does not represent a discussion of all commercially available **C** compilers. It does represent a review of those compilers supplied to us with no restrictions on their use or on our comments, and which we also found to be attractive in performance and in price-value. The compilers reviewed briefly here are the commercially available versions as of July 1983. They were obtained directly from the authors or publishers. No standard UNIX compilers are included here. Compilers for the 8080/Z80 and 8086/8088 microprocessor families are discussed. As all **C** compilers at this time for the 68000 or Z8000 run under UNIX, these processors are not covered here. The compilers divide neatly into two classes:

1. Those which support the full language and have a UNIX-style system library.
2. Those which provide either partial language support, or which fail to comply in style with the UNIX library. Some of these compilers are still useful for serious work. Unfortunately, circumventing their limitations is difficult for a beginner.

The **C** compiler situation is bright for 8086/8088 family of microprocessors; four compilers are available to run either under MS-DOS or CP/M-86. Support for the 8080/Z80 family of microprocessors is not as complete. Only one compiler for the 8080/Z80 gives support complete enough to be ranked Class 1, as defined here.

Class 1: Full Language/UNIX Library Compatibility

The compilers in this group are adequate for demanding software development. All of the constructions used in this book will work with little or no change on these compilers, making it relatively easy to learn to program in **C**. They are all excellent examples of compiler construction for small machines.

Computer Innovations C86

Running under MS-DOS and CP/M-86, C86 produces code for the 8086/8088 family of microprocessors. C86 supports the entire **C** language and a large part of the standard UNIX library. All standard I/O functions are supported. The system library supports the 8087 numeric data processor by linking an additional library. A rich set of mathematical functions is provided in the library. The compiler optionally accepts identifier names up to 31 significant characters in length, which aids maintaining large programs, but can lead to non-portable code.

The compiler is divided into three sections, each of which is run to produce a relocatable object module. As of this writing, the object module produced under MS-DOS is in the Microsoft standard format. Assembly code and **C** code may be freely mixed. The compiler uses the standard MS-DOS linker. Under CP/M-86, the compiler uses a custom format.

Under MS-DOS, an optimizing version is available that generates either code for the "small" (64K bytes code and 64K bytes data) or for the "large" (many code and data segments).

Under CP/M-86, the maximum program size is 64K bytes of code and 64K bytes of data. An overlay linker is provided to allow larger programs to be developed.

The system library includes numerous special functions for each of the operating systems, allowing access to system and interrupt level operations without resorting to assembly language. Assembly language modules may be linked after conversion with a supplied utility to the custom object format.

Full source code for the system library functions is provided. Librarian utilities for both source code and object modules are also supplied.

Some programs in the book need minor conversion to run with C86. The include files **ctype.h** and **math.h** are not provided. The character classification and conversion functions are provided in the system library. Math functions must be declared explicitly before use rather than with **math.h**. Or, you may write your own **math.h** file and include it in your programs at compile time.

C86's **fscanf** function returns zero on end-of-file. This is nonstandard and affects the **TXTRDR2** and **TXTRDR3** code. Change the end-of-file test condition to zero from **EOF** when using C86.

Lattice C and Microsoft C

Also running under MS-DOS and CP/M-86, Microsoft C, which is derived from Lattice C, produces code for the 8086/8088 family of microprocessors. Lattice C and Microsoft C support the entire C language and a large part of the standard UNIX library. All standard I/O functions are supported. In this discussion, because of the similarities between the two brands, we refer to the two compilers together.

The compiler is divided into two sections, each of which is run to produce a relocatable object module. The object module is in the standard format for MS-DOS. This allows free mixing of assembly language and C code. A librarian for object modules is provided.

The compiler provides rapid compilation and produces fast, small programs. Diagnostic messages are among the most clear and helpful of any of the C compilers we have tested on microcomputers.

The maximum size of programs is 64K bytes of code and 64K bytes of data. Under MS-DOS, the standard linker supplied with the operating system is used for program development. PLINK2, an overlay linker, is provided for use under CP/M-86.

Lattice/Microsoft C uses special buffering methods to speed input/output operations. This presents a problem when reading from and writing to the console. No characters are written to the console until a newline is written, ending the line. Programs in the first half of the book that prompt without a newline may cause problems; add a newline to the prompt. Backspaces are not processed as expected. The manual describes special techniques for doing input and output to the console. Console input/output can present a problem to the beginning programmer.

A **math.h** include file is not provided; few mathematical functions are provided. Explicit declaration of mathematical functions is required.

Mark Williams C

Running under CP/M-86, Mark Williams C also produces code for the 8086/8088 family of microprocessors. Mark Williams C supports the entire C language and a large part of the standard UNIX library. All standard I/O functions are supported. Several C language extensions available under Berkeley UNIX are supported, including the **enum** data type. The compiler is run by invoking a single command which compiles and/or assembles and links all source files listed.

The compiler is divided into four sections, each of which is run to produce a relocatable object module. The object module uses a custom format. A linker is provided.

This compiler provides superb diagnostic messages. A **strict** compilation mode is available that provides a level of program checking unavailable with any other microcomputer C compiler. The checking is similar in many ways to the UNIX *lint* program checker.

The maximum size of programs is 64K bytes of code and 64K bytes of data.

The compiler adheres strictly to the UNIX standard. No special conversion should be needed for most programs.

Digital Research C (DRC)

Running under CP/M-86 and MS-DOS, DRC produces code for the 8086/8088 family of microprocessors. DRC supports the entire C language and a large part of the standard UNIX library. All standard I/O functions are supported.

The compiler is divided into three sections, each of which is run to produce the relocatable object module. The object module produced complies with the new Digital Research object format for CP/M-86. A relocating assembler and linker are provided in the package.

DRC produces C programs in several different 8086 memory models. In the largest model, programs can be constructed with up to 64K bytes of stack, 64K bytes of data, and as much code as can be addressed by the machine. Unfortunately, the execution speed of the code produced by DRC for programs described in Part Two of this book is several times slower than for the other compilers discussed above.

The compiler adheres strictly to the UNIX standard. No conversion should be needed for most programs.

Aztec C

Aztec C is the only full-language compiler we have obtained that runs under CP/M-80 and that also has a standard UNIX system library. Aztec C produces code for the 8080/Z80 family of microprocessors. A separate Z80-only compiler is provided. The system library contains a good part of the standard UNIX library; it is not as robust in functions as the compilers listed above. Most standard I/O functions are supported. **alloc** is provided, but the companion function **free** is not. (**free** is not used in this book.)

The compiler is a single program which writes a file of assembly language as its output. An assembler provided with the package translates this assembly language into a custom object format. A custom linker reads object modules from either C or custom assembly language files. A librarian for object modules is included, along with full source code for the system libraries.

The maximum size of programs is 60K bytes of code and data. The linker supports overlays.

Aztec C requires more effort to convert UNIX programs than do the other full-language compilers. Aztec C provides both a **stdio.h** and a special **libc.h** file. **libc.h** is closer to the UNIX standard include file. **ctype.h** and **math.h** are not included. Some character classification and conversion functions are not included in the standard library.

Missing functions, including **free**, can be written in **C**, compiled, and then merged back into the standard library with no problem. While simple for an experienced programmer, a beginner may have trouble.

Unlike the 8086 compilers, the 8080 microprocessor architecture does not provide an efficient way to recover from stack overflow or underflow. The 8086 compilers usually recover neatly from errors of including too many or too few actual parameters in a function call, or errors in the type of the actual parameters in a function call. Code produced by all the 8080 compilers is highly sensitive to these errors. Being less forgiving, these compilers are more difficult for a beginner than are the 8086 compilers.

Class 2: Partially Compatible Compilers

There are many compilers for the 8080/Z80 family of processors that support a subset of the C language and are partially compatible with the UNIX standard library. In spite of these limitations, two of these compilers provide a good level of support.

Usual Limitations

Almost without exception, these compilers provide the same level of support. The following language features are usually missing in this group:

- **long**, **float**, and/or **double** support. Sometimes a data type itself is supported, but no standard operators apply to the type. Usually some special library functions are needed to use the data type.
- **typedefs**. All **typedef** declarations must be replaced by hand or, preferably, by **#define** substitutions.
- Casts. Casts must be removed from programs. This is not as serious as it might be; the **long**, **float**, and **double** data types which often need explicit casts are not usually available with these compilers.
- Bit fields and **unions**. None of the programs in this book use these features of **C**.
- Code macros. **#define**s with parameters are not usually allowed.
- **alloc/free**. Many of these compilers do not provide an **alloc/free** function set compatible with UNIX.

Most of the features lacking are advanced-language features. Note, though, that none of the programs in Part Two of this book can be compiled directly by a compiler with these limitations. Porting a program in the face of these deficiencies is trying, and is a job best left to an experienced programmer.

Software Toolwork's C/80

This compiler offers excellent value for those who want to try programming in C without making a large purchase for a compiler. C/80 supports the standard C language except for **typedef**s, **float**s, and **double**s, code macros, and bit fields. It operates under CP/M-80 and produces code for the 8080/Z80 family of microprocessors. The support library is not extensive, but the functions supplied do adhere to the UNIX system library. It is not difficult for an experienced programmer to write code in C to fill in the missing functions.

C/80 compiles into assembly language. The assembly language source is assembled into a relocatable object module by Microsoft M80, or is assembled directly to an executable form by the absolute assembler that is supplied with C/80.

The maximum size of programs is 60K bytes of code and data.

BDS C

BDS C has been commercially available for over three years and is a mature, stable product. It supports the standard C language except for **typedef**s, **float**s, and **double**s, code macros, bit fields, initializers, and explicit declaration of storage classes. The omission of initializers and storage classes is serious and requires special efforts for program conversion. Several of the normal I/O functions are non-standard; **fopen**, for example, returns an **int** and takes a special second argument.

BDS C operates under CP/M-80 and produces code for the 8080/Z80 family of microprocessors. The support library is a large subset of the UNIX library. Many functions especially suited to the CP/M-80 environment are included. BDS C is the only microcomputer C compiler to come with a symbolic debugger. While no operators for **float**s and **double**s are supplied, the support library does have library functions for doing limited floating-point arithmetic.

The BDS C compiler is split into two phases. The output is an object module in a custom format. An overlay linker is provided.

BDS C compiles and links with amazing speed on eight-bit microcomputers. The maximum size of programs is 60K bytes of code and data.

Conversion For Subset Compilers

It is clearly not possible to convert directly programs which use data types like **float** when the compiler does not support them. Even programs such as **TXTRDR3** are hard to convert exactly; **TXTRDR3** only uses floating-point arithmetic for summary calculations.

typedef support can be faked by using **#define** substitutions for the **typedef** name. Casts can simply be removed for all pointer operations, as pointers and integers are the same size on 8080/Z80 machines. This is a dangerous practice, and can lead to non-portable programs when moved to a machine where pointers and integers are not the same size.

Lack of initializers can be difficult to handle. Array and string initialization is a powerful feature in **C**, and much uninspiring **C** code can result from removing initializers. In general, a variable can be initialized either with an initializer or with an assignment statement at the beginning of the function using the variable. This replacement must be done painstakingly by hand.

Summary of Special Compiler Features and Limitations

1. **Long Identifier Names**—Standard UNIX compilers retain the first eight characters of identifier names. All compilers in this group retain eight characters except C/80 which requires names to be unique within seven characters. All compilers truncate long names.

   C/86 optionally allows 31 character names, as does Berkeley UNIX.

2. **Character Class Functions and ctype.h**—The Lattice/Microsoft, Mark Williams, and Digital Research compilers use **ctype.h** the same way UNIX does. C/86 provides the character class and conversion functions in the system library, and does not use **ctype.h**. C/80 does not supply many of these functions in the system library. BDS C provides some functions, but does not use **ctype.h**.

3. **Mathematical Functions and math.h**—Only the Mark Williams and Digital Research compilers provide a good selection of mathematical functions and a **math.h** include file. C/86 provides mathematical functions, but no include file. A programmer using C/86 can either explicitly declare functions used or create a **math.h** file. Other compilers do not provide mathematical functions, although a skilled programmer could create a library of functions with Lattice/Microsoft C.

4. **Output to the Printer**—Most microcomputer **C** compilers provide a special device name for output to the printer. Opening a file with this filename opens the printer for output. This table provides a guide:

   ```
   C/86              prn:
   Lattice/
      Microsoft      prn:
   Mark Williams     lst:
   DRC               lst:
   C/80              lst:
   BDS C             lst:
   ```

5. **Newline Translation**—CP/M, CP/M-86, and MS-DOS differ from UNIX in using an ASCII CR and LF characters to end a line instead of a single ASCII LF. UNIX C assumes a single ASCII LF ends a line; UNIX C programs can interchangeably refer to newlines ('\n') and ASCII LF characters.

   Most microcomputer compilers do newline translation on input and output from text files. When an ASCII CR-LF sequence is read from a file, it is translated into a single newline character. When a newline is written, it is translated back to a CR-LF sequence. Most times this is adequate.

Programs dealing with files with binary information rather than textual information must suppress this translation mechanism. C86 and Mark Williams C provide a special option to the **fopen** mode that turns off translation. Lattice/Microsoft C provides a global variable that is set to a special value to stop translation. As these details are constantly in flux, check the compiler documentation.

6. index—The **index** function described in *The C Programming Language* is not the same definition as Berkeley UNIX uses. This book has adhered to the *The C Programming Language* rather than UNIX when talking about **index**. Check the compiler documentation for **index** before using it. Most compilers considered here use the Berkeley UNIX definition, including C86, Mark Williams C, and Lattice/Microsoft C.

7. unsigned and long—All the Class 1 compilers provide the **unsigned** and **long** data types. Some 8080 compilers not discussed here do not support **long** but usually do support **unsigned**. Use **unsigned** rather than **long** to get some extra precision. Many programs simply cannot be converted to a compiler that does not provide support for **long**s.

Appendix B

ctype.h

The following is a group of **#define** instructions that are sometimes provided as
ctype.h. It is a file of code macros that define character classification and conversion functions. If your compiler does not include this useful file, it can be created
from the code given here. Insert a **#include ctype.h** file directive a program you
write requiring these facilities. Appendix C shows the same group as real functions.
Note: backslashes are used as a continuation character to fit the limitations of the
printed page.

```
#define TRUE      1
#define FALSE     0

#define isascii(ch) (((ch) < 128) ? TRUE : FALSE)
#define isalpha(ch) (((ch) >= 'A' && (ch) <= 'Z') ||\
                    ((ch) >= 'a' && (ch) <= 'z')) ? TRUE : FALSE)
#define isupper(ch) (((ch) >= 'A' && (ch) <= 'Z') ? TRUE : FALSE)
#define islower(ch) (((ch) >= 'a' && (ch) <= 'a') ? TRUE : FALSE)
#define isdigit(ch) (((ch) >= '0' && (ch) <= '9') ? TRUE : FALSE)
#define isalnum(ch) ((isalpha(ch) || isdigit(ch)) ? TRUE : FALSE)
#define isspace(ch) (((ch) == ' ' || (ch) == '\t' ||\
                    (ch) == '\n') ? TRUE : FALSE)
#define ispunct(ch) (((ch) >= '!' && (ch) <= '/') ||\
                    ((ch) >= ':' && (ch) <= '@') ||\
                    ((ch) >= '[' && (ch) <= '`') ||\
                    ((ch) >= '{' && (ch) <= '~')) ? TRUE : FALSE)
#define isprint(ch) (((ch) >= ' ' && (ch) <= '~') ? TRUE : FALSE)
#define iscntrl(ch) (((ch) >= 0 && (ch) < ' ') ? TRUE : FALSE)
#define tolower(ch) (((ch) >= 'A' && (ch) <= 'Z') ? \
                    (ch) - 'A' + 'a' : (ch))
#define toupper(ch) (((ch) >= 'a' && (ch) <= 'z') ?\
                    (ch) - 'a' + 'A' : (ch))
#define toascii(ch) return((ch) & 0x7F)
```

The standard UNIX definitions for these macros make use of a special array defined
in the system library that contains the character attributes. Microcomputer C's that
supply a **ctype.h** file also provide the special attribute array. The macro definitions
using the attribute array are less easily understood than these definitions, but they
execute faster.

Appendix C

ctype.c

The standard character classification and converstion functions are listed here as C source code. Compare the difference between the source code and the macro definitions in Appendix B.

```
#define TRUE    1
#define FALSE   0

isascii(ch)
char    ch ;
{
    return((ch < 128) ? TRUE : FALSE) ;
}

isalpha(ch)
char    ch ;
{
    return((ch >= 'A' && ch <= 'Z') || (ch >= 'a' && ch <= 'z'))
        ? TRUE : FALSE) ;
}

isupper(ch)
char    ch ;
{
    return((ch >= 'A' && ch <= 'Z') ? TRUE : FALSE) ;
}

islower(ch)
char    ch ;
{
    return((ch >= 'a' && ch <= 'z') ? TRUE : FALSE) ;
}

isdigit(ch)
char    ch ;
{
    return((ch >= '0' && ch <= '9') ? TRUE : FALSE) ;
}

isalnum(ch)
char    ch ;
{
    return((isalpha(ch) || isdigit(ch)) ? TRUE : FALSE) ;
}
```

```
isspace(ch)
char      ch ;
{
    return((ch == ' ' || ch == '\t' || ch == '\n') ? TRUE : FALSE)
}

ispunct(ch)
char      ch ;
{
    return((ch >= '!' && ch <= '/') ||
           (ch >= ':' && ch <= '@') ||
           (ch >= '[' && ch <= '`') ||
           (ch >= '{' && ch <= '~')) ? TRUE : FALSE) ;
}

isprint(ch)
char      ch ;
{
    return((ch >= ' ' && ch <= '~') ? TRUE : FALSE) ;
}

iscntrl(ch)
char      ch ;
{
    return((ch >= 0 && ch < ' ') ? TRUE : FALSE) ;
}

tolower(ch)
char      ch ;
{
    return((ch >= 'A' && ch <= 'Z') ? ch - 'A' + 'a' : ch) ;
}

toupper(ch)
char      ch ;
{
    return((ch >= 'a' && ch <= 'z') ? ch - 'a' + 'A' : ch) ;
}

toascii(ch)
char      ch ;
{
    return(ch & 0x7F) ;
}
```

Appendix D

math.h

Many microcomputer C's do not provide mathematical functions in the system library. An experienced programmer can write these functions in **C** if the compiler supports the **float** and **double** data types.

The following is the usual content of the **math.h** include file. Digital Research C and Mark Williams C already provide this include file. C/86 provides mathematical functions but no **math.h** file. C/86 users may include this file in programs that use mathematical functions.

If your compiler does not provide the mathematical functions, you must write the functions yourself. After writing the functions, include this file to declare the functions before using them in a program:

```
extern double sin(), cos(), tan();
extern double asin(), acos(), atan(), atan2();
extern double ldexp(), frexp(), modf();
extern double floor(), ceil();
extern double log(), log10(), exp(), sqrt(), pow();
extern double sinh(), cosh(), tanh();

#define fabs(d) ((d) < 0.0 ? -(d) : (d))
#define HUGE    5.2e+151
#define LOGHUGE 349.3
#define TINY    7.5e-155
#define LOGTINY -354.8
```

Index

Le

Prentice/Hall PHI International

Englewood Cliffs, N.J.   London   New Delhi   Rio de Janerio
Singap...   ...ellington

Library of Congress Cataloging in Publication Data

Wortman, Leon A., 1921–
  The C programming tutor.

  Includes index.
  1. C (Computer program language) I. Sidebottom, Thomas O., 1956–
II. Title.
QA76.73C15W67 1984 001.64'24 83-21436

ISBN 0-13-110024-6

Prentice-Hall International, Inc., London
Prentice-Hall Canada, Inc., Scarborough, Ontario
Prentice-Hall of Australia, Pty., Ltd., Sydney
Prentice-Hall of India Private Limited, New Delhi
Prentice-Hall of Japan, Inc., Tokyo
Prentice-Hall of Southeast Asia Pte. Ltd., Singapore
Whitehall Books, Limited, Petone, New Zealand
Editora Prentice-Hall Do Brasil LTDA., Rio de Janeiro

Printed in Great Britain by BPCC Wheatons Ltd, Exeter

10 9 8 7 6